CIMA Exam Practice Kit

F2 – Financial Management

CIMA Exam Practice Kit

F2 – Financial Management

Cathy Sibley

Amsterdam • Boston • Heidelberg • London • New York • Oxford
Paris • San Diego • San Francisco • Singapore • Sydney • Tokyo

CIMA Publishing
An imprint of Elsevier
Linacre House, Jordan Hill, Oxford OX2 8DP
30 Corporate Drive, Burlington, MA 01803

Copyright © 2009, Elsevier Ltd. All rights reserved

No part of this publication may be reproduced in any material form (including photocopying or storing in any medium by electronic means and whether or not transiently or incidentally to some other use of this publication) without the written permission of the copyright holder except in accordance with the provisions of the Copyright, Designs and Patents Act 1988 or under the terms of a licence issued by the Copyright Licensing Agency Ltd, 90 Tottenham Court Road, London, England W1T 4LP. Applications for the copyright holder's written permission to reproduce any part of this publication should be addressed to the publisher

Permissions may be sought directly from Elsevier's Science and Technology Rights Department in Oxford, UK: phone: (+44) (0) 1865 843830; fax: (+44) (0) 1865 853333; e-mail: permissions@elsevier.com. You may also complete your request on-line via the Elsevier homepage (http://www.elsevier.com), by selecting 'Customer Support' and then 'Obtaining Permissions'

Notice
No responsibility is assumed by the publisher for any injury and/or damage to persons or property as a matter of products liability, negligence or otherwise, or from any use or operation of any methods, products, instructions or ideas contained in the material herein.

British Library Cataloguing in Publication Data
A catalogue record for this book is available from the British Library

Library of Congress Cataloging in Publication Data
A catalog record for this book is available from the Library of Congress

978-1-85617-732-0

For information on all CIMA publications visit our website at www.elsevierdirect.com

Typeset by Macmillan Publishing Solutions
(www.macmillansolutions.com)

Printed and bound in Great Britain

09 10 11   11 10 9 8 7 6 5 4 3 2 1

Working together to grow
libraries in developing countries

www.elsevier.com | www.bookaid.org | www.sabre.org

ELSEVIER   BOOK AID International   Sabre Foundation

Contents

Syllabus Guidance, Learning Objectives and Verbs	xiii
Learning Outcomes, Syllabus Content and Examination Format	xvi

1	**Accounting for Investments**	**1**
	Accounting for investments	3
	Investment in associates	3
	Investment in subsidiaries	4
	The requirement to prepare consolidated financial statements	5
	Exclusion from preparing consolidated accounts	5
	IFRS 3 *Business combinations*	5
	Fair values in acquisition accounting	6
	Investment in joint ventures	6
	Medium answer questions	7
	Question 1	7
	Question 2	7
	Answer to medium answer questions	8
	Answer 1	8
	Answer 2	8
	Simple Investments	8
	Investment in associate	9
	Investment in subsidiary	9
	Investment in joint ventures	9
2	**The Consolidated Statement of Financial Position**	**11**
	The basic mechanics of consolidation	13
	Ownership and control	13
	Key workings	14
	The treatment of goodwill and non-controlling interest (IFRS 3 revised)	14
	Treatment of unrealised profits	15
	Medium answer questions	15
	Question 1 – DNT	15
	Question 2 – AB	15
	Question 3 – ABC	16
	Question 4 – XYZ	17
	Question 5	18
	Answer to medium answer questions	18
	Answer 1 – DNT	18
	Answer 2 – AB	19
	Answer 3 – ABC	20

	Treatment of costs	21
	Answer 4 – XYZ	21
	Answer 5	22
3	**The Consolidated Statements of Comprehensive Income and Changes in Equity**	**23**
	Intra-group trading and unrealised profits	25
	Intra-group asset transfers	26
	The impact of fair value adjustments and changes in accounting policy	26
	The statement of comprehensive income	26
	The statement of changes in equity	27
	Medium answer questions	27
	Question 1	27
	Question 2	28
	Question 3	28
	Answer to medium answer questions	29
	Answer 1	29
	Answer 2	30
	Answer 3	31
4	**Associates and Joint Ventures**	**33**
	IAS 28 Accounting for Associates – the basics	35
	Equity accounting	36
	Goodwill on acquisition	36
	Equity accounting – intra-group issues	36
	IAS 31 Interests in Joint ventures	37
	Accounting for jointly controlled operations	37
	Accounting for jointly controlled assets	38
	Accounting for jointly controlled entities	38
	Medium answer questions	39
	Question 1 – ST	39
	Answers to medium answer questions	40
	Answer 1 – ST	40
	Long answer questions	41
	Question 1 – AT	41
	Question 2 – AD	42
	Question 3 – AJ	44
	Answers to long answer questions	46
	Answer 1 – AT	46
	Answer 2 – AD	48
	Answer 3 – AJ	50
5	**Statement of Cash Flow**	**53**
	The basics	55
	Group issues	55
	Medium answer questions	56
	Question 1	56
	Answer to medium answer questions	57
	Answer 1	57
	Long answer questions	57

	Question 1 – EAG	57
	Question 2 – AH	59
	Question 3 – WORLDWIDE	61
Answer to long answer questions		64
	Answer 1 – EAG	64
	Answer 2 – AH	66
	Answer 3 – WORLDWIDE	67

6 Changes in Group Structure — 71

- Piecemeal acquisitions — 73
  - Increasing a stake from a simple investment to a subsidiary — 73
  - From associate to subsidiary — 74
  - Increasing a controlling interest — 74
  - Disposals in the period — 74
- Business reorganisations — 75
  - Possible scenarios — 75
- A subsidiary becomes a sub-subsidiary — 75
- A sub-subsidiary becomes a subsidiary — 76
- The addition of a new parent company — 76
- A subsidiary moved along — 76
- Medium answer questions — 77
  - Question 1 — 77
- Answers to medium answer questions — 78
  - Answer 1 — 78
- Long answer questions — 79
  - Question 1 — 79
- Answers to long answer questions — 81
  - Answer 1 — 81

7 Foreign Currency Translation — 83

- Single transactions in foreign currencies — 85
- Functional and presentational currencies — 85
  - Functional currency — 85
  - Presentation currency — 86
- Translating foreign operations — 86
- Hedging — 87
- Medium answer questions — 87
  - Question 1 – Sizewell Ltd — 87
  - Question 2 – Home — 88
- Answers to medium answer questions — 89
  - Answer 1 – Sizewell Ltd — 89
  - Answer 2 – Home — 91
- Long answer questions — 91
  - Question 1 — 91
  - Question 2 — 93
- Answers to long answer questions — 95
  - Answer 1 — 95
  - Answer 2 — 97

8 Complex Group Structures — 99
- The concept of the sub-subsidiary — 101
- Key differences for sub-subsidiary — 102
- Mixed group — 102
- Indirect investment in associates or joint ventures — 103
- Medium answer questions — 103
  - Question 1 — 103
  - Question 2 — 104
- Answers to medium answer questions — 105
  - Answer 1 — 105
  - Answer 2 — 106
- Long answer questions — 108
  - Question 1 – Big, Small and Tiny — 108
- Answer to long answer questions — 109
  - Answer 1 — 109

9 Substance Over Form — 113
- The concept of substance over form and off-statement of financial position financing — 115
- IAS 18 – *Revenue* — 116
- Recognition and derecognition of assets and liabilities — 116
- Specific examples of substance over form — 116
  - Sale and repurchase agreements — 116
  - Consignment stock — 116
  - Factoring of receivables — 117
  - Securitised assets and loan transfers — 117
- Special purpose entities (SPEs) — 117
- Medium answer questions — 118
  - Question 1 – Juncus plc — 118
  - Question 2 – LMN — 118
- Long answer questions — 119
  - Question 3 – Ned — 119
  - Question 4 — 120
- Answer to medium answer questions — 122
  - Answer 1 – Juncus plc — 122
  - Answer 2 – LMN — 124
- Answer to long answer questions — 125
  - Answer 3 – Ned — 125
  - Answer 4 — 127

10 Accounting for Financial Instruments — 131
- Core definitions — 133
- IAS 32 *Classification rules* — 134
  - Debt or equity? — 134
- Manipulation of gearing — 134
- Specific examples of financial instruments and their treatment — 135
- Hybrid instruments — 135
- Initial recognition — 136
  - Finanical assets — 136
  - Financial liabilities — 137

	Subsequent measurement of financial instruments	137
	Financial assets	137
	Treatment of gains and losses	137
	Financial liabilities	137
	Derivatives	138
	Impairment	138
	Hedging	138
	IFRS 7 *Financial Instruments: Disclosures*	139
	Medium answer questions	139
	Question 1	139
	Question 2 – PX plc	140
	Question 3	140
	Question 4	141
	Answers to medium answer questions	141
	Answer 1	141
	Answer 2 – PX plc	142
	Answer 3	143
	Answer 4	143
11	**Employee Benefits**	**145**
	IAS 19 – *Accounting for employee benefits*	147
	Accounting for pensions	148
	Income statement	148
	Statement of financial position	149
	Accounting for share-based payments	149
	Types of share-based payments	149
	Medium answer questions	149
	Question – BGA	149
	Question 2 – CBA	150
	Question 3	150
	Question 4	151
	Answer to medium answer questions	151
	Answer 1 – BGA	151
	Answer 2 – CBA	152
	Answer 3	152
	Answer 4	153
12	**Financial Reporting in an Environment of Price Changes**	**155**
	Defects of historical cost accounting	157
	Capital	158
	Replacement cost accounting	158
	Exit values	158
	Current cost accounting	158
	Current purchasing power (CPP) accounting	160
	The 'real terms' system	160
	Financial reporting in hyperinflationary economies	160
	Dealing with hyperinflation	161
	Medium answer questions	161
	Question 1 – DCB	161
	Question 2	162

x Contents

Answer to medium answer questions	162
Answer 1 – DCB	162
Answer 2	163

13 Interpretation of Accounting Ratios — 165

The stakeholders	167
The basis of effective analysis	167
Ratios	168
Performance ratios	168
Activity ratios	168
Return on capital ratios	168
Liquidity ratios	169
Valuation and investor ratios	169
Cash flow ratios	169
Capital structure ratios	170
Service industries	170
Long answer questions	171
Question 1 – BZJ	171
Question 2 – AXZ	173
Question 3 – DPC	174
Question 4 – BHG	176
Question 5 – BSP	177
Answers to long answer questions	179
Answer 1 – BZJ	179
Appendix	181
Answer 2 – AXZ	181
Appendix	184
Answer 3 – DPC	184
Answer 4 – BHG	186
Answer 5	188

14 Analysis of Financial Statements: Earnings per Share — 193

Basic EPS	195
Diluted EPS	196
EPS disclosure	196
Medium answer questions	197
Question 1 – JKL plc	197
Question 2	197
Question 3 – AGZ	198
Question 4 – CB	198
Question 5 – BAQ	199
Answers to medium answer questions	201
Answer 1 – JKL plc	201
Answer 2	202
Answer 3 – AGZ	203
Answer 4 – CB	203
Answer 5 – BAQ	204

15 Interpretation of Financial Statements — 207

Basic ground rules	209
Limitations of financial reporting information	210
Limitations of ratio analysis	210

	Creative accounting	210
	IFRS 8 *Operating Segments*	211
	Long answer questions	213
	Question 1 – DM	213
	Question 2 – STV	215
	Question 3 – ABC	216
	Question 4	218
	Question 5 – SBD	219
	Question 6 – SBD	222
	Answers to long answer questions	225
	Answer 1 – DM	225
	Summary	225
	Appendix: Ratio calculations	226
	Answer 2 – STV	226
	Appendix: Key ratios	228
	Answer 3 – ABC	229
	Answer 4	231
	Appendix	232
	Accounting ratios	232
	Answer 5	234
	Conclusion	235
	Appendix	235
	Answer 6 – SBD	236
	Conclusion	238
	Appendix	238
16	**Scope of External Reporting**	**239**
	The operating and financial review	241
	OFR: the ASB's reporting statement of best practice	241
	Advantages and drawbacks of the OFR	242
	Mangement commentary	243
	Social accounting and reporting	243
	Accounting for the impact of an entity on the environment around it	244
	Accounting for human resource issues	244
	Intellectual capital reporting	245
	Human asset accounting	245
	The global reporting initiative	245
	Medium answer questions	247
	Question 1	247
	Question 2	247
	Question 3	247
	Question 4	247
	Answers to medium questions	248
	Answer 1	248
	Answer 2	249
	Answer 3	250
	Answer 4	250
17	**International Issues in Financial Reporting**	**253**
	Progress towards convergence	255
	Short-term convergence projects	255
	Long-term projects	256

Remaining differences between US GAAP and IFRS	256
Barriers to harmonisation	257
Medium answer questions	258
Question 1	258
Question 2	258
Question 3	258
Question 4	259
Question 5 – Titanium plc	259
Answers to medium answer questions	260
Answer 1	260
Answer 2	261
The convergence project: progress to date	261
Answer 3	262
Answer 4	262
Answer 5 – Titanium plc	263

Exam Q & As   **265**

Syllabus Guidance, Learning Objectives and Verbs

A The syllabus

The syllabus for the CIMA Professional Chartered Management Accounting qualification 2010 comprises three learning pillars:

- Enterprise pillar
- Financial pillar
- Operational pillar

Subjects within each learning pillar of the qualification are set at three levels, Operational level, Managerial level and Strategic level. The pass mark is 50%.

For further syllabus information please see CIMA's website www.cimaglobal.com.

B Aims of the syllabus

The aims of the syllabus for the CIMA Professional Chartered Management Accounting qualification 2010 are:

- To provide for the Institute, an adequate basis for assuring society that those admitted to membership are competent to act as management accountants for entities, whether in manufacturing, commercial or service organisations, in the public or private sectors of the economy.
- To enable the Institute to examine whether prospective members have an adequate knowledge, understanding and mastery of the stated body of knowledge and skills.
- To enable the Institute to assess whether prospective members have completed initial professional development and acquired the necessary work-based practical experience and skills.

C Study weightings

Within a syllabus subject, a percentage weighting is shown against each section topic and is intended as a guide to the proportion of study time each topic requires.

It is essential that all topics in the syllabus are studied, since any single examination question may examine more than one topic, or carry a higher proportion of marks than the percentage study time suggested.

D Learning Outcomes

Each subject within the three learning pillars of the syllabus is divided into a number of broad syllabus topics. The topics contain one or more lead learning outcomes, related component learning outcomes and indicative knowledge content.

A learning outcome has two main purposes:

(a) to define the skill or ability that a well-prepared candidate should be able to exhibit in the examination;
(b) to demonstrate the approach likely to be taken by examiners in examination questions.

The learning outcomes are part of a hierarchy of learning objectives. The verbs used at the beginning of each learning outcome relate to a specific learning objective e.g.

> *Evaluate* performance using fixed and flexible budget reports

The verb '*evaluate*' indicates a high, level 5, learning objective. Because learning objectives are hierarchical, it is expected that at this level, students will have knowledge of fixed and flexible budget techniques, to be able to apply them and assess performance using relevant reports.

The following table lists the learning objectives and the verbs that appear in the syllabus learning outcomes and examination questions:

Learning Objective	Verbs Used	Definition
1 Knowledge		
What you are expected to know	List	Make a list of
	State	Express, fully or clearly, the details/facts of
	Define	Give the exact meaning of
2 Comprehension		
What you are expected to understand	Describe	Communicate the key features of
	Distinguish	Highlight the differences between
	Explain	Make clear or intelligible/state the meaning or purpose of
	Identify	Recognise, establish or select after consideration
	Illustrate	Use an example to describe or explain something
3 Application		
How you are expected to apply your knowledge	Apply	Put to practical use
	Calculate	Ascertain or reckon mathematically
	Demonstrate	Prove with certainty or exhibit by practical means
	Prepare	Make or get ready for use
	Reconcile	Make or prove consistent/compatible
	Solve	Find an answer to
	Tabulate	Arrange in a table

4 Analysis		
How you are expected to analyse the detail of what you have learned	Analyse	Examine in detail the structure of
	Categorise	Place into a defined class or division
	Compare and contrast	Show the similarities and/or differences between
	Construct	Build up or compile
	Discuss	Examine in detail by argument
	Interpret	Translate into intelligible or familiar terms
	Prioritise	Place in order of priority or sequence for action
	Produce	Create or bring into existence
5 Evaluation		
How you are expected to use your learning to evaluate, make decisions or recommendations	Advise	Counsel, inform or notify
	Evaluate	Appraise or assess the value of
	Recommend	Propose a course of action

Learning Outcomes, Syllabus Content and Examination Format

Paper F2 – Financial Management

Syllabus Overview

Paper F2 extends the scope of Paper F1 Financial Operations to more advanced topics in financial accounting (preparation of full consolidated financial statements and issues of principle in accounting standards dealing with more complex areas) and to developments in external reporting. With the advanced level of financial accounting and reporting achieved in this paper, the analysis and interpretation of accounts becomes more meaningful and this constitutes a substantial element.

Syllabus Structure

The syllabus comprises the following topics and study weightings:

A	Group Financial Statements	35%
B	Issues in Recognition and Measurement	20%
C	Analysis and Interpretation of Financial Accounts	35%
D	Developments in External Reporting	10%

Assessment Strategy

There will be a written examination paper of 3 hours, plus 20 minutes of pre-examination question paper reading time. The examination paper will have the following sections:

Section A – 50 marks
Five compulsory medium answer questions, each worth 10 marks. Short scenarios may be given, to which some or all questions relate.

Section B – 50 marks
One or two compulsory questions. Short scenarios may be given, to which questions relate.

Learning Outcomes and Indicative Syllabus Content

F2 – A. Group Financial Statements (35%)

Learning Outcomes
On completion of their studies students should be able to:

Lead	Component	Indicative Syllabus Content
1. Prepare the full consolidated statements of a single company and the consolidated statements of financial position and comprehensive income for a group (in relatively complex circumstances). (3)	(a) prepare a complete set of consolidated financial statements, as specified in IAS 1(revised), in a form suitable for publication for a group of companies; (b) identify and demonstrate the impact on group financial statements where: there is a non-controlling interest; the interest in a subsidiary or associate is acquired or disposed of part way through an accounting period (to include the effective date of acquisition and dividends out of pre-acquisition profits); shareholdings, or control, are acquired in stages; intra-group trading and other transactions occur; the value of goodwill is impaired; (c) explain and apply the concept of a joint venture and how their various types are accounted for.	• Relationships between investors and investees, meaning of control and circumstances in which a subsidiary is excluded from consolidation. (A) • The preparation of consolidated financial statements (including the group cash flow statement and statement of changes in equity) involving one or more subsidiaries, sub-subsidiaries and associates (IAS 1(revised), 7 & 27, IFRS 3). (A) • The treatment in consolidated financial statements of non-controlling interests, pre- and post-acquisition reserves, goodwill (including its impairment), fair value adjustments, intra-group transactions and dividends, piece-meal and mid-year acquisitions, and disposals to include sub-subsidiaries and mixed groups. (A, B) • The accounting treatment of associates and joint ventures (IAS 28 & 31) using the equity method and proportional consolidation method. (A, C)
2. Explain the principles of accounting for capital schemes and foreign exchange rate changes.	(a) explain the principles of accounting for a capital reconstruction scheme or a demerger; (b) explain foreign currency translation principles, including the difference between the closing rate/net investment method and the historical rate method; (c) explain the correct treatment for foreign loans financing foreign equity investments.	• Accounting for reorganisations and capital reconstruction schemes. (A) • Foreign currency translation (IAS 21), to include overseas transactions and investments in overseas subsidiaries. (B, C)

F2 – B. Issues in Recognition and Measurement (20%)

Learning Outcomes

On completion of their studies students should be able to:

Lead	Component	Indicative Syllabus Content
1. Discuss accounting principles and their relevance to accounting issues of contemporary interest. (4)	(a) discuss the problems of profit measurement and alternative approaches to asset valuations; (b) discuss measures to reduce distortion in financial statements when price levels change; (c) discuss the principle of substance over form applied to a range of transactions; (d) discuss the possible treatments of financial instruments in the issuer's accounts (i.e. liabilities versus equity, and the implications for finance costs); (e) identify discuss circumstances in which amortised cost, fair value and hedge accounting are appropriate for financial instruments, explain the principles of these accounting methods and discuss considerations in the determination of fair value; (f) discuss the recognition and valuation issues concerned with pension schemes (including the treatment of actuarial deficits and surpluses) and share-based payments.	• The problems of profit measurement and the effect of alternative approaches to asset valuation; current cost and current purchasing power bases and the real terms system; Financial Reporting in Hyperinflationary Economies (IAS 29). (A, B) • The principle of substance over form and its influence in dealing with transactions such as sale and repurchase agreements, consignment stock, debt factoring, securitised assets, loan transfers and public and private sector financial collaboration. (C) • Financial instruments classified as liabilities or shareholders funds and the allocation of finance costs over the term of the borrowing (IAS 32 & 39). (D, E) • The measurement, including methods of determining fair value, and disclosure of financial instruments (IAS 32 & 39, IFRS 7). (D, E) • Retirement benefits, including pension schemes – defined benefit schemes and defined contribution schemes, actuarial deficits and surpluses (IAS 19). (F) • Share-based payments (IFRS 2): types of transactions, measurement bases and accounting; determination of fair value. (F)

F2 – C. Analysis and Interpretation of Financial Accounts (35%)

Learning Outcomes
On completion of their studies students should be able to:

Lead	Component	Indicative Syllabus Content
1. Produce a ratio analysis from financial statements and supporting information, and explain its limitations. (4)	(a) calculate and interpret a full range of accounting ratios; (b) explain and discuss the limitations of accounting ratio analysis and analysis based on financial statements.	• Ratios in the areas of performance, profitability, financial adaptability, liquidity, activity, shareholder investment and financing, and their interpretation. (A) • Calculation of Earnings per Share under IAS 33, to include the effect of bonus issues, rights issues and convertible stock. (A) • The impact of financing structure, including use of leasing and short-term debt, on ratios, particularly gearing. (A) • Limitations of ratio analysis (e.g. comparability of businesses and accounting policies). (B)
2. Analyse and evaluate performance and position, and discuss the results. (4)	(a) analyse financial statements in the context of information provided in the accounts and corporate report; (b) evaluate performance and position based on analysis of financial statements; (c) prepare and discuss segmental analysis, with inter-firm and international comparisons taking account of possible aggressive or unusual accounting policies and pressures on ethical behaviour; (d) discuss the results of an analysis of financial statements and its limitations, in a concise report.	• Interpretation of financial statements via the analysis of the accounts and corporate reports. (A, B) • The identification of information required to assess financial performance and the extent to which financial statements fail to provide such information. (A, B, D) • Interpretation of financial obligations included in financial accounts (e.g. redeemable debt, earn-out arrangements, contingent liabilities). (A, B, D) • Segment analysis: inter-firm and international comparison (IFRS 8). (C) • The need to be aware of aggressive or unusual accounting policies ('creative accounting'), e.g. in the areas of cost capitalisation and revenue recognition, and threats to the ethics of accountants from pressure to report 'good results'. (C) • Reporting the results of analysis. (D)

F2 – D. Developments in External Reporting (10%)

Learning Outcomes On completion of their studies students should be able to:		Indicative Syllabus Content
Lead	**Component**	
1. Explain and discuss contemporary developments in financial and non-financial reporting. (4)	(a) discuss pressures for extending the scope and quality of external reports to include prospective and non-financial matters, and narrative reporting generally; (b) explain how information concerning the interaction of a business with society and the natural environment can be communicated in the published accounts; (c) identify and discuss social and environmental issues which are likely to be the most important to stakeholders in an organisation; (d) explain the process of measuring, recording and disclosing the effect of exchanges between a business and society – human resource accounting; (e) identify and discuss major differences between IFRS and US GAAP, and the measures designed to contribute towards their convergence.	• Increasing stakeholder demands for information that goes beyond historical financial information and frameworks for such reporting, including, as an example of national requirements and guidelines, the UK's Business Review and the Accounting Standard Board's best practice standard, RS1, and the Global Reporting Initiative. (A, B) • Environmental and social accounting issues, differentiating between externalities and costs internalised through, for example, capitalisation of environmental expenditure, recognition of future environmental costs by means of provisions, taxation and the costs of emissions permit trading schemes. (B, C) • Non-financial measures of social and environmental impact. (B, C) • Human resource accounting. (D) • Major differences between IFRS and US GAAP, and progress towards convergence. (E)

Accounting for Investments

Accounting for Investments

LEARNING OUTCOMES

After studying this chapter students should be able to:

- explain the relationships between investors and investees;
- explain the different levels of investment and the conditions required for significant influence, control and joint control;
- explain the circumstances in which a subsidiary is excluded from consolidation;
- explain and apply the principles of recognition of goodwill based on the fair value of assets at the date of acquisition.

Accounting for investments

The accounting in the investees' *individual accounts* for all investments and for *simple investments* (commonly less than 20% of the total equity share capital of the entity invested in), the accounting treatment will be determined by applying the recognition, measurement and disclosure requirements of the accounting standards that specifically deal with investments:

- IAS 32 *Financial instruments: presentation*
- IAS 39 *Financial instruments: recognition and measurement*
- IFRS 7 *Financial instruments: disclosure*

The provisions of these standards are dealt with in more detail in Chapter 10.

Investment in associates

If an investor holds, directly or indirectly, 20% of the voting rights of an entity then it is normally considered an associated entity and is accounted for in accordance with IAS 28 *Accounting for associates*. IAS 28 states that there is a presumption that the investor has significant influence over the entity, unless it can be clearly demonstrated that this is not the case.

The existence of significant influence by an investor is usually evidenced in one or more of the following ways:

- representation on the board of directors;
- participation in policy-making processes;
- material transactions between the investor and the entity;
- interchange of managerial personnel;
- provision of essential technical information.

The investment in the associate is equity accounted (given in greater detail in Chapter 4) and the investment shown in the statement of financial position will include the investing entity's share of the gains of the associate from the date the investment was made. The investing entity will show the share of realised and recognised gains it is entitled to by virtue of this investment rather than just the dividend received.

Investment in subsidiaries

The accounting standard that sets out the requirements for recognition of an entity as a subsidiary is IAS 27 *Consolidated and separate financial statements*. This standard was revised in January 2008, but its basic principles have been part of IFRS for many years.

First, some relevant definitions taken from the standard:

 A *parent* is an entity that has one or more subsidiaries.
A *subsidiary* is an entity, including an unincorporated entity such as a partnership, which is controlled by another entity (known as the parent).

The key concept in determining whether or not an investment constitutes a subsidiary is that of *control*.

Control is the power to govern the financial and operating policies of an entity so as to obtain benefit from its activities.

There is a presumption that control exists where the investor entity owns over half of the voting power of the other entity.

In most cases, control can be easily determined by looking at the percentage ownership of the ordinary share capital in the investee entity. However, there are exceptions. A parent/subsidiary relationship can exist even where the parent owns less than 50% of the voting power of the subsidiary since the key to the relationship is control. IAS 27 supplies the following instances:

When there is:

(a) power over more than half of the voting rights by virtue of an agreement with other investors;

(b) power to govern the financial and operating policies of the entity under a statute or agreement;
(c) power to appoint or remove the majority of the members of the board of directors or equivalent governing body and control of the entity is by that board or body; or
(d) power to cast the majority of votes at meetings of the board of directors or equivalent governing body and control of the entity is by that board or body.

> *In the Financial Management examination, questions may be set that test understanding of the principle of control, and it is possible that you will be required to explain these conditions in a written question.*

The requirement to prepare consolidated financial statements

Where a parent/subsidiary relationship exists, IAS 27 requires that the parent should prepare consolidated financial statements.

Exclusion from preparing consolidated accounts

A full set of financial statements in addition to those already prepared is, of course, quite an onerous requirement. IAS 27 includes some exemptions, as follows:

A parent need not present consolidated financial statements if and only if:

(a) the parent is itself a wholly owned subsidiary, or is a partially owned subsidiary of another entity and its other owners, including those not otherwise entitled to vote, have been informed about, and do not object to, the parent not presenting consolidated financial statements;
(b) the parent's debt or equity instruments are not traded in a public market (a domestic or foreign stock exchange or an over-the-counter market, including local and regional markets);
(c) the parent did not file, nor is it in the process of filing, its financial statements with a securities commission or other regulatory organisation for the purpose of issuing any class of instruments in a public market;
(d) the ultimate or any intermediate parent of the parent produces consolidated financial statements available for public use that comply with IFRS.

The only other exemption from the requirement to consolidate is in respect of an investment in subsidiary that has been acquired exclusively with the intention of reselling it. The provisions of **IFRS 5** *Non-current assets held for sale and discontinued operations* apply.

IFRS 3 *Business combinations*

IFRS 3 requires that entities should account for business combinations by applying the **acquisition method of accounting**. This involves recognising and measuring the identifiable assets acquired, the liabilities assumed and any non-controlling interest in the acquiree entity (the recognition and measurement of non-controlling interests will be explained in

Chapter 3). Measurement should be at fair value on the date of acquisition. Where 100% of the equity of a subsidiary is acquired, goodwill on acquisition is calculated as follows:

> π Goodwill on acquisition is the aggregate of:
> Consideration, measured at fair value
> LESS
> Net assets acquired (the fair value of identifiable assets acquired less liabilities assumed)

The goodwill arises at the date of acquisition and will not change unless impairment is identified, whereby it will be held net of impairment losses (which should be recognised in accordance with IAS 36 *Impairment of assets*).

Fair values in acquisition accounting

IFRS 3 requires that whenever a group entity is consolidated for the first time the purchase consideration and the group share of the net assets of the acquired entity are measured at fair values. The difference between these two figures is goodwill. The purpose of a fair-value exercise is to apportion the consideration given by the parent to purchase the shares in the newly acquired entity to the net assets of the newly acquired entity for consolidation purposes. Any difference between the fair value of the consideration given and the fair values of the net assets acquired is goodwill on acquisition.

Fair value is defined in IFRS 3 as the amount for which an asset could be exchanged or a liability settled between knowledgeable, willing parties in an arm's-length transaction.

Investment in joint ventures

Where an entity enters into an arrangement whereby control over an economic activity is shared between it and other parties, a joint venture arrangement exists. A joint venture can take a number of forms (covered in depth in Chapter 4), however one of those is where a new entity is formed and since that entity is under joint control it will be consolidated.

Again the method of accounting reflects the level of the investment made – it is greater than significant influence (associate) but not as much as full control (subsidiary). The joint venture will be consolidated but not using the full consolidation method. Instead IAS 31 *Interests in joint ventures* requires that joint ventures be proportionally consolidated. This will involve only aggregating the parent's share of the JV's assets, liabilities, revenues and expenses.

Medium answer questions

Question 1

You are the chief accountant of XYZ Group responsible for production of the consolidated financial statements. The CEO has asked you to explain why another set of financial statements is necessary and whether XYZ Group could avoid the preparation of consolidated financial statements as it appears to be an expensive and time-consuming process.

Requirements

(a) Explain the main principles of the consolidation of a subsidiary and why it is necessary.
(5 marks)

(b) Briefly explain the exclusions from the requirement to prepare consolidated accounts
(5 marks)
(Total = 10 marks)

Question 2

Entities will often invest in the equity of other businesses. The extent of the equity shareholding will determine how the investment should be accounted for. The accounting treatment applied for investments is intended to reflect the importance of the investment in the financial statements of the investee and how the future performance and financial position might be affected by these investments.

Requirement

Briefly describe the different levels of investment that an entity can make and how they would be accounted for.
(10 marks)

Answer to medium answer questions

Answer 1

(a) There are two main reasons for the preparation of consolidated financial statements:
   (i) Reflecting the substance of the relationship between parent and subsidiary recognising that although they may well be completely separate legal entities they are on single economic entity.
   (ii) A regulatory requirement. IAS 27 requires that the parent should prepare consolidated financial statements where a parent/subsidiary relationship exists.

IFRS 3 requires that entities should account for business combinations by applying the acquisition method of accounting. This involves consolidating the income statement and statement of financial position of the parent and subsidiary, in effect adding them together line by line to reflect the single economic entity.

Where the cost of the investment in the subsidiary exceeds the fair value of the identifiable net assets goodwill is created and recognised in the consolidated financial statement. The goodwill is reviewed for impairment where appropriate.

To reflect the single economic entity position all transactions and balances between group companies are eliminated before consolidation takes place (e.g. receivables and payables balances from intra-group trading).

(b) A parent need not present consolidated financial statements if and only if:
   (a) the parent is itself a wholly owned subsidiary, or is a partially owned subsidiary of another entity and its other owners, including those not otherwise entitled to vote, have been informed about, and do not object to, the parent not presenting consolidated financial statements;
   (b) the parent's debt or equity instruments are not traded in a public market (a domestic or foreign stock exchange or an over-the-counter market, including local and regional markets);
   (c) the parent did not file, nor is it in the process of filing, its financial statements with a securities commission or other regulatory organisation for the purpose of issuing any class of instruments in a public market;
   (d) the ultimate or any intermediate parent of the parent produces consolidated financial statements available for public use that comply with IFRS.
   (e) The only other exemption from the requirement to consolidate is in respect of an investment in subsidiary that has been acquired exclusively with the intention of reselling it.

Answer 2

Simple Investments

This would commonly be a holding of less than 20% of the total equity share capital of the entity invested in. There would generally be no significant influence or control and so the accounting treatment will be determined by applying the recognition, measurement and disclosure requirements of the accounting standards that specifically deal with investments:

- IAS 32 *Financial instruments: presentation*
- IAS 39 *Financial instruments: recognition and measurement*
- IFRS 7 *Financial instruments: disclosure*

Investment in associate

If an investor holds, directly or indirectly, 20% of the voting rights of an entity then it is normally considered an associated entity and is accounted for in accordance with IAS 28 *Accounting for associates*. IAS 28 states that there is a presumption that the investor has significant influence over the entity, unless it can be clearly demonstrated that this is not the case.

The key concept in the definition is 'significant influence'. IAS 28 explains that significant influence is the power to participate in the financial and operating policy decisions of the entity but is not control over those policies.

The impact of this level of investment on the investing entity is likely to be greater than that of a simple investment. There is greater exposure to the results of the associate and a decline in its value will have a greater negative impact on the statement of financial position of the investing entity.

Investment in subsidiary

It is often the case that businesses conduct part of their operations by making investments in other business entities. In order to fulfil the needs of investors and other users, additional information is likely to be required, and therefore the IASB has in issue several accounting standards setting out the principles and practices that must be followed.

IAS 27 *Consolidated and separate financial statements* – sets out the requirements for recognition of an entity as a subsidiary. The key concept in determining whether or not an investment constitutes a subsidiary is that of *control*. *Control* is the power to govern the financial and operating policies of an entity so as to obtain benefit from its activities. There is a presumption that control exists where the investor entity owns over half of the voting power of the other entity.

However, there are exceptions. A parent/subsidiary relationship can exist even where the parent owns less than 50% of the voting power of the subsidiary since the key to the relationship is control.

IFRS 3 requires that entities should account for business combinations by applying the **acquisition method of accounting**. This involves adding together the parent and subsidiary's financial statements.

Investment in joint ventures

Where an entity enters into an arrangement whereby control over an economic activity is shared between it and other parties, a joint venture arrangement exists. A joint venture can take a number of forms, however one of those is where a new entity is formed and since that entity is under joint control it will be consolidated.

Again the method of accounting reflects the level of the investment made – it is greater than significant influence (associate) but not as much as full control (subsidiary). The joint venture will be consolidated but not using the full consolidation method. Instead IAS 31 *Interests in joint ventures* requires that joint ventures be proportionally consolidated. This will involve only aggregating the parent's share of the JV's assets, liabilities, revenues and expenses.

This answer is comprehensive and not representative of what is required from an exam standard 10 mark question.

The Consolidated Statement of Financial Position

The Consolidated Statement of Financial Position

2

LEARNING OUTCOMES

After studying this chapter students should be able to:
- prepare a consolidated statement of financial position;
- account for non-controlling interests;
- account for the effects of intra-group balances and transactions in the consolidated statement of financial position;
- apply the concepts of fair value at the date of acquisition.

The basic mechanics of consolidation

- The investment in Subsidiary in the Parents's statement of financial position is replaced by adding the 100% Subsidiary's net assets to the Parents's line-by-line in the consolidated statement of financial position to show a single economic entity and total group resources.

Ownership and control

- Ownership – if the parent acquires less than 100% of the voting ordinary shares of the subsidiary then a non-controlling interest exists, i.e. that part of the Subsidiarys's net assets not owned by the Parent.
- Control – usually if the Parent owns > 50% of the voting ordinary shares of the Subsidiary.
- Other factors should be considered when establishing whether or not control has been obtained e.g. influence over the board or level of other investors influence

Key workings

- Group structure.
- Net assets at both the date of acquisition, needed for the calculation of goodwill, and at the statement of financial position date, needed for the calculation of the non-controlling interest.
- Goodwill – the difference between the cost of the investment and the fair value of the acquiree's identifiable assets, liabilities and contingent liabilities.
- Non-controlling interest – their share of the net assets at the statement of financial position date.
- Retained profits

	$
P (100%)	X
S (share of post-acquisition)	X
Goodwill impaired to date	(X)
	X

The treatment of goodwill and non-controlling interest (IFRS 3 revised)

Goodwill on consolidation – proportionate share of net assets approach

	$	$
Consideration		X
Net assets at date of acquisition:		
Share capital ($1 shares)	X	
Retained earnings	X	
	X	
Group share (%)		X
Goodwill		X

Non-controlling interest – proportionate share of net assets approach

	$
NCI share of subsidiary's net assets at statement of financial position date	X

Goodwill on consolidation – fair value approach

	$	$
Consideration		X
Net assets at date of acquisition:		
Share capital ($1 shares)	X	
Retained earnings	X	
	X	
Less NCI at fair value	(X)	
Group share		X
Goodwill		X

Non-controlling interest – fair value approach

	$
NCI share of subsidiary's net assets at statement of financial position date	X
NCI share of goodwill less impairment	X
	X

Treatment of unrealised profits

- Unrealised profits remaining at the statement of financial position date need to be eliminated as they do not represent a genuine profit to the group, which must be viewed as a single entity.
- Inventory – eliminate the unrealised profit against the reserves of the seller, to ensure the non-controlling interest bear their share, and from the inventory total in the consolidated statement of financial position.
- Property, plant and equipment – adjust the reserves of the seller and deduct from the property, plant and equipment total in the consolidated statement of financial position.
- The inflated transfer price of property, plant and equipment will also lead to excess depreciation being charged in the books of the recipient. This excess will need to be added back to the non-current asset carrying value and to the accumulated profits of the receiving entity.

Medium answer questions

Question 1 – DNT (Nov '08)

At its year end on 31 August 2008, DNT held investments in two subsidiaries, CM and BL. Details of the investments were as follows:

1. Several years ago DNT purchased 850,000 of CM's 1 million ordinary $1 shares when CM's retained earnings were $1,775,000 (there were no other reserves). At 31 August 2008, CM's retained earnings were $2,475,000.
2. On 31 May 2008, DNT purchased 175,000 of BL's 250,000 $1 ordinary shares. At 1 September 2007, BL's retained earnings were $650,000 (there were no other reserves). During the year ended 31 August 2008, BL made a loss after tax of $40,000. It can be assumed that BL's revenue and expenses accrue evenly throughout the year.

No adjustments to fair value of the subsidiaries' net assets were required at either of the acquisitions.

On 1 March 2007 CM sold an item of machinery to DNT for $75,000. The carrying amount of the item at the date of sale was $60,000, and CM recorded a profit on disposal of $15,000. The remaining useful life of the item at the date of sale was 2.5 years. The group depreciation policy in respect of machinery is the straight line basis with a proportionate charge in the years of acquisition and of disposal.

DNT's retained earnings balance at 31 August 2008 was $2,669,400.

Requirement

Calculate the amounts of consolidated retained earnings and non-controlling interest for inclusion in the DNT group's statement of financial position at 31 August 2008.

(10 marks)

Question 2 – AB (May '07)

On 1 November 2005, AB purchased 75% of the issued share capital of CD at a cost of $204,000. CD's issued share capital at the date of acquisition was $50,000 in $1 shares, and its retained earnings were $142,000 (there were no other reserves).

At that date, the carrying value of CD's property, plant and equipment was $150,000, split as follows:

	$
Land and buildings (including land at cost of $35,000)	105,000
Plant and equipment	45,000
	150,000

The fair value exercise carried out at acquisition showed that the fair value of CD's land and buildings was $125,000, of which $45,000 was attributable to land. The carrying value of plant and equipment approximated to fair value, and no adjustment was considered necessary. An intangible asset representing intellectual property rights, which had previously been unrecognised by CD, was recognised at a value of $10,000 at the date of acquisition. The directors decided that this asset should be amortised at the rate of 2.5% each month on the straight line basis. The intangible asset and the revaluation of land and buildings are recognised as consolidation adjustments only; they are not recognised in CD's own financial statements.

At 1 November 2005, the remaining useful life of CD's buildings was estimated at 21.5 years. Depreciation on buildings is calculated each month on the straight line basis.

A further revaluation exercise was conducted at 1 November 2006. The fair value of CD's land and buildings had increased by a further $20,000, half attributable to land and half to buildings. The estimate of the remaining useful life of the buildings was consistent with the estimate on 1 November 2005. AB's group policy is to adopt the revaluation model in respect of land and buildings.

At the group's year end on 30 April 2007, the retained earnings of AB were $365,000 and the retained earnings of CD were $183,000. During the financial year, CD had started supplying goods to AB at a mark-up of 17% on cost. AB's inventories at 30 April 2007 included $6,000 in respect of goods supplied by CD.

Since 1 November 2005, CD has been AB's only subsidiary. It is the group's policy to value non-controlling interests at fair value. It is the group's policy to value non-controlling interests at its proportionate share of the fair value of the subsidiary's identifiable net assets.

Requirement

Calculate the amounts to be included in the consolidated statement of financial position of the AB group at 30 April 2007 for:

(i) Goodwill (assuming that there has been no impairment of goodwill since acquisition);
(ii) Consolidated retained earnings;
(iii) Non-controlling interest.

Work to the nearest $. **(10 marks)**

Question 3 – ABC (Nov '05)

ABC is currently expanding its portfolio of equity interests in other entities. On 1 January 2005, it made a successful bid for a controlling interest in DEF, paying a combination of shares and cash in order to acquire 80% of DEF's 100,000 issued equity shares. The terms of the acquisition were as follows.

In exchange for each $1 ordinary share purchased, ABC issued one of its own $1 ordinary shares and paid $1.50 in cash. In addition to the consideration paid, ABC agreed to pay a further $1 per share on 1 January 2007, on condition that the profits of DEF for the year ended 31 May 2006 will exceed $6,000,000. ABC's directors consider that it is more likely than not that the additional consideration will be paid. The market value of a $1 share in ABC at 1 January 2005 was $3.50, rising to $3.60 at ABC's 31 May 2005 year end.

Total legal, administrative and share issue costs associated with the acquisition were $60,000: this figure included $20,000 paid to external legal and accounting advisers, an estimated $10,000 in respect of ABC's own administrative overhead and $30,000 in share issue costs.

The carrying value of DEF's net assets at 1 January 2005 was $594,000. Carrying value was regarded as a close approximation to fair value, except in respect of the following:

1. The carrying value of DEF's property, plant and equipment at 1 January 2005 was $460,000. Market value at that date was estimated at $530,000.
2. DEF had a contingent liability in respect of a major product warranty claim with a fair value of $100,000.
3. The cost of reorganising DEF's activities following acquisition was estimated at $75,000.
4. DEF's inventories included goods at an advanced stage of work-in-progress with a carrying value of $30,000. The sales value of these goods was estimated at $42,000 and further costs to completion at $6,000.
5. It is the group's policy to value non-controlling interests at fair value. The fair value of the NCI at the date of acquisition was $.

Requirement

Calculate goodwill on the acquisition of DEF, in accordance with the requirements of IFRS 3 *Business Combinations*, explaining your treatment of the legal, administrative, share issue and reorganisation costs. **(10 marks)**

Question 4 – XYZ

XYZ is a listed entity engaged in the provision of recruitment services, preparing financial statements to 30 June each year. Part of the directors' long term strategy is to identify opportunities for the takeover of other related businesses. In 1997, the directors decided to expand their operations into the second major city of the country in which XYZ operates by taking over an existing recruitment agency. On 1 July 1997, XYZ paid $14,700,000 for 80% of the shares in the successful AB Agency. At that date, AB had 1,000,000 shares in issue at a nominal value of $1 each, and accumulated profits were $2,850,000. At the date of acquisition, AB's brand name was valued by specialists at $2,900,000 and following the acquisition it has been recognised in the consolidated financial statements of XYZ. Apart from accumulated profits, AB has no other reserves.

AB has continued to be very successful and, therefore, XYZ's directors have been seeking further acquisitions. On 1 April 2003, XYZ gained control of a small on-line recruitment business, paying $39.60 per share to acquire 60,000 out of 100,000 issued shares in the CD Agency. The nominal value of each share in CD is $1. CD's accumulated profits at 1 July 2002 were $700,000; at 30 June 2003, they were $780,000. CD paid no dividends during the year ended 30 June 2003. CD's profits can be assumed to accrue evenly over time. Since acquisition CD has continued to produce growth in both profit and market share.

XYZ's directors estimate that the useful economic life of goodwill arising upon each of these acquisitions is ten years. Goodwill on the acquisition of AB had been impaired by

18 Exam Practice Kit: Financial Management

$6,510,000 and on the acquisition of CD by $372,000. XYZ has no investments other than those in AB and CD.

It is the group's policy to value non-controlling interests at its proportionate share of the fair value of the subsidiary's identifiable net assets.

Requirements

(a) Calculate the balance of goodwill on acquisition to be included in the consolidated financial statements of XYZ for the year ended 30 June 2004. **(6 marks)**

(b) Discuss the effects on the measurement of goodwill in XYZ's consolidated statement of financial position if the option to value non-controlling interest under IFRS3 – *Business combinations (Revised)*, had been adopted in respect of these acquisitions.
(4 marks)
(Total = 10 marks)

Question 5

Fair values in acquisition accounting is dealt with in IFRS 3 *Business Combinations*.

Requirements

(a) Explain why such an accounting standard was needed for fair values. **(4 marks)**

(b) Describe the main provisions of IFRS 3 as they relate to fair value. **(6 marks)**
(Total = 10 marks)

Answer to medium answer questions

Answer 1 – DNT (Nov '08)

Consolidated retained earnings

	$
DNT's retained earnings	2,669,400
Group share of CM's post-acquisition earnings (W2)	582,250
Consolidation adjustment: additional depreciation (W3)	9,000
Group share of BL's post-acquisition loss (W4)	(7,000)
	3,253,650

Non-controlling interest

	$
CM: share capital (1,000,000 − 850,000)	150,000
CM: retained earnings (2,475,000 − 15,000) × 15%	369,000
BL: share capital (250,000 − 175,000)	75,000
BL: retained earnings (650,000 − 40,000) × 30%	183,000
	777,000

Workings

1. DNT's holding in CM: 850,000/1,000,000 = 85%
   DNT's holding in BL: 175,000/250,000 = 70%

2. *Group share of CM's post-acquisition earnings*

	$
Post-acquisition earnings (2,475,000 – 1,775,000)	700,000
Less: profit on intra-group disposal	(15,000)
	685,000
85% of post acquisition earnings	582,250

3. *Additional depreciation adjustment*
   Required in respect of the additional depreciation on the item of machinery. 1.5 years (out of a remaining life of 2.5 years) have elapsed since the intra-group purchase.
   ($75,000 – 60,000) × 1.5/2.5   9,000

4. *Group share of BL's post-acquisition loss*
   3/12 × 40,000 × 70%   7,000

Answer 2 – AB (May '07)

(i) **Goodwill**

	$	$
Investment at cost		204,000
Less: Acquired		
Share capital	50,000	
Retained earnings	142,000	
Fair value adjustment – land and buildings	20,000	
Fair value adjustment – intangible assets	10,000	
	222,000	
Group share: $222,000 × 75%		(166,500)
Goodwill		37,500

(ii) **Consolidated retained earnings**

Workings:

1. *Post-acquisition amortisation of intangible:*
   (2.5% × 18 months) × $10,000 = $4,500

2. *Depreciation of building revaluation:*
   In respect of fair value adjustment at acquisition:
   (1.5/21.5 × $10,000) $698
   In respect of post-acquisition revaluation:
   (0.5/20.5 × $10,000) $244

3. *Provision for unrealised profit*
   $6,000 × 17/117 = $872

	$	$
AB's retained earnings		365,000
CD's post-acquisition retained earnings:		
As stated	183,000	
Less: Pre-acquisition	(142,000)	
	41,000	
Group share $41,000 × 75%		30,750
		395,750
Amortisation of intangible (W1)	4,500	
Depreciation of building (W2) ($698 + $244)	942	
Provision for unrealised profit (W3)	872	
	6,314	
Group share $6,314 × 75%		(4,735)
Consolidated retained earnings		391,015

(iii) Non-controlling interest

	$	$
Share of share capital 25% × $50,000		12,500
Share of retained earnings 25% × $183,000		45,750
Share of FV adjustments 25% × ($10,000 + $20,000 + $20,000)		12,500
Amortisation of intangible (W1)	4,500	
Depreciation of building (W2) ($698 + $244)	942	
Provision for unrealised profit (W3)	872	
	6,314	
Non-controlling interest share $6,314 × 25%		(1,579)
		69,171

Answer 3 – ABC (Nov '05)

Goodwill on the acquisition of DEF

		$
Cost of combination		480,000
Less: fair value of net assets acquired	456,000	
Less: fair value of NCI at acquisition	(90,000)	
		(366,000)
Goodwill		114,000

Cost of combination

	$
Shares at market value (80,000 × $3.50)	280,000
Cash (80,000 × $1.50)	120,000
Deferred consideration (80,000 × $1)	80,000
	480,000

Fair value of net assets acquired

		$
Carrying value of DEF's net assets		594,000
Adjustments:		
	Property, plant and equipment (530,000 − 460,000)	70,000
	Contingent liability	(100,000)
	Work-in-progress [(42,000 − 6,000) − 30,000]	6,000
		570,000

Treatment of costs

IFRS 3 *Business Combinations (revised)* no longer allows costs of acquisition to be included in the cost of the business combination.

- The legal and accountancy fees are directly attributable costs but should be expenses to the income statement.
- The administrative overheads are expensed to the income statement.
- The costs of the share issue are not directly attributable to the acquisition and therefore are not included. IFRS 3 explains that these are part of the issue transaction and should be deducted from the proceeds of the share issue.
- IFRS 3 also states that provisions for reorganisation costs can only be recognised as part of the net assets acquired if these were liabilities of the subsidiary at the date of acquisition. This is not the case here because the reorganisation results from the acquisition. Therefore the costs are not included in the fair value calculation.

Answer 4 – XYZ

(a) (W1) *Goodwill on AB acquisition (80% acquired)*

	$000
Acquisition at cost	14,700
Share capital acquired (1,000 × 80%)	(800)
Share of accumulated profits at date of acquisition	
(2,850 × 80%)	(2,280)
Share of brand (2,900 × 80%)	(2,320)
Goodwill on acquisition	9,300
At 30 June 2004	
Impairment	(6,510)
	2,790

(W2) *Goodwill on CD acquisition (60% acquired)*

	$000
Acquisition at cost ($39.60 × 60,000 shares)	2,376
Share capital acquired	(60)
Share of accumulated profits at date of acquisition	
(700 + [9/12 × {780 − 700}]) × 60%	(456)
Goodwill on acquisition	1,860
At 30 June 2004	
Impairment	(372)
	1,488

The balance of goodwill on acquisition to be included in XYZ's consolidated financial statements at 30 June 2004 is $4,278,000 ($2,790,000 + $1,488,000).

(b) In taking the option to value non-controlling interest at fair value rather than as a proportional share of net assets at the end of the year the value of non-controlling interest will include their share of goodwill on the acquisition of the respective subsidiary.

The fair value of an entity is actually the net assets and the goodwill inherent within a business. Inherent goodwill of course is not included in the statement of financial position at any time but when a parent acquires a subsidiary it gives a reliable value to that goodwill.

In the past only the parent or groups share of the goodwill has been included in the consolidated statement of financial position which many have argued is inconsistent with the consolidation process where 100% of subsidiary and parent assets and liabilities are consolidated line by line.

In adopting the fair value method, total goodwill is included in the consolidated statement of financial position and is then shared with the non-controlling interest in addition to their share of the net assets.

The result is a more consistent approach to the inclusion of goodwill with the consolidation process.

Answer 5

(a) The objective of IFRS3 is to ensure that when a business entity is acquired by another, all the assets and liabilities that existed in the acquired entity at the date of acquisition are recorded at fair values reflecting their condition at that date. The difference between the fair values of the net assets and the cost of the acquisition is recognised as goodwill or negative goodwill.

There is therefore a clear need for guidance as to which assets and liabilities would be permitted to be included in a fair value exercise and how these would be valued. This should help to ensure consistency and comparability in the calculations of fair values.

(b) The main relevant provisions of IFRS3 are as follows:
1. The assets and liabilities of a subsidiary acquires should be valued at their fair values. However, only those assets/liabilities that existed at the date of acquisition should be recognised. No attempt should be made to provide for any liability which would result from the acquirer's future intentions for the acquiree.
2. The acquiree should be valued using the acquirer's accounting policies.
3. The fair value of liabilities should also exclude provisions for future operating losses and reorganisation/restructuring costs.
4. The method of calculation of assets should be as follows:

    Non-monetary assets   at lower of replacement cost or recoverable amount reflecting the current condition of the assets.

    Monetary assets   should be based on amounts expected to be received with the possibility of discounting long-term assets to their present value.

5. The fair value of the purchase consideration should represent the actual cash paid plus the present value of any deferred consideration plus the market value of the shares taken up on acquisition.

3

The Consolidated Statements of Comprehensive Income and Changes in Equity

The Consolidated Statements of Comprehensive Income and Changes in Equity

3

LEARNING OUTCOMES

After studying this chapter students should be able to:
- prepare a consolidated income statement and a consolidated statement of comprehensive income;
- prepare a consolidated statement of changes in equity;
- account for intra-group transactions;
- apply the concepts of fair value at the point of acquisition.

Intra-group trading and unrealised profits

- Intra-group trading must be eliminated in full.
- When goods sold intra-group remain within the inventory of the recipient group company, at the period end any unrealised profit must be eliminated from the books of the selling company.
- When there is a provision for unrealised profit brought forward from the previous period the adjustment to the current income statement will represent the movement on the provision.

Intra-group asset transfers

- Again consistency is needed with the statement of financial position.
- Eliminate any profit or loss arising on the transfer of the asset, and adjust the depreciation charge to reflect a figure based on the original cost of the asset.

The impact of fair value adjustments and changes in accounting policy

- At the date of acquisition the assets of S are revised to their fair values – this has a knock-on effect for depreciation charges.
- Realigning the accounting policies of S to be consistent with those of P will frequently have a knock-on effect for the income statement.

The statement of comprehensive income

Statement of Comprehensive Income

	$
Revenue	X
Cost of sales	(X)
Gross profit	X
Other income	X
Distribution costs	X
Administrative expenses	X
Other expenses	X
Finance costs	X
Share of profit of associates	X
Profit before tax	X
Income tax expense	X
PROFIT FOR THE YEAR	X
Other comprehensive income:	
Exchange differences on translating foreign operations	X
Available-for-sale financial assets	X
Cash flow hedges	X
Gains on property revaluation	X
Actuarial gains/(losses) on defined benefit pension plans	X
Share of other comprehensive income of associates	X
Income tax relating to components of other comprehensive income	X
Other comprehensive income for the year, net of tax	X
TOTAL COMPREHENSIVE INCOME FOR THE YEAR	X
Profit attributable to:	
Owners of the parent	X
Non-controlling interests	X
	X
Total comprehensive income attributable to:	
Owners of the parent	X
Non-controlling interests	X
	X

The statement of changes in equity

Summarised consolidated statement of changes in equity for the year ended.......

	Attributable to equity holders of parent $000	Non-controlling interest $000	Total $000
Balance at start	X	X	X
Profit for the period:			
Parent	X	X	X
Minority			
Dividends:			
Parent	X		
Non-controlling interest		X	X
Balance at close	X	X	X

Medium answer questions

Question 1 (May '08)

Summarised statements of changes in equity for the year ended 31 March 2008 for AAY and its only subsidiary, BBZ, are shown below:

	AAY $000	BBZ $000
Balance at 1 April 2007	662,300	143,700
Profit for the period	81,700	22,000
Dividends	(18,000)	(6,000)
Balance at 31 March 2008	726,000	159,700

Notes:

1. AAY acquired 80% of the issued share capital of BBZ on 1 April 2005, when BBZ's total equity was $107.7 million. The first dividend BBZ has paid since acquisition is the amount of $6 million shown in the summarised statement above. The profit for the period of $81,700 in AAY's summarised statement of changes in equity above does **not** include its share of the dividend paid by BBZ.

2. The only consolidation adjustment required is in respect of intra-group trading. BBZ regularly supplies goods to AAY. The amount included in the inventory of AAY in respect of goods purchased from BBZ at the beginning and end of the accounting period was as follows:

        1 April 2007 $2 million
        31 March 2008 $3 million

BBZ earns a profit on intra-group sales of 25% on cost.

Requirement

Prepare a summarised consolidated statement of changes in equity for the AAY Group for the year ended 31 March 2008.

(Total = 10 marks)

Question 2 (Nov '07 Revised)

On 1 September 2006, BLT held 60% of the ordinary share capital of its only subsidiary CMU. The consolidated equity of the group at that date was $576,600, of which $127,000 was attributable to the non-controlling interest.

On 28 February 2007, exactly halfway through the financial year, BLT bought a further 20% of the ordinary share capital of CMU. In the year ended 31 August 2007 BLT's profits for the period were $98,970 and CMU's were $30,000. BLT paid a dividend of $40,000 on 1 July 2007. There were no other movements in equity. It can be assumed that profits accrue evenly throughout the year.

Requirements

(a) Prepare a consolidated statement of changes in equity for the BLT group for the year ended 31 August 2007.

(5 marks)

(b) Discuss the requirement to produce a statement of comprehensive income and statement of changes in equity and the distinction between the items that should be included in each.

(5 marks)
(Total = 10 marks)

Question 3 (May '05 Revised)

RW holds 80% of the 1,000,000 ordinary shares of its subsidiary, SX. Summarised income statements of both entities for the year ended 31 December 2004 are shown below:

	RW $000	SX $000
Revenue	6,000	2,500
Cost of sales	(3,000)	(1,200)
Gross profit	3,000	1,300
Operating costs	(1,500)	(500)
Profit before tax	1,500	800
Income tax expense	(300)	(250)
Profit for the period	1,200	550

RW purchased 800,000 of SX's $1 shares in 2003 for $3.2 million, when SX's reserves were $2.4 million. It is group policy to value non-controlling interests at its proportionate share of the fair value of the subsidiary's identifiable net assets. Goodwill has been impaired by 10%.

RW has invested in available for sale investments which have the following values:

	$000
31 December 2003	1,200
31 December 2004	1,000

RW has a defined benefit pension scheme in operation for its employees. It is group policy to recognise actuarial gains and losses immediately. The actuarial gain for the year ended 31 December 2004 was $250,000.

Requirement

Prepare the summarised consolidated statement of comprehensive income statement for RW for the year ended 31 December 2004.

(Total = 10 Marks)

✓ Answer to medium answer questions

Answer 1 (May '08)

AAY Group: Summarised consolidated statement of changes in equity for the year ended 31 March 2008

	Attributable to equity holders of parent $000	Non-controlling interest $000	Total $000
Balance at 1 April 2007 (W1)	345,390	14,330	359,720
Profit for the period:			
Parent (40,850 + 8,720 (W3))	49,570		
NCI (W3)		4,360	51,750
Dividends:			
Parent	(9,000)		
NCI (6,000 × 20%)		(600)	(9,600)
Balance at 31 March 2008	385,960	15,910	401,870

Workings:

1. *Opening balances*

			Equity holders of parent $000	NCI $000
AAY			331,150	
BBZ Opening balance		71,850		
Less: PUP (W2)		(200)		
		7,650		
Attributable to NCI: 20% × 71,650				14,165
Attributable to parent:				
Post-acquisition: (71,650 − 53,850) × 80%			14,240	
Total			345,390	14,330

2. *Unrealised profit*

		$000
PUP on opening inventory:	25/125 × $1 m	200
PUP on closing inventory:	25/125 × $1.5 m	300

Movement in the year: increase in provision required of 300 − 200 = 100.

3. BBZ's profit for the period

	$000
Profit in own financial statements	11,000
Less: increase in provision for unrealised profit	(100)
Profit after consolidation adjustment	10,900
Attributable to:	
Equity holders of parent: 80% × 10,900	8,720
Non-controlling interest: 20% × 10,900	2,180

Answer 2 (Nov '07 Revised)

(a) **BLT Group: Statement of changes in equity for the year ended 31 August 2007**

	Attributable to equity holders of parent $	Non-controlling interest $	Total $
Brought forward	449,600	127,000	576,600
Profit for the period (W1)	119,970	9,000	128,970
Transfer in respect of shares purchased by BLT (W2)	66,500	(66,500)	
Dividend	(40,000)		(40,000)
Carried forward	596,070	69,500	665,570

(W1) Profit shares
NCI share of profit
$30,000 × 6/12 × 40% 6,000
$30,000 × 6/12 × 20% 3,000
                      9,000
Group share
$98,970 + ($30,000 − 9,000) = $119,970

(W2) Transfer in respect of share purchase
Value of non-controlling interest at date of transfer: $127,000 + 6,000 = $133,000
50% of shareholding transferred: $133,000/2 = $66,500

(b) **Presentation of the income statement and statement of changes in equity (SOCIE)**

Prior to the issue of the revised IAS 1, entities were required to present an income statement that included items of income and expense recognised in profit or loss. Any other items of income and expenditure, i.e. those not recognised in profit or loss, were to be presented in the SOCIE, together with owner changes in equity (such as increases in share capital and dividends paid).

IAS 1 (revised) draws a distinction between owner changes in equity and all other items of income and expense (which are known as 'comprehensive income'). IAS 1 (revised) requires that all non-owner changes in equity should be presented either in:

- A single statement of comprehensive income

Or
- Two statements, one being an income statement and the other a statement of comprehensive income.

The SOCIE is to be used exclusively for presenting changes in owner equity.

The lower part of the single statement or the statement of comprehensive income are used to present items of income or expense that IFRS require to be recognised outside profit or loss such as translation differences relating to foreign operations and gains or losses on available-for-sale investments.

Answer 3 (May '05 Revised)

RW: Consolidated income statement for the year ending 31 December 2004

	$000
Revenue [6,000 + 2,500]	8,500
Cost of sales [3,000 + 1,200]	(4,200)
Gross profit	4,300
Operating costs [1,500 + 500 + 48]	(2,048)
Profit before tax	2,252
Income tax [300 + 250]	(550)
Profit for the period	1,702
Other comprehensive income:	
Loss on available for sale investments (1,200−1,000)	(200)
Actuarial gains on defined benefit pension	250
Total comprehensive income	1,752
Attributable to:	
Equity holders of the parent	1,587
Non-controlling interest	165
	1,752

Workings

1. *Goodwill on consolidation*

	$000
Purchase consideration	3,200
Share of net assets acquired [1,000 + 2,400] × 80%	(2,720)
Goodwill	480
Less impairment (10% × 480)	(48)

2. *Non-controlling interest*

	$000
To 1 July 2004: [550/2] × 20%	55
1 July – 31 December 2004: [550/2] × 40%	110
	165

4

Associates and Joint Ventures

Associates and Joint Ventures

4

LEARNING OUTCOMES

After studying this chapter students should be able to:

► explain the conditions required to be an associate of another entity and the accounting treatment for associates;

► explain the conditions required to account for an operation as a joint venture, the different forms the venture can take, and how they should be accounted for;

► prepare consolidated financial statements including an associate;

► prepare consolidated financial statements including a joint venture.

IAS 28 Accounting for Associates – the basics

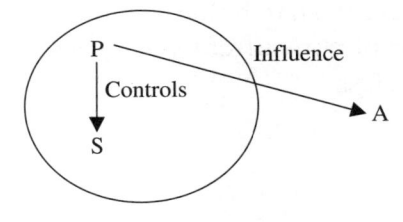

The IAS 28 defines an associate as:

> An entity, including an unincorporated entity such as a partnership, over which the investor has significant influence and that is neither a subsidiary nor an interest in a joint venture.

The key concept in the definition is 'significant influence'. IAS 28 says that significant influence is the power to participate in the financial and operating policy decisions of the entity but is not control over those policies. The existence of significant influence by an investor is usually evidenced in one or more of the following ways:

- representation on the board of directors;
- participation in policy-making processes;
- material transactions between the investor and the entity;

- interchange of managerial personnel;
- provision of essential technical information.

If an investor holds, directly or indirectly, 20 per cent of the voting rights of an entity, IAS 28 states that there is a presumption that the investor has significant influence over the entity, unless it can be clearly demonstrated that this is not the case.

Equity accounting

IAS 28 requires that associates are accounted for using equity accounting. This is not a method of consolidation, the assets and liabilities of the associate are not aggregated on a line-by-line basis in the group accounts. Instead, only selected items are included in the consolidated financial statement.

The consolidated statement of comprehensive income:

- The investor will include **its share of the results of the associate for the period** in its consolidated statement of comprehensive income (or income statement depending on how the statements have been prepared).
- The share of results is based on the associate's profit after tax, but is included in the consolidated profit before tax in the group accounts.
- The investor will also include its share of any other comprehensive income of the associate in the 'other comprehensive income' section of the income statement.
The consolidated statement of financial position.
- The investor will include one figure within non-current assets in the consolidated statement of financial position, entitled **Investment in associat**e. The balance to be included under this heading is calculated as follows:

    Investment at cost; plus
    Share of profits or losses since acquisition; plus
    Share of any other changes to shareholders' funds e.g., other comprehensive income (maybe from revaluation of non-current assets); less
    Impairment of goodwill; less
    Dividends received.

Goodwill on acquisition

Note that the starting point for this calculation is cost of investment. This means the value of any goodwill on acquisition is already included. Goodwill is part of the value of investment. It may have to be calculated if any impairment is to be recorded, however it will not appear under the heading of goodwill in the group statement of financial position. The impairment will simply be deducted from the value of the investment.

Equity accounting – intra-group issues

- In the consolidated statement of financial position intercompany accounts are not eliminated, as the associate is not part of the single entity.
- Consequently the group can have receivables and payables with the associate, and sell to or make purchases from the associate.

- However, the ability of the P to influence the associate dictates that unrealised profits on inventory or non-current assets must be eliminated.
- Unlike a subsidiary only the group's share of the unrealised profit is adjusted as the statement of financial position does not reflect 100% of the associates net assets.
- The consolidated statement of financial position will disclose dividends receivable from associates separately as a current asset.
- The consolidated income statement must NOT include dividends from the associate as these will effectively be paid from the parent's share of the associate's profits. The inclusion of both profits and dividends would be double counting.

IAS 31 Interests in Joint ventures

The IAS states that a joint venture is:

> A contractual arrangement whereby two or more parties undertake an economic activity that is subject to joint control.

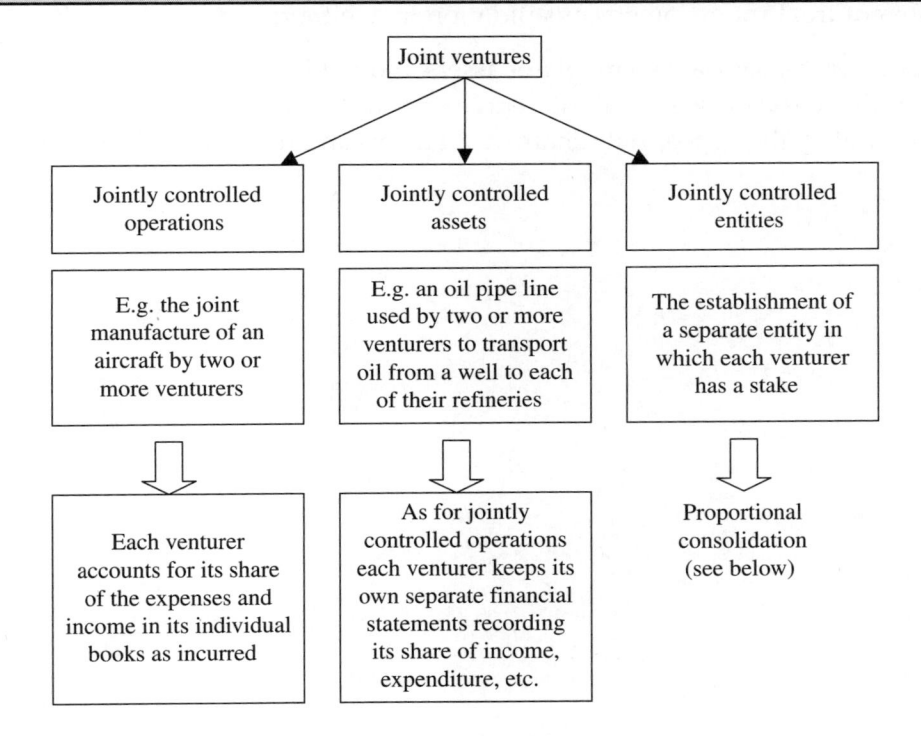

```
                        Joint ventures
           ┌─────────────────┼─────────────────┐
    Jointly controlled  Jointly controlled  Jointly controlled
       operations           assets              entities

    E.g. the joint      E.g. an oil pipe line   The establishment of
    manufacture of an   used by two or more     a separate entity in
    aircraft by two or  venturers to transport  which each venturer
    more venturers      oil from a well to each has a stake
                        of their refineries

    Each venturer       As for jointly          Proportional
    accounts for its    controlled operations   consolidation
    share of the        each venturer keeps     (see below)
    expenses and        its own separate
    income in its       financial statements
    individual books    recording its share
    as incurred         of income,
                        expenditure, etc.
```

Accounting for jointly controlled operations

Some joint ventures do not involve the establishment of an entity that is separate from the venturers themselves, but rather the joint uses of the assets and other resources of the individual venturer. In such situations the *individual* financial statements of each entity will show:

- the assets that it controls and the liabilities that it incurs;
- the expenses that it incurs and its share of the income that it earns from the sale of goods or services by the joint venture.

No further adjustments will be required in the consolidated financial statements.

Accounting for jointly controlled assets

Accounting is very similar to jointly controlled operations in that, both in the separate financial statements of the venturers and in their consolidated financial statements each venturer will recognise:

- its share of the jointly controlled assets and jointly incurred liabilities, classified according to their nature;
- any liabilities that it has incurred;
- its share of the income generated by the venture, less any joint expenses of the venture;
- any expenses that it has incurred itself in respect of its interest in the joint venture.

Accounting for jointly controlled entities

The recommended treatment for such joint ventures in the consolidated financial statements is that the venturer should use **proportionate consolidation**. IAS 31 states that this best represents the economic reality of the arrangement, which is that the venturer has control over its share of future economic benefits through its shares of the assets and liabilities of the joint venture. Proportionate consolidation may either:

- aggregate the appropriate share of net assets and net income with those of the group on a line-by-line basis (as we did in our earlier example); or
- show separately the appropriate share of net assets and net income on a line-by-line basis.

Medium answer questions

Question 1 – ST (May '06)

The income statements of ST and two entities in which it holds investments are shown below for the year ended 31 January 2006:

	ST $000	UV $000	WX $000
Revenue	1,800	1,400	600
Cost of sales	(1,200)	(850)	(450)
Gross profit	600	550	150
Operating expenses	(450)	(375)	(74)
Profit from operations	150	175	76
Finance cost	(16)	(12)	–
Interest income	6	–	–
Profit before tax	140	163	76
Income tax expense	(45)	(53)	(26)
Profit for the period	95	110	50

Notes

1. *investments by ST*
   Several years ago ST acquired 70% of the issued ordinary share capital of UV. On 1 February 2005, ST acquired 50% of the issued share capital of WX, an entity set up under a contractual arrangement as a joint venture between ST and one of its suppliers. The directors of ST have decided to adopt a policy of proportionate consolidation wherever appropriate and permitted by International Financial Reporting Standards.

2. *UV's borrowings*
   During the financial year ended 31 January 2006, UV paid the full amount of interest due on its 6% debenture loan of $200,000. ST invested $100,000 in the debenture when it was issued three years ago.

3. *Intra-group trading*
   During the year, WX sold goods to ST for $20,000. Half of the goods remained in ST's inventories at 31 January 2006. WX's gross profit margin on the sale was 20%.

Requirement

Prepare the consolidated income statement of the ST group for the year ended 31 January 2006.

(Total = 10 marks)

40 Exam Practice Kit: Financial Management

Answers to medium answer questions

Answer 1 – ST (May '06)

ST Group: consolidated income statement for the year ended 31 January 2006

	$000
Revenue (1,800 + 1,400 + [{600 − 20}/2]	3,490
Cost of sales (1,200 − [20/2] + 850 + [450/2] + 1 [W1])	(2,266)
Gross profit	1,224
Operating expenses (450 + 375 + [74/2])	(862)
Profit from operations	362
Finance cost (16 + [12 − 6])	(22)
Profit before tax	340
Income tax expense (45 + 53 + [26/2])	(111)
Profit for the period	229

	$000
Attributable to:	
Equity holders of the parent	196
Non-controlling interest (110 [profit of UV for the period] × 30%)	33
	229

(W1) Provision for unrealised profit
$10,000 × 20% = $2,000.
50% of this is treated as realised, and the remainder ($1,000) as unrealised.

Long answer questions

Question 1 – AT (May '07)

AT holds investments in three other entities. The draft income statements for the four entities for the year ended 31 March 2007 are as follows:

	AT $000	BU $000	CV $000	DW $000
Revenue	2,450	1,200	675	840
Cost of sales	(1,862)	(870)	(432)	(580)
Gross profit	588	330	243	260
Distribution costs	(94)	(22)	(77)	(18)
Administrative expenses	(280)	(165)	(120)	(126)
Interest received	–	2	–	–
Finance costs	(26)	–	–	–
Profit before tax	188	145	46	116
Income tax	(40)	(50)	(12)	(37)
Profit for the period	148	95	34	79

Notes

1. *Investments in BU, CV and DW*
   Several years ago AT purchased 75% of the ordinary shares of BU. On 30 September 2006 it purchased a further 5% of BU's ordinary shares. In 2003 AT, together with two other investor entities, set up CV. Each of the three investors owns one-third of the ordinary shares in CV. All managerial decisions relating to CV are made jointly by the three investor entities. On 1 January 2007, AT purchased 35% of the ordinary shares in DW. AT exerts significant influence over the management of DW, but does not control the entity.

2. *Intra-group trading*
   BU supplies inventories to AT, earning a gross profit margin of 20% on such sales. During the financial year ended 31 March 2007, BU supplied a total of $80,000 at selling price to AT. Of these items, 25% remained in AT's inventories at the year end. AT supplies a range of administrative services to BU, at cost. $12,000 is included in BU's administrative expenses, and in AT's revenue, in respect of such services supplied during the year ended 31 March 2007.

3. The group has a policy of adopting proportional consolidation wherever permitted by International Financial Reporting Standards.

4. Revenue and profits accrue evenly throughout the year, unless otherwise stated.

5. *Finance costs*
   The finance costs in AT's income statement are in respect of short-term bank borrowings only. Finance costs in respect of its long-term borrowings have not yet been included, and an appropriate adjustment must be made. On 1 April 2004, AT issued bonds at par in the amount of $1,000,000. Issue costs were $50,000. The bonds carry a coupon rate of interest

of 5% each year, payable on the last day of the financial year. The interest actually paid on 31 March 2007 has been debited to a suspense account, which is included under current assets in AT's draft statement of financial position. The bonds will be repaid on 31 March 2009 at a premium of $162,000.

The effective interest rate associated with the bonds is 9%, and the liability is measured, in accordance with IAS 39 *Financial Instruments: Recognition and Measurement*, at amortised cost.

6. *Financial asset*

   From time to time BU uses available cash surpluses to make short-term investments in financial assets. Such assets are 'held-for-trading' and are invariably sold within a few months. At 31 March 2007, BU held 4,000 shares in a listed entity, EX. The shares had been purchased on 20 January 2007 at a price of 1332¢ per share. At 31 March 2007, the market price per share was 1227¢. No adjustment has been made to the draft income statement above in respect of this financial asset.

Requirement

Prepare the consolidated income statement for the AT group for the financial year ended 31 March 2007. Show full workings.

(Total = 25 marks)

Note: 8 marks are available for the adjustments in respect of notes 5 and 6.

Work to nearest $100. For the purposes of this question it is not necessary to make any adjustments to income tax.

Question 2 – AD (Nov '06)

The statements of financial position of three entities, AD, BE and CF at 30 June 2006, the year end of all three entities, are shown below:

	AD		BE		CF	
	$000	$000	$000	$000	$000	$000
ASSETS						
Non-current assets						
Property, plant and equipment	1,900		680		174	
Financial assets						
Investments in equity						
Shares	880		104		–	
Other (see note 3)	980		–		–	
		3,760		784		174
Current assets						
Inventories	223		127		60	
Trade receivables	204		93		72	
Other financial asset (see note 4)	25		–		–	
Cash	72		28		12	
		524		248		144
		4,284		1,032		318

EQUITY AND LIABILITIES
Equity
Called up share capital

($1 shares)	1,000		300		100
Reserves	2,300		557		122
		3,300		857		222
Non-current liabilities		600		–		–
Current liabilities					
Trade payables	247		113		84
Income tax	137		62		12
		384		175		96
		4,284		1,032		318

Notes

1. *Investment by AD in BE*

   AD acquired 80% of the ordinary shares of BE on 1 July 2003 for $880,000 when BE's reserves were $350,000. Goodwill on acquisition continues to be unimpaired. It is the group's policy to value non-controlling interests at fair value. The fair value of the NCI at the date of acquisition was $.

2. *Investment by AD in CF*

   AD acquired 40% of the ordinary shares of CF on 1 January 2006 for $104,000. AD appoints one of CF's directors and, since the acquisition, has been able to exert significant influence over CF's activities. CF's reserves at the date of acquisition were $102,000.

3. *Non-current financial asset*

   AD's other non-current financial asset is a debenture with a fixed interest rate of 5%. AD invested $1 million in the debenture at par on its issue date, 1 July 2004. The debenture is redeemable at a premium on 30 June 2008; the applicable effective interest rate over the life of the debenture is 8%. The full annual interest amount was received and recorded by AD in June 2005 and June 2006, and the appropriate finance charge was recognised in the financial year ended 30 June 2005. However, no finance charge has yet been calculated or recognised in respect of the financial year ended 30 June 2006.

4. *Current financial asset*

   The current financial asset of $25,000 in AD represents a holding of shares in a major listed company. AD maintains a portfolio of shares held for trading. At 30 June 2006, the only holding in the portfolio was 4,000 shares in DG, a major listed company with 2.4 million ordinary shares in issue. The investment was recognised on its date of purchase, 13 May 2006, at a cost of 625¢ per share. At 30 June 2006, the fair value of the shares had risen to 670¢ per share.

5. *Intra-group trading*

   BE supplies goods to both AD and CF. On 30 June 2006, CF held inventories at a cost of $10,000 that had been supplied to it by BE. BE's profit margin on the selling price of these goods is 30%.

   On 30 June 2006, AD's inventories included no items supplied by BE. However, BE's receivables on 30 June 2006 included $5,000 in respect of an intra-group balance relating to the supply of goods to AD. No equivalent balance was included in AD's payables because it had made a payment of $5,000 on 27 June 2006, which was not received and recorded by BE until after the year end.

Requirements

(a) Explain the accounting treatment in the statement of financial position and income statement for the financial assets described in notes 3 and 4 above, as required by IAS 39 *Financial Instruments: Recognition and Measurement*.

(5 marks)

(b) Prepare the consolidated statement of financial position for the AD Group at 30 June 2006.

(20 marks)

(Total = 25 marks)

Question 3 – AJ (May '05)

AJ is a law stationery business. In 20X2 the majority of the entity's board of directors were replaced. The new board decided to adopt a policy of expansion through acquisition. The statement of financial positions as at 31 March 20X5 of AJ and of two entities in which it holds significant investments are shown below:

	AJ		BK		CL	
	$'000	$'000	$'000	$'000	$'000	$'000
ASSETS						
Non-current assets						
Property, plant and equipment	12,500		4,700		4,500	
Investments	18,000		–		1,300	
		30,500		4,700		5,800
Current assets						
Inventories	7,200		8,000		–	
Trade receivables	6,300		4,300		3,100	
Financial assets	–		–		2,000	
Cash	800		–		900	
		14,300		12,300		6,000
		44,800		17,000		11,800
EQUITY AND LIABILITIES						
Equity						
Called up share capital ($1 shares)		10,000		5,000		2,500
Retained earnings		14,000		1,000		4,300
		24,000		6,000		6,800
Non-current liabilities						
Loan notes		10,000		3,000		–
Current liabilities						
Trade payables	8,900		6,700		4,000	
Tax	1,300		100		600	
Short-term borrowings	600		1,200		400	
		10,800		8,000		5,000
		44,800		17,000		11,800

Notes

1. *Investment by AJ in BK*

   On 1 April 20X2, AJ purchased $2 million loan notes in BK at par.

   On 1 April 20X3, AJ purchased 4 million of the ordinary shares in BK for $7.5 million in cash, when BK's retained earnings were $1.5 million.

   At the date of acquisition of the shares, BK's property, plant and equipment included land recorded at cost of $920,000. At the date of acquisition the land was valued at $1,115,000. No other adjustments in respect of fair value were required to BK's assets and liabilities upon acquisition. BK has not recorded the revaluation in its own accounting records.

2. *Investment by AJ in CL*

   On 1 October 20X4, AJ acquired 1 million shares in CL, a book distributor, when the retained earnings of CL were $3.9 million. The purchase consideration was $4.4 million. Since the acquisition, AJ has the right to appoint one of the five directors of CL. The remaining shares in CL are owned principally by three other investors.

   No fair value adjustments were required in respect of CL's assets or liabilities upon acquisition.

3. *Goodwill on consolidation*

   Since acquiring its investment in BK, AJ has adopted the requirements of IFRS 3 *Business Combinations* in respect of goodwill on consolidation. During March 20X5, it has conducted an impairment review of goodwill. As a result the value of goodwill on consolidation in respect of BK is now $1.7 million.

4. *Intra-group trading*

   BK supplies legal books to AJ. On 31 March 20X5, AJ's inventories included books purchased at a total cost of $1 million from BK. BK's mark-up on books is 25%.

5. It is the group's policy to value non-controlling interests at its proportionate share of the fair value of the subsidiary's identifiable net assets.

Requirements

(a) Explain, with reasons, how the investments in BK and CL will be treated in the consolidated financial statements of the AJ group.

(5 marks)

(b) Prepare the consolidated statement of financial position for the AJ group at 31 March 20X5.

(20 marks)

(Total = 25 marks)

Answers to long answer questions

Answer 1 – AT (May '07)

AT Group: consolidated income statement for the year ended 31 March 2007

	$000	Ref to working
Revenue	3,783	(1)
Cost of sales	(2,800)	(3)
Gross profit	983	
Distribution costs	(141.7)	(4)
Administrative expenses	(473)	(4)
Interest received	2	
Loss on investment in financial asset	(4.2)	(5)
Finance costs	(118.2)	(6)
Share of profit of associate	6.9	(7)
Profit before tax	254.8	
Income tax expense	(94)	(8)
Profit for the period	160.8	

Attributable to:

	$000	Ref to working
Equity holders of the parent	141.1	
Non-controlling interest	19.7	(9)
	160.8	

Workings:

1. *Revenue*

	$000
AT	2,450
BU	1,200
CV (1/3 × 675)	225
	3,875
Less: Intra-group sales of inventories	(80)
Less: Intra-group sales of administrative services	(12)
	3,783

2. *Provision for unrealised profit*

Closing intra-group inventories = $80,000 × 25% = 20,000.
Unrealised profit = 20% × $20,000 = $4,000.

3. *Cost of sales*

	$000
AT	1,862
BU	870
CV (1/3 × 432)	144
	2,876

Add: Provision for unrealised profit (W2)		4
Less: Intra-group sales of inventories		(80)
		2,800

4. *Distribution costs and administrative expenses*

	Distribution costs $000	Administrative expenses $000
AT	94	280
BU	22	165
CV (1/3 × 77)/(1/3 × 120)	25.7	40
	141.7	485
Less: Intra-group purchases of administrative services	–	(12)
	141.7	473

5. *Loss on investment in financial asset*

Loss on investment in EX: 4,000 shares at (1332¢ − 1227¢) = $4,200.

6. *Finance costs*

Y/e 31 March	Principal b/fwd	Effective interest @ 9%	Interest charge	C/fwd
2005	950.0	85.5	(50)	985.5
2006	985.5	88.7	(50)	1,024.5
2007	1,024.5	92.2	(50)	1,066.4
2008	1,066.4	96.0	(50)	1,112.4
2009	1,112.4	100.1	(50)	1,162.5

The amount for inclusion in the income statement for the year ended 31 March 2007 is $92.2 + interest of $26 on short-term borrowings. Total = $118.2.

7. *Share of profit of associate*

Profit after tax × 3/12 × 35% = $79 × 3/12 × 35% = $6.9

8. *Income tax*

	$000
AT	40
BU	50
CV (1/3 × 12)	4
	94

9. *Non-controlling interest*

	6 months to 30 September 2006	6 months to 31 March 2007
Adjusted profit of BU:		
Profit for the period, as stated	95	
Less: Provision for unrealised profit	(4)	
	91	
Split 1 : 1	45.5	45.5
Less: Loss on financial asset		(4.2)
	45.5	41.3

Answer 2 – AD (Nov '06)

(a) The financial asset falls into the category of loans and receivables, and, according to the Standard, should be accounted for using the amortised cost method. The effective nterest rate inherent in the financial instrument is used to calculate the annual amount of interest receivable, which is credited to the income statement. If an annual amount of interest is receivable, this is credited to the financial asset (with the related debit to cash or receivable).

The other current asset in this case falls into the category of 'held-for-trading' and should be accounted for at fair value through profit and loss account. Where securities are actively traded, the statement of financial position amount (at fair value) is likely to differ from the amount at which the asset was originally recognised. Fair value differences are debited or credited to profit or loss, and appear in the income statement.

(b) AD: Consolidated statement of financial position at 30 June 2006

	$	$
ASSETS		
Non-current assets		
Property, plant and equipment (1,900 + 680)	2,580,000	
Goodwill (W1)	330,000	
Investment in associate (W5)	110,800	
Financial asset (W2)	1,062,400	
		4,083,200
Current assets		
Inventories (223 + 127)	350,000	
Trade receivables (204 + 93 − 5)	292,000	
Other current assets (W3)	26,800	
Cash in transit	5,000	
Cash (72 + 28)	100,000	
		773,800
		4,857,000
EQUITY AND LIABILITIES		
Equity		
Share capital	1,000,000	
Consolidated reserves (W7)	2,556,600	
		3,556,600
Non-controlling interest (W6)		141,400
Non-current liabilities		600,000
Current liabilities		
Trade payables (247 + 113)	360,000	
Income tax (137 + 62)	199,000	
		559,000
		4,857,000

Workings:

1. *Goodwill on acquisition of BE*

	$	$
Cost of investment		880,000
Net assets at FV (300,000 + 350,000)	650,000	
Less FV of NCI at acquisition	(100,000)	
		(550,000)
		330,000

2. *Financial asset*

Calculation of finance charge for year ended 30 June 2006:

	$
1 July 2004 Proceeds of instrument	1,000,000
Year 1 finance charge 8%	80,000
Less: Interest received ($1,000,000 × 5%)	(50,000)
At 30 June 2005	1,030,000
Year 2 finance charge ($1,030,000 × 8%)	82,400
Less: Interest received ($1,000,000 × 5%)	(50,000)
At 30 June 2006	1,062,400

The balance is currently stated at $980,000 (i.e. $1,030,000 brought forward less the interest receipt of $50,000). The following adjustment is required:

DR Financial asset 82,400

CR Interest receivable 82,400

The credit to interest receivable increases retained earnings by $82,400 (see W7)

3. *Other current assets*

Increase in fair value: 670¢ − 625¢ = 45¢ × 4,000 shares = $1,800

DR Other current assets 1,800

CR Fair value adjustments 1,800

The credit to fair value adjustments increases retained earnings by $1,800 (see W7)

4. *Provision for unrealised profit*

Unrealised profit in BE: ($10,000 × 30%) × 40% = $1,200

This is deducted from the investment in associate (W5).

5. *Investment in associate*

	$
Cost of investment	104,000
Add: Share of post-acquisition profit ($20,000 × 40%)	8,000
	112,000
Less: PURP (W4)	(1,200)
	110,800

6. Non-controlling interest

	$
Fair value of NCI at acquisition	100,000
20% post-acquisition reserves 20% × (557,000 − 350,000)	41,400
	141,400

7. Consolidated reserves

	$
AD's reserves	2,300,000
Group share of post-acquisition earnings in BE: ($557,000 − 350,000) × 80%	165,600
Group share of post-acquisition earnings in CF: ($122,000 − 102,000) × 40%	8,000
Financial asset interest credit (W2)	82,400
Fair value increase – other financial asset (W3)	1,800
	2,557,800
Less: Group share of provision for unrealised profit (W4)	(1,200)
	2,556,600

Answer 3 – AJ (May '05)

(a) AJ owns 80% of the shares of BK, which points to the existence of a parent/subsidiary relationship. Provided that AJ controls the activities of BK (and there is nothing to suggest that it does not have control) AJ will account for its investment in BK as a subsidiary and will prepare consolidated financial statements, using the acquisition method.

AJ acquired 40% of the shares in CL. An investment of 40% in another entity would normally indicate that the investor has a significant influence over (but not control of) the entity's activities. The fact that AJ has the power to appoint one director to the board tends to support this conclusion. Also, the fact that three other investors hold most of the remainder of the shares makes it unlikely that another investor in CL would be able to control the entity's activities. AJ will account for CL as an associate using the equity accounting method.

(b) **AJ: Consolidated statement of financial position at 31 March 20X5**

	$000	$000
Non-current assets		
Property, plant and equipment [12,500 + 4,700 + 195 (FV)]	17,395	
Goodwill	1,700	
Investment in associate (W3)	4,560	
Other financial assets (W1)	4,100	
		27,755

Current assets

Inventories [7,200 + 8,000 + 200 (W4)]	15,000	
Trade receivables (6,300 + 4,300)	10,600	
Cash	800	
		26,400
		54,155 |-
Capital and reserves		
Share capital	10,000	
Consolidated reserves (W6)	13,156	
		23,156
Non-controlling interest (W5)		1,199
Non-current liabilities		
Loan notes [10,000 + 3,000 + 2,000 (intra-group)]		11,000
Current liabilities		
Trade payables (8,900 + 6,700)	15,600	
Tax (1,300 + 100)	1,400	
Short-term borrowings (600 + 1,200)	1,800	
		18,800
		54,155 |-

Workings:

1. *AJ's investments*

	$000
As stated	18,000
Purchase of BK's loan notes	(2,000)
Purchase of BK's shares	(7,500)
Purchase of CL's shares	(4,400)
Balance: other financial assets	4,100

2. *Goodwill on consolidation of BK*

	$000
Purchase consideration	7,500
Share of net assets acquired:	
[5,000 + 1,500 + 195 (FV adjustment)] × 80%	(5,356)
Goodwill as originally calculated	2,144
Impairment loss (balancing figure)	(444)
Goodwill carried forward	1,700

3. *Investment in associate*

	$000
Purchase consideration	4,400
Group share of post-acquisition profits [($4,300 − $3,900) × 40%]	160
	4,560

4. *Intra-group trading*

Total provision for unrealised profit (PURP) = $1 million × 25/125 = $200,000

	$000	$000
DR Minority share (20%)	40	
DR Consolidated reserves	160	
CR Consolidated inventories		200

5. *Non-controlling interest*

	$000
Share of net assets in BK: (6,000 + 195) × 20%	1,239
Less: PURP (W4)	(40)
	1,199

6. *Consolidated reserves*

	$000
AJ	14,000
BK – share of post-acquisition loss: (1,500 − 1,000) × 80%	(400)
CL – share of post-acquisition profits: (4,300 − 3,900) × 40%	160
Impairment loss (W2)	(444)
PURP (W4)	(160)
	13,156

5

Statement of Cash Flow

Statement of Cash Flow   5

Learning Outcome

After studying this chapter students should be able to:
▶ prepare a consolidated statement of cash flow in a form suitable for publication for a group of companies.

The basics

- The standard headings under which cash flows are reported are:
  - operating activities
  - investing activities
  - financing activities
  - net change in cash and cash equivalents for the period.
- Cash comprises cash in hand and demand deposits.
- Cash equivalents are short term, highly liquid investments that are readily convertible into known amounts of cash and which are subject to an insignificant risk of changes in value.

Group issues

- Consistent with the consolidated income statement and statement of financial position, the consolidated statement of cash flow must reflect only those cash flows that are external to the group.
- Dividends paid to non-controlling interests should be disclosed within the statement of cash flow under financing activities.
- Dividends received from associates should be shown within investing activities.

- When an investment is acquired during the financial period only post-acquisition cash flows should be shown in the statement of cash flow.
- Cash expensed in the purchase of an investment should be netted against cash and overdrafts in the books of the investment at the acquisition date and the net figure shown within investing activities.
- When a new investment is acquired do not double count the cash flows relating to items already reflected in the books of the subsidiary at the purchase date (this is not an issue for associates and trade investments as they are not consolidated on a line-by-line basis).
- When the financial data of the investment has to be translated from a foreign currency, the exchange differences arising do not constitute cash flows and will need to be taken into consideration when identifying the 'pure' cash flows to be included in the statement of cash flow.

Medium answer questions

Question 1

GPX's financial statements included the following figures

	30.09.08 $	30.09.09 $
Investment in associate	6,600,000	6,750,000
Property, plant and equipment – NBV	207,000	228,000
Non-controlling interest	77,600	64,700
Pre-tax share of profit in the associate was		420,000
Related tax charge		180,000
Depreciation charge		32,000
NCI share of subsidiary's profits		6,500

There were no impairments to the investment in associate, or acquisitions or disposals of shares during the financial year. During the year the GPX group disposed of plant for proceeds of $8,500 that had cost $62,000 several years ago and which was fully written down at 1 October 2008. There were no other disposals. GPX had disposed of its holding of 75% of the ordinary share capital of its subsidiary NJZ. At the date of disposal the net assets of NJZ totalled $64,000.

Requirement

Calculate the following figures for GPX Groups Consolidated Statement of Cash flow for the year ended 30 September 2009

(i) dividends received from associate
(ii) cash outflow in respect of purchases of property, plant and equipment
(iii) dividends paid to non-controlling interest

Answer to medium answer questions

Answer 1

GPX

		$000
Opening investment in associate		6,600
Add: share of profit of associate	(420 − 180)	240
Cash flow (dividend paid) (balancing figure)		(90)
Closing investment in associate		6,750

	$000
Opening balance	207
Less: Depreciation	(32)
Add: Purchases (balancing figure)	53
Closing balance	228

	$
Balance brought forward	77,600
Disposal: 25% × 64,000	(16,000)
Share of profit for the period	6,500
Dividend paid (balancing figure)	(3,400)
Balance carried forward	64,700

Long answer questions

Question 1 – EAG (May '08)

Extracts from the consolidated financial statements of the EAG Group for the year ended 30 April 2008 are as follows:

EAG Group: Consolidated income statement for the year ended 30 April 2008

	$ million
Revenue	30,750.0
Cost of sales	(26,447.5)
Gross profit	4,302.5
Distribution costs	(523.0)
Administrative expenses	(669.4)
Finance cost	(510.9)
Share of profit of associate	1.6
Profit on disposal of associate	3.4
Profit before tax	2,604.2
Income tax	(723.9)
Profit for the period	1,880.3
Attributable to:	
Equity holders of the parent	1,652.3
Non-controlling interest	228.0
	1,880.3

EAG Group: Statement of financial position at 30 April 2008

	2008	2008	2007	2007
	$ million	$ million	$ million	$ million
ASSETS				
Non-current assets				
Property, plant and equipment	22,225.1		19,332.8	
Goodwill	1,662.7		1,865.3	
Intangible assets	306.5		372.4	
Investment in associate	–		13.8	
		24,194.3		21,584.3
Current assets				
Inventories	5,217.0		4,881.0	
Trade receivables	4,633.6		4,670.0	
Cash	62.5		88.3	
		9,913.1		9,639.3
		34,107.4		31,223.6
EQUITY AND LIABILITIES				
Equity				
Share capital	4,300.0		3,600.0	
Retained earnings	14,643.7		12,991.4	
		18,943.7		16,591.4
Non-controlling interest		2,010.5		1,870.5
Non-current liabilities				
Long-term borrowings		6,133.9		6,013.0
Current liabilities				
Trade payables	5,579.3		5,356.3	
Short-term borrowings	662.4		507.7	
Income tax	777.6		884.7	
		7,019.3		6,748.7
		34,107.4		31,223.6

Notes

1. Depreciation of $2,024.7 million was charged in respect of property, plant and equipment in the year ended 30 April 2008.
2. On 1 January 2008 EAG disposed of the investment in associate for $18 million. The share of profit in the income statement relates to the period from 1 May 2007 to 31 December 2007. A dividend was received from the associate on 1 June 2007. There were no other disposals, and no acquisitions, of investments in the accounting period.
3. Goodwill in one of the group's subsidiaries suffered an impairment during the year. The amount of the impairment was included in cost of sales.
4. The long-term borrowings are measured at amortised cost. The borrowing was taken out on 1 May 2006, and proceeds of $6,000 million less issue costs of $100,000 were

received on that date. Interest of 5% of the principal is paid in arrears each year, and the borrowings will be redeemed on 30 April 2011 for $6.55 million. All interest obligations have been met on the due dates. The effective interest rate applicable to the borrowings is 7%. The finance cost in the income statement includes interest in respect of both the long-term and the short-term borrowing. Short-term borrowing comprises overdrafts repayable on demand.

5. Amortisation of 25% of the opening balance of intangibles was charged to cost of sales. A manufacturing patent was acquired for a cash payment on 30 April 2008.
6. An issue of share capital at par was made for cash during the year.
7. Dividends were paid to non-controlling interests during the year, but no dividend was paid to the equity holders of the parent entity.

Requirement

Prepare the consolidated statement of cash flow of the EAG Group for the financial year ended 30 April 2008. The statement of cash flow should be presented in accordance with the requirements of IAS 7 *Cash Flow Statements*, and using the indirect method. Notes to the financial statement are NOT required, but full workings should be shown. **(25 marks)**

Question 2 – AH (Nov '05)

Extracts from the consolidated financial statements of the AH Group for the year ended 30 June 2005 are given below:

AH Group: Consolidated income statement for the year ended 30 June 2005

	2005 $000
Revenue	85,000
Cost of sales	59,750
Gross profit	25,250
Operating expenses	5,650
Profit from operations	19,600
Finance cost	1,400
Profit before disposal of property	18,200
Disposal of property (note 2)	1,250
Profit before tax	19,450
Income tax	6,250
Profit for the period	13,200
Attributable to:	$000
Non-controlling interest	655
Group profit for the year	12,545
	13,200

AH Group: Extracts from statement of changes in equity for the year ended 30 June 2005

	Share capital $000	Share premium $000	Consolidated revenue reserves $000
Opening balance	18,000	10,000	18,340
Issue of share capital	2,000	2,000	
Profit for period			12,545
Dividends			(6,000)
Closing balance	20,000	12,000	24,885

AH Group: Statement of financial position, with comparatives, at 30 June 2005

	2005 $000	2005 $000	2004 $000	2004 $000
ASSETS				
Non-current assets				
Property, plant and equipment	50,600		44,050	
Intangible assets (note 3)	6,410		4,160	
		57,010		48,210
Current assets				
Inventories	33,500		28,750	
Trade receivables	27,130		26,300	
Cash	1,870		3,900	
		62,500		58,950
		119,510		107,160
EQUITY AND LIABILITIES				
Equity				
Share capital	20,000		18,000	
Share premium	12,000		10,000	
Consolidated revenue reserves	24,885		18,340	
		56,885		46,340
Non-controlling interest		3,625		1,920
Non-current liabilities				
Interest-bearing borrowings		18,200		19,200
Current liabilities				
Trade payables	33,340		32,810	
Interest payables	1,360		1,440	
Tax	6,100		5,450	
		40,800		39,700
		119,510		107,160

Notes:

1. Several years ago, AH acquired 80% of the issued ordinary shares of its subsidiary, BI. On 1 January 2005, AH acquired 75% of the issued ordinary shares of CJ in exchange for a fresh issue of 2 million of its own $1 ordinary shares (issued at a premium of

$1 each) and $2 million in cash. The net assets of CJ at the date of acquisition were assessed as having the following fair values:

	$000
Property, plant and equipment	4,200
Inventories	1,650
Receivables	1,300
Cash	50
Trade payables	(1,950)
Tax	(250)
	5,000

2. During the year, AH disposed of a non-current asset of property for proceeds of $2,250,000. The carrying value of the asset at the date of disposal was $1,000,000. There were no other disposals of non-current assets. Depreciation of $7,950,000 was charged against consolidated profits for the year.
3. Intangible assets comprise goodwill on acquisition of BI and CJ (2004: BI only). Goodwill has remained unimpaired since acquisition.

Requirement

Prepare the consolidated statement of cash flow of the AH Group for the financial year ended 30 June 2005 in the form required by IAS 7 *Cash Flow Statements*, and using the indirect method. Notes to the statement of cash flow are NOT required, but full workings should be shown. **(25 marks)**

Question 3 – WORLDWIDE (Nov '02)

You are the Consolidation Accountant of Worldwide, an entity with subsidiaries located throughout the world. You are currently involved in preparing the consolidated financial statements for the year ended 30 September 2002. Your assistant has prepared the consolidated income statement, the consolidated statement of changes in equity, and the consolidated statement of financial position, together with some supporting schedules. The material your assistant has prepared is given below:

Worldwide – consolidated income statement for the year ended 30 September 2002

	$ million
Revenue	4,000
Cost of sales	(2,200)
Gross profit	1,800
Other operating expenses	(789)
Profit from operations	1,011
Gain on sale of subsidiary (note 1)	50
Finance cost (note 2)	(200)
Profit before tax	861
Income tax expense	(180)
Profit after tax	681
Profit attributable to non-controlling interests	(128)
Profit attributable to equity holders of the parent	553

Worldwide – consolidated statement of changes in equity for the year ended 30 September 2002

	$ million
Balance at 1 October 2001	3,307
Currency translation differences (note 3)	47
Profit for the period attributable to equity holders of the parent	553
Dividends paid:	
– ordinary shares	(240)
Issue of share capital	1,000
Balance at 30 September 2002	4,667

Worldwide – consolidated statements of financial position at 30 September

	2002		2001	
	$ million	$ million	$ million	$ million
Assets:				
Non-current assets:				
Property, plant and equipment (note 4)	5,900		4,100	
Goodwill on consolidation	52		72	
		5,952		4,172
Current assets:				
Inventories	950		800	
Trade receivables	1,000		900	
Cash and cash equivalents	80		98	
		2,030		1,798
		7,982		5,970
Equity and liabilities:				
Equity attributable to equity holders of the parent:				
Share capital (ordinary shares)		3,500		2,500
Retained earnings		1,167		807
		4,667		3,307
Non-controlling interests		543		500
Non-current liabilities:				
Interest-bearing borrowings	1,779		1,340	
Deferred tax	278		218	
		2,057		1,558
Current liabilities:				
Trade payables	495		425	
Accrued interest	25		20	
Income tax	130		120	
Overdrafts	65		40	
		715		605
		7,982		5,970

Notes:

1. *Gain on sale of subsidiary*
   On 1 April 2002, Worldwide disposed of a 75%-owned subsidiary located in the same country for $250 million in cash. The statement of financial position of the subsidiary drawn up at the date of disposal showed the following:

	$ million
Property, plant and equipment	200
Inventory	100
Trade receivables	110
Cash	10
Trade payables	(80)
Income tax	(25)
Interest-bearing borrowings	(75)
	240

   This subsidiary had been acquired on 1 April 1994 for a cash payment of $110 million when its net assets had a fair value of $120 million.

2. *Finance cost*
   During the year, Worldwide constructed a factory in its country of incorporation. Construction commenced on 1 November 2001 and the factory was ready for use on 1 June 2002. However, production did not begin at the factory until 1 August 2002. The construction of the factory was financed by general borrowings denominated in $s. Your assistant has included the finance cost relating to the period from 1 November 2001 to 1 June 2002 in the cost of property, plant and equipment rather than taking it to the income statement. The amount of finance cost that was treated in this way is $10 million. The figure was arrived at by applying a relevant capitalisation rate to expenditure on the factory in the period 1 November 2001 to 1 June 2002.

3. *Currency translation differences*

	Total $ million	Group share $ million
Arising on retranslation of opening net assets:		
Property, plant and equipment	25	20
Inventory	20	15
Trade receivables	20	16
Trade payables	(9)	(6)
	56	45
Arising on retranslation of profit for the period	16	12
Offset of exchange loss on Worldwide borrowings (see below)	(10)	(10)
	62	47

   Worldwide has taken out a number of borrowings denominated in foreign currencies to partly finance the equity investments in its foreign subsidiaries. Your assistant has offset the exchange differences arising on the retranslation of these borrowings against the exchange differences arising on the retranslation of the net investments in the relevant subsidiaries. The exchange gain on retranslation of the income statement (from average rate for the year to the closing rate) relates to operating profit excluding depreciation.

4. Property, plant and equipment

- During the period, the depreciation charged in the consolidated income statement was $320 million.
- Apart from the disposal mentioned in note 1, the Worldwide group disposed of property, plant and equipment having a net book value of $190 million for cash proceeds of $198 million. The profit on this disposal has been credited to 'other operating expenses' in the consolidated income statement.
- During the period, the Worldwide group entered into a significant number of new finance leases. Additions to property, plant and equipment include $250 million capitalised under finance leases.

Requirement

Prepare the consolidated cash flow statement of the Worldwide group for the year ended 30 September 2002. You should use the indirect method. Notes to the cash flow statement are NOT required. **(25 marks)**

✓ Answer to long answer questions

Answer 1 – EAG (May '08)

EAG Group: consolidated statement of cash flow for the year ended 30 April 2008

	$ million	$ million	Ref to workings
Cash flows from operating activities			
Profit before taxation		2,604.2	
Adjustments for:			
Depreciation	2,024.7		
Impairment of goodwill (1,865.3 − 1,662.7)	202.6		
Amortisation of intangibles	93.1		
Interest expense	510.9		
Profit on disposal of associate	(3.4)		
Share of profit of associate	(1.6)		
		2,826.3	
		5,430.5	
Increase in inventories (5,217.0 − 4,881.0)		(336.0)	
Decrease in receivables (4,670.0 − 4,633.6)		36.4	
Increase in payables (5,579.3 − 5,356.3)		223.0	
Cash generated from operations		5,353.9	
Interest paid		(390.0)	3
Income taxes		(831.0)	4
Net cash from operating activities		4,132.9	
Cash flows from investing activities			
Purchase of property, plant and equipment	(4,917.0)		1
Purchase of intangibles	(27.2)		5
Proceeds from sale of associate	18.0		
Dividend received from associate	0.8		2
		(792.5)	

Cash flows from financing activities
Proceeds from issue of share capital (4,300.0 − 3,600.0)	700.0	
Dividends paid to non-controlling interest	(88.0)	6
Net cash used in financing activities		612.0
Net decrease in cash and cash equivalents		(180.5)
Cash at the beginning of the period (88.3 − 507.7)		(419.4)
Cash at the end of the period (62.5 − 662.4)		(599.9)

Workings

1. *Non-current assets and depreciation*

	$ million
Net book value b/fwd	19,332.8
Depreciation	(2,024.7)
Additions (balancing figure)	4,917.0
Net book value c/fwd	22,225.1

2. *Investment in associate*

	$ million
Balance b/fwd	13.8
Share of profit to 31.12.07	1.6
Disposal proceeds	(18.0)
Dividend received 1.6.07 (balancing figure)	(0.8)
Profit on disposal	3.4

3. *Interest*

   The interest charged and the amortised cost of the financial instrument, over its five-year life, are as follows:

Date	Balance b/fwd	Interest at 7%	Interest paid 5%	Balance c/fwd
1.5.2006	5,900.0	413.0	(300.0)	6,013.0
1.5.2007	6,013.0	**420.9**	(300.0)	6,133.9
1.5.2008	6,133.9	429.4	(300.0)	6,263.3
1.5.2009	6,263.3	438.4	(300.0)	6,401.7
1.5.2010	6,401.7	448.1	(300.0)	6,549.8

Figure in bold is the interest charged against profit for the year ended 30 April 2008.

	$ million
Total finance cost in income statement	510.9
Less: Interest on long-term borrowings	(420.9)
Balance = Interest on short-term borrowings	90.0

Total cash outflow in respect of interest: 90.0 + 300.0 = 390.0

4. *Income taxes*

	$ million
Balance b/fwd	884.7
Income statement: provision	723.9
Paid (balancing figure)	(831.0)
Balance c/fwd	777.6

5. *Intangibles*

	$ million
Balance b/fwd	372.4
Amortisation (372.4 × 25%)	(93.1)
Purchase of patent (balancing figure)	27.2
Balance c/fwd	306.5

6. *Non-controlling interest*

	$ million
Balance b/fwd	1,870.5
Profit attributable to minority	228.0
Dividend paid (balancing figure)	(88.0)
Balance c/fwd	2,010.5

Answer 2 – AH (Nov '05)

Consolidated cash flow statement for the year ended 30 June 2005

	$000	$000
Operating activities		
Profit from operations		19,600
Adjustments for:		
Depreciation		7,950
Decrease in trade and other receivables (27,130 – 26,300 – 1,300)		470
Increase in inventories (33,500 – 28,750 – 1,650)		(3,100)
Decrease in trade payables (33,340 – 32,810 – 1,950)		(1,420)
Cash generated from operations		23,500
Interest paid (W1)		(1,480)
Income taxes paid (W2)		(5,850)
Net cash from operating activities		16,170
Investing activities		
Acquisition of subsidiary net of cash acquired (2,000 – 50)	(1,950)	
Purchase of property, plant and equipment (W3)	(11,300)	
Proceeds from sale of property	2,250	
Net cash used in investing activities		(11,000)
Financing activities		
Repayment of long-term borrowings (18,200 – 19,200)	(1,000)	
Dividend paid	(6,000)	
Dividend paid to non-controlling interest (W4)	(200)	
Net cash used in financing activities		(7,200)
Net decrease in cash and cash equivalents		(2,030)
Cash and cash equivalents at 1 July 2004		3,900
Cash and cash equivalents at 30 June 2005		1,870

Workings

1. *Interest paid*

	$000
Balance b/fwd	1,440
Income statement	1,400
Interest paid (balancing figure)	(1,480.0)
Balance c/fwd	1,360

2. *Income taxes paid*

	$000
Balance b/fwd	5,450
Income statement	6,250
Acquisition of subsidiary	250
Cash paid (balancing figure)	(5,850)
Balance c/fwd	6,100

3. *Property, plant and equipment*

	$000
Net book value b/fwd	44,050
Depreciation	(7,950)
Acquired with subsidiary	4,200
Disposals	(1,000)
Additions (balancing figure)	11,300
Net book value c/fwd	50,600

4. *Non-controlling interest*

	$000
Balance b/fwd	1,920
Income statement	655
Acquisition of subsidiary (25% × 5,000)	1,250
Cash paid (balancing figure)	(200)
Balance c/fwd	3,625

Answer 3 – WORLDWIDE (Nov '02)

Consolidated cash flow statement for the year ended 30 September 2002

	$ million	$ million
Cash flows from operating activities		
Profit before tax		861
Adjustments for:		
Depreciation		320
Exchange differences on translation of profit		16
Exchange differences on translation of working capital (20 + 20 − 9)		31
Profit on sale of property, plant and equipment (198 − 190)		(8)
Gain on sale of subsidiary		(50)
Finance expense		200

Operating profit before working capital changes	1,370	
Increase in inventories (950 − 800 + 100)	(250)	
Increase in receivables (1,000 − 900 + 110)	(210)	
Decrease in trade payables (450 − 400 + 80)	130	
Cash generated from operations	1,040	
Interest paid (W2)	(205)	
Income taxes paid (W3)	(85)	
Net cash from operating activities		750
Cash flows from investing activities		
Receipts from sale of property, plant and equipment	198	
Payments to purchase property, plant and equipment (W4)	(2,225)	
Sale of investment in subsidiary net of cash sold (250 − 10)	240	
Net cash used in investing activities		(1,787)
Cash flows from financing activities		
Proceeds from issue of share capital	1,000	
Proceeds from new interest-bearing borrowings (W5)	274	
Equity dividends paid	(240)	
Dividend paid to non-controlling shareholders (W7)	(40)	
Net cash from financing activities		994
Net decrease in cash and cash equivalents		(43)
Cash and cash equivalents at beginning of period (98 − 40)		58
Cash and cash equivalents at end of period (80 − 65)		15

Workings

1. *Goodwill (proof)*

Goodwill

	$ million		$ million
Balance b/d	72	Written off on disposal (note)	20
		Balance c/d	52
	72		72

Note: Goodwill written off on disposal

	$ million
Cost of investment	110
Net assets acquired (75% × 120)	(90)
	20

2. *Interest payable*

Interest payable

	$ million		$ million
Cash paid (balancing figure)	205	Balance b/d	20
Balance c/d	25	Income statement	200
		Capitalised in non-current assets	10
	230		230

3. *Income taxes*

Income taxes

	$ million		$ million
Disposal	25	Balance b/d (current)	120
Cash paid (balancing figure)	**85**	Balance b/d (deferred)	218
Balance c/d (current)	130	Income statement	180
Balance c/d (deferred)	278		
	518		518

4. *Property, plant and equipment*

Property, plant and equipment

	$ million		$ million
Balance b/d	4,100	Disposals (subsidiary)	200
Interest capitalised	10	Disposals (other)	190
Exchange differences	25	Depreciation	320
Cash paid (balancing figure)	**2,225**	Balance c/d	5,650
	6,360		6,360

5. *Interest bearing borrowings*

Interest bearing borrowings

	$ million		$ million
Disposal of subsidiary	75	Balance b/d	1,365
Balance c/d	1,574	Exchange loss	10
		Increase (balancing figure)	**274**
	1,649		1,649

6. *Dividends payable to non-controlling interest*

Dividends payable to non-controlling interest

	$ million		$ million
Disposal of subsidiary		Balance b/d	500
(25% × 240)	60	Income statement	128
Cash paid (balancing figure)	**40**	Share of exchange differences	15
Balance c/d	543		643
	643		

6
Changes in Group Structure

Changes in Group Structure 6

> **LEARNING OUTCOME**
>
> After studying this chapter students should be able to:
> - demonstrate the impact on group financial statements when a subsidiary is acquired or disposed part way through an accounting period, and where shareholdings, or control, are acquired in stages.

Piecemeal acquisitions

> IFRS 3 prescribes the following treatment for a business combination achieved in stages:
> '... each exchange transaction shall be treated separately by the acquirer, using the cost of the transaction and fair value information at the date of each exchange transaction, to determine the amount of any goodwill associated with that transaction. This results in a step-by-step comparison of the cost of the individual investments with the acquirer's interest in the fair values of the acquiree's identifiable assets, liabilities and contingent liabilities at each step'.

Increasing a stake from a simple investment to a subsidiary

From the group's perspective the simple investment is derecognised at the date that control is gained.

The simple investment is accounted for in accordance with IAS 39 and will generally be an available for sale investment (no intention to sell at the time of initial investment)

The gains resulting from the fair value assessments will in line with IAS 39, be recognised in equity.

On derecognition the gains up to that date must be included in the consolidated retained earnings. We must remember, however, to remove the total gains on the simple investment that would have been included in retained earnings to date to avoid double counting.

From associate to subsidiary

Where a piecemeal acquisition takes a stake from that of associate to a subsidiary, the principles of the accounting treatment remain the same as above.

The fair value of the investment previously held in this case would be the carrying value of the associate. The date that control is gained is the trigger for any fair value adjustment.

Increasing a controlling interest

The treatment is different where the parent already holds a controlling interest in the subsidiary as it is merely increasing this interest.

No gain or loss on derecognition is recorded, instead it is treated as a transaction between owners and any adjustment is to parent's equity (the parent's interest has increased and the non-controlling interest has decreased).

The calculation would be as follows:

FV of consideration paid	(X)
Decrease in NCI in net assets at date of acquisition	X
Decrease in NCI goodwill (only if NCI is held at FV and goodwill has been calculated on their share)	X
= adjustment to parent's equity	(X)

Disposals in the period

	Consolidated income statement /TCI	Consolidated statement of financial position
Full disposal	• Consolidate sub and show NCI up to date of disposal • Include profit or loss on disposal	• No consolidation as disposed of at year end date
Sub to associate	• Consolidate sub and show NCI up to date of disposal • Include profit or loss on disposal • Equity account for associate from disposal date to year end (time apportion results)	• Calculate FV of remaining investment (this will act as open value of investment) • The investment is equity accounted at year end date

Sub to trade investment	• Consolidate sub and show NCI up to date of disposal • Include profit or loss on disposal • Include dividend income from date of disposal to year end date	• Calculate FV of remaining investment (this will act as opening cost of investment) • Account for investment under IAS 39.
Sub to reduced sub	• Full consolidation for whole period • Time apportion the NCI based on % holding x number of months • **No** profit or loss on disposal	• Full consolidation • NCI at % held at year end dat • Calculate adjustment to parent's equity

Business reorganisations

Possible scenarios

To eliminate a debit balance on the profit and loss reserve.

The breach of debt covenants results in lenders enforcing a reorganisation.

A predatory group that has made many acquisitions wants to streamline the group structure.

A new structure to facilitate a flotation.

A new structure to facilitate the disposal of a company whilst retaining other investments.

A subsidiary becomes a sub-subsidiary

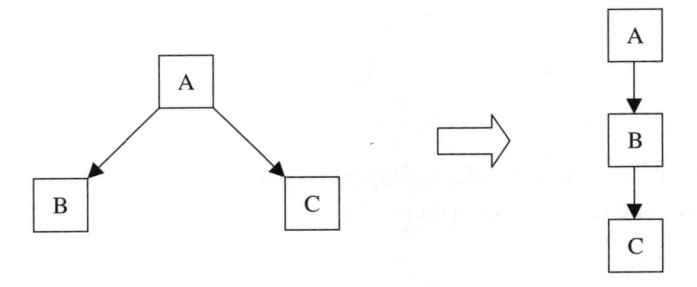

- This strategy might be employed if the directors of A want to create a sub-group.
- The overall effect on the A group is nil.

A sub-subsidiary becomes a subsidiary

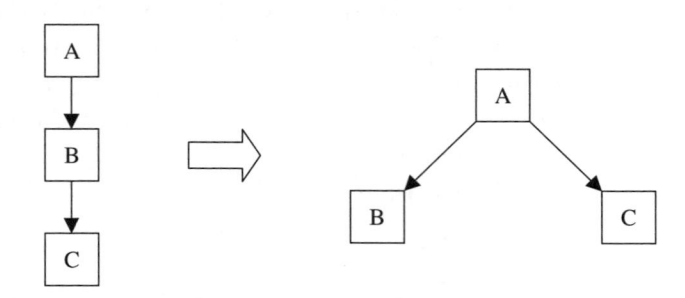

- This strategy might be employed if the directors of A want to dispose of B whilst retaining C.
- It is not possible for this type of reorganisation to be effected by A issuing shares to B in exchange for the shares in C ... it is illegal for a parent to issue shares to its subsidiary.
- Consequently the transfer is achieved by B making a dividend in specie represented by the shares of C.

The addition of a new parent company

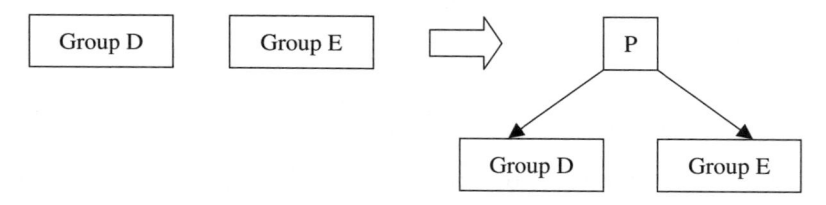

- The shareholders of the parent company of each group conduct a share for share exchange in the new parent bringing all the resources under central control.

A subsidiary moved along

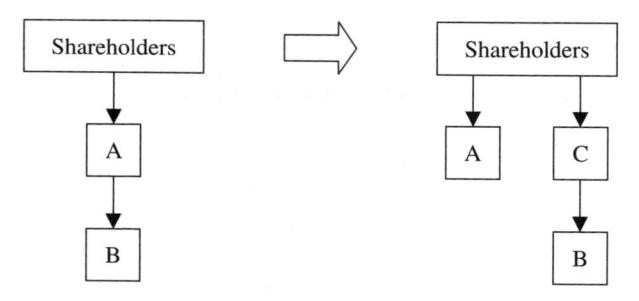

- Company A has effectively made a disposal of the shares in B to the shareholders of A which constitutes a dividend in specie.

Medium answer questions

Question 1 (May '05)

RW holds 80% of the 1,000,000 ordinary shares of its subsidiary, SX. Summarised income statements of both entities for the year ended 31 December 2004 are shown below:

	RW $000	SX $000
Revenue	6,000	2,500
Operating costs	(4,500)	(1,700)
Profit before tax	1,500	800
Income tax expense	(300)	(250)
Profit for the period	1,200	550

RW purchased 800,000 of SX's $1 shares in 2003 for $3.2 million, when SX's reserves were $2.4 million. Goodwill has been carried at cost since acquisition and there has been no subsequent impairment.

On 1 July 2004, RW disposed of 400,000 shares in SX for $3 million. SX's reserves at 1 January 2004 were $2.9 million, and its profits accrued evenly throughout the year. RW is liable to income tax of $50,000 on the disposal of its investment in SX. The effects of the disposal are not reflected in the income statements shown above.

It is the group's policy to value non-controlling interests at its proportionate share of the fair value of the subsidiary's identifiable net assets.

The fair value of the investment in shares retained is $1 m

Requirement

Prepare the summarised consolidated income statement for RW for the year ended 31 December 2004.

(Total = 10 marks)

Answers to medium answer questions

Answer 1 (May '05)

RW: Consolidated income statement for the year ending 31 December 2004

	$000
Revenue [6,000 + 6/12 × 2,500]	7,250
Operating costs [4,500 + 6/12 × 1,700]	(5,350)
	1,900
Profit on disposal of investment (W3)	180
Share of associates profits	
40% × (6/12 × 550)	110
Profit before tax	2,190
Income tax [300 + 6/12 × 250] + 50	(475)
	1,715
Attributable to:	
Equity holders of the parent	1,660
Non-controlling interest (W3)	55
	1,715

Workings

1. *Goodwill on consolidation*

	$000
Purchase consideration	3,200
Share of net assets acquired [1,000 + 2,400] × 80%	(2,720)
Goodwill	480

2. *Consolidated profit on disposal of investment*

	$000	$000
FV of consideration received (proceeds)		3,000
Plus FV of 40% retained		1,000
Less share of FV of the consolidated carrying value of the sub at date control is lost		
Share capital	1,000	
Retained earnings at 1 January 2004	2,900	
Less earnings from 1 January to 1 July 2004 (6/12 × 550)	275	
	4,175	
Group share	80%	(3,340)
Goodwill (W2)		(480)
Consolidated profit on disposal		180

3. *Non-controlling interest*

   20% Sub PAT for first 6 mths 20% × (6/12 × 550)   55

Long answer questions

Question 1 (May '06)

The statements of financial position of AZ and two entities in which it holds substantial investments at 31 March 2006 are shown below:

	AZ $000	AZ $000	BY $000	BY $000	CX $000	CX $000
Non-current assets:						
Property, plant and equipment	10,750		5,830		3,300	
Investments	7,650		–		–	
		18,400		5,830		3,300
Current assets:						
Inventories	2,030		1,210		1,180	
Trade receivables	2,380		1,300		1,320	
Cash	5,630		50		140	
		10,040		2,560		2,640
		28,440		8,390		5,940
Equity:						
Called up share capital ($1 shares)	8,000		2,300		2,600	
Preferred share capital	–		1,000			
Reserves	10,750		3,370		2,140	
		18,750		6,670		4,740
Current liabilities:						
Trade payables	3,770		1,550		1,080	
Income tax	420		170		120	
Suspense account	5,500		–		–	
		9,690		1,720		1,200
		28,440		8,390		5,940

Notes

1. *Investments by AZ in BY*

    Several years ago AZ purchased 80% of BY's ordinary share capital for $3,660,000 when the reserves of BY were $1,950,000. It is the group's policy to value non-controlling interests at its proportionate share of the fair value of the subsidiary's identifiable net assets and there has been no subsequent impairment.

    At the same time as the purchase of the ordinary share capital, AZ purchased 40% of BY's preferred share capital at par. The remainder of the preferred shares are held by several private investors.

2. *Investment by AZ in CX*

    Several years ago AZ purchased 60% of CX's ordinary share capital for $2,730,000 when the reserves of CX were $1,300,000. It is the group's policy to value non-controlling interests at its proportionate share of the fair value of the subsidiary's identifiable net assets and there has been no subsequent impairment.

On 1 October 2005, AZ disposed of all of its ordinary shares in CX, thus losing control of CX's operations. The proceeds of disposal, $5,500,000, were debited to cash and credited to a suspense account. No other accounting entries have been made in respect of the disposal. An investment gains tax of $200,000 on the profit on disposal will become payable by AZ within the twelve months following the statement of financial position date of 31 March 2006, and this liability should be accrued. CX's reserves at 1 April 2005 were $1,970,000. The entity's profits accrued evenly throughout the year.

3. *Additional information*

   No fair value adjustments were required in respect of assets or liabilities upon either of the acquisitions of ordinary shares. The called up share capital of both BY and CX has remained the same since the acquisitions were made.

4. *Intra-group trading*

   During the year ended 31 March 2006, BY started production of a special line of goods for supply to AZ. BY charges a mark-up of 20% on the cost of such goods sold to AZ. At 31 March 2006, AZ's inventories included goods at a cost of $180,000 that had been supplied by BY.

Requirements

(a) Calculate the profit or loss on disposal after tax of the investment in CX that will be disclosed in:
   (i) AZ's own financial statements;
   (ii) the AZ group's consolidated financial statements. **(6 marks)**

(b) Calculate the consolidated reserves of the AZ group at 31 March 2006. **(5 marks)**

(c) Prepare the consolidated statement of financial position of the AZ group at 31 March 2006. **(14 marks)**

Full workings should be shown. **(Total = 25 marks)**

Answers to long answer questions

Answer 1 (May '06)

(a) AZ originally acquired 60% of 2,600,000 shares: 1,560,000. On 1 October 2005, it disposed of 520,000 shares – that is one third of its holding. After the disposal, AZ retained ownership of 40% of the ordinary share capital of CX.

(i) Profit or loss on disposal in AZ's own financial statements:

	$000
Proceeds of sale	5,500
Cost:	(2,730)
Profit before tax	2,770
Tax charge:	(200)
Profit after tax	2,570

(ii) Profit on disposal in the AZ group's consolidated financial statements

Workings

1. *Goodwill on the acquisition of CX*

	$000
Cost of investment	2,730
Less: Acquired (2,600 + 1,300 = 3,900 × 60%)	(2,340)
Goodwill on acquisition	390

2. *CX's net assets at the date of disposal*

	$000
Reserves on 1 April 2005	1,970
½ × profit for the year (2,140 − 1,970)/2	85
	2,055

	$000
Proceeds of sale	5,500
Less: share of net assets relating to the disposal (2,055 [W2] + 2,600)	(4,655)
Less: unimpaired goodwill relating to the disposal	(390)
Consolidated profit on disposal before tax	455
Tax charge (as in part (i))	(200)
Consolidated profit on disposal after tax	255

(b) (W1) Provision for unrealised profit

	selling price
Cost structure: cost + (20% × cost) =	$30,000
Unrealised profit = 20/120 × 180 =	
Of this, 20% is attributable to the NCI:	$6,000
The remainder reduces consolidated reserves:	$24,000

82 Exam Practice Kit: Financial Management

Consolidated reserves

	$000
Reserves of AZ	10,750
Post-acquisition reserves of BY:	
($3,370 − 1,950) × 80%	1,136
Profit on disposal (see part (a)(i))	2,570
Provision for unrealised profit (W1)	(24)
	14,432

(c) **AZ: Consolidated statement of financial position at 31 March 2006**

	$000	$000
Non-current assets:		
Property, plant and equipment [10,750 + 5,830]	16,580	
Goodwill (W1)	260	
Other investments (W2)	860	
		17,700
Current assets:		
Inventories [2,030 + 1,210 − 30 PURP]	3,210	
Trade receivables [2,380 + 1,300]	3,680	
Cash [5,630 + 50]	5,680	
		12,570
		30,270
Equity:		
Share capital	8,000	
Consolidated reserves (part (b))	14,432	
		22,432
Non-controlling interest (W4)		1,728
Current liabilities:		
Trade payables (3,770 + 1,550)	5,320	
Income tax (420 + 170 + 200 [part a)i)]	790	
		6,110
		30,270

Workings

1. *Goodwill on the acquisition of BY*

	$000
Cost of investment	3,660
Less: acquired (1,950 + 2,300) × 80%	(3,400)
Goodwill on acquisition	260

2. *Investments*

	$000
As stated in AZ's statement of financial position	7,650
Less: investment at cost in BY's ordinary shares	(3,660)
Less: investment at cost in BY's preferred shares	(400)
Less: investment at cost in CX's ordinary shares	(2,730)
Balance = other investments	860

3. *Non-controlling interest*

	$000
In BY's preferred shares	600
In BY's other net assets (2,300 + 3,370) × 20%	1,134
Provision for unrealised profit (part b))	(6)
	1,728

7

Foreign Currency Translation

Foreign Currency Translation

7

> **LEARNING OUTCOMES**
>
> After studying this chapter students should be able to:
> - explain foreign currency translation principles;
> - explain the correct treatment for foreign loans financing foreign equity investments.

Single transactions in foreign currencies

A single foreign currency transaction is one that is denominated in a foreign currency, or requires settlement in a foreign currency. Examples include:

- purchase or sale of goods or services where the price is denominated in a foreign currency;
- borrowing or lending of funds denominated in a foreign currency;
- acquisition or disposal of assets denominated in a foreign currency.

IAS 21 requires that the transaction should be recorded by translating the foreign currency amount into the entity's functional currency using the spot exchange rate at the date of the transaction (spot rate is the exchange rate for immediate delivery of the currency).

Functional and presentational currencies

Functional currency

Where an entity operates in several different national environments it may not always be a straightforward matter to determine its functional currency. Entities need to consider the following issues in determining their functional currency:

- Which currency principally influences selling prices for goods and services?
- Which country's competitive forces and regulations principally determine the selling prices of the entity's goods and services?
- In which currency are funds for financing activities (debt and equity instruments) generated?

- In which currency are receipts from operations generally kept?
- Which currency influences labour, material and other costs of providing goods or services?

Where consideration of the different factors does not result in a clear identification of the functional currency, the issue becomes a matter of judgement for management.

Presentation currency

The functional currency of an entity is a matter of fact, although identifying it may not be straightforward. By contrast, the entity's presentational currency is a matter of choice. IAS 21 permits an entity to present its financial statements in any currency it chooses; this may differ from the entity's functional currency. Why would an entity choose a presentation currency that is different from its functional currency? One of the following reasons may apply:

- The entity's functional currency is relatively obscure. The entity may then choose to report in a currency such as US dollars or Euros in order to make its financial statements more transparent.
- The entity's principal investors tend to function in another currency from the entity's own functional currency.
- The entity may be seeking investment from potential investors whose functional currency is not the same as the entity's functional currency.

Translating foreign operations

Sometimes, foreign operations such as subsidiaries, branches, associates and joint ventures operate using a different functional currency from that of the reporting entity. Where this is the case, the results, assets and liabilities of the foreign operation must be translated into a presentation currency, that is, the currency of the reporting entity.

The method employed is as follows:

(a) assets and liabilities should be translated using the closing rate at the date of the statement of financial position;
(b) income and expenses should be translated at the exchange rates in force at the date of the transactions; (for practical reasons, an average rate for the period may be used instead*)
(c) all resulting exchange differences are recognised as part of equity, until such time as the investment in the foreign operation is realised.

Consolidation techniques are the same for foreign operations as for operations reporting under the same functional currency as the investor. The requirements of IFRS 3 *Business Combinations*, IAS 28 *Investments in Associates*, IAS 31 *Interests in Joint Ventures* and IAS 27 *Consolidated and Separate Financial Statements* apply equally to foreign operations.

Goodwill arising on the consolidation of a foreign operation should be recognised according to the requirements of IFRS 3. Such goodwill is treated as being an investment by the reporting entity in an asset, and it should be translated along with all other investee's assets at the closing rate. Fair value adjustments to the carrying amounts of assets and liabilities in the foreign operation should also be translated at the closing rate.

*However, if there are significant fluctuations in the exchange rate during an accounting period, it may not be acceptable to use the average rate.

Hedging

Hedging establishes a relationship between a hedging instrument and a hedged item.

A *hedged item* in the context of this chapter is a net investment in a foreign operation.

A *hedging instrument*, in the context of this chapter, is a financial liability (loan) whose cash flows are expected to offset cash flows of a designated hedge item.

Provided that the hedge is designated as such, the exchange movements on both the investment and the hedge can be recognised as part of equity. If hedging were not permitted, gains or losses on the investment in the foreign operation would be recognised as part of equity (as required by IAS 21) but gains or losses on the loan would be recognised in profit for the year. Hedging allows for recognition of the substance of the relationship between the investment and the loan that finances it.

Medium answer questions

Question 1 – Sizewell Ltd

Sizewell Ltd trades in the UK, and on 1 January 20X4 it acquired a subsidiary, Trent GmbH, in Germany. The statement of financial position of the two companies as at 31 December 20X4 were as follows:

	Sizewell Ltd		Trent GmbH	
	£000	£000	€000	€000
Assets				
Non-current assets				
Property, plant and equipment		150		25
Investment in Trent Gmbh		70		–
		220		25
Current assets				
Inventory	80		17	
Receivables	24		10	
Cash	36	140	2	29
Total assets		360		54
Equity and liabilities				
Capital and reserves		100		20
Ordinary share capital		210		20
Accumulated profits		310		40
Non-current liabilities				
Loan		20		9
Current liabilities				
Trade payables				
		360		54

Further information:

- At the date of acquisition the accumulated profits of Trent GbmH were €10,000.
- Sizewell Ltd acquired 80% of the share capital of Trent GbmH.
- Trent GbmH has retained control over its day-to-day operations with Sizewell Ltd deliberately adopting a hands-off approach.

88 Exam Practice Kit: Financial Management

- It is the group's policy to value non-controlling interests at its proportionate share of the fair value of the subsidiary's identifiable net assets.
- A range of exchange rates are available:

1 January 20X4	£1 = €1.8
Average for 20X4	£1 = €1.64
31 December 20X4	£1 = €1.6

Requirement

Prepare the consolidated statement of financial position of Sizewell Ltd for the year ended 31 December 20X4.
(10 marks)

Question 2 – Home (May '06)

The income statements for Home and its wholly owned subsidiary Foreign for the year ended 31 July 2006 are shown below:

	Home $000	Foreign Crowns 000
Revenue	3,000	650
Cost of sales	(2,400)	(550)
Gross profit	600	100
Distribution costs	(32)	(41)
Administrative expenses	(168)	(87)
Finance costs	(15)	(10)
Profit (Loss) before tax	385	(38)
Income tax	(102)	10
Profit (Loss) for the period	283	(28)

Notes

1. The presentation currency of the group is the $ and Foreign's functional currency is the Crown.
2. Home acquired 100% of the ordinary share capital of Foreign on 1 August 2004 for 204,000 Crowns. Foreign's share capital at that date comprised 1,000 ordinary shares of 1 Crown each, and its reserves were 180,000 Crowns. In view of its subsidiary's losses, Home's directors conducted an impairment review of the goodwill at 31 July 2006. They concluded that the goodwill had lost 20% of its value during the year (before taking exchange differences into account). The impairment should be reflected in the consolidated financial statements for the year ended 31 July 2006.
3. On 1 June 2006, Home purchased an item of plant for 32,000 Florins. At the year end, the payable amount had not yet been settled. No exchange gain or loss in respect of this item is reflected in Home's income statement above.
4. Exchange rates are as follows:

On 1 August 2004:	1.7 Crowns = $1
On 31 July 2006:	2.2 Crowns = $1
Average rate for year ended 31 July 2006:	2.4 Crowns = $1
On 1 June 2006:	1.5 Florins = $1
On 31 July 2006:	1.6 Florins = $1

5. During the year, Foreign made sales of 50,000 Crowns to Home. None of the items remained in inventory at the year end.
6. It is the group's policy to value non-controlling interests at its proportionate share of the fair value of the subsidiary's identifiable net assets.

Requirement

Prepare the consolidated income statement for the Home group for the year ended 31 July 2006. (Work to the nearest $100) **(10 marks)**

Answers to medium answer questions

Answer 1 – Sizewell Ltd

Consolidated statement of financial position as at 31 December 20X4

	£000	£000
Assets		
Non-current assets		
Property, plant and equipment		165.625
Intangibles [W1]		63.75
		229.375
Current assets		
Inventory	90.625	
Receivables	30.25	
Cash	37.25	
		158.125
Total assets		387.5
Equity and liabilities		
Capital and reserves		
Ordinary share capital		100
Accumulated profits [W4]		223.75
		323.75
Non-controlling interest [W2 and W3]		5
		328.75
Non-current liabilities		
Loan		33.125
Current liabilities		
Trade payables		25.625
		387.5

Workings

1. *Goodwill*

	£000	£000
Cost of investment [70 × €1.8]		126
Share capital at acquisition	20	
Reserves at acquisition	10	
	30	
80% stake		(24)
		102
Translated at the closing rate	[£1 = €1.6]	€63.75

2. *Translation of Trent GbmH statement of financial position*

	€000	Trent GmbH Rate [£1 =]	£000	£000
Assets				
Non-current assets				
Property, plant and equipment	25	1.6		15.625
				15.265
Current assets				
Inventory	17	1.6	10.625	
Receivables	10	1.6	6.25	
Cash	2	1.6	1.25	
Total assets	54			18.125
Equity and liabilities				33.75
Capital and reserves				
Ordinary share capital	20	1.8		11.111
Accumulated profits: Pre-acq.	10	1.8		5.555
Accumulated profits: Post-acq.	10	Bal fig		8.334
				25
Non-current liabilities				
Loan	5	1.6		3.125
Current liabilities				
Trade payables	9	1.6		5.625
	54			33.75

3. *Non-controlling interest*
   20% × €25,000 = €5,000

4. *Consolidated accumulated profits*

	£000
Sizewell Ltd	210
Trent GbmH [80% × 8.334]	6.667
Goodwill exchange gain [W5]	7.083
	223.75

There was no indication of a goodwill impairment since acquisition.

5. *Gain for the year on the retranslation of goodwill*

	£000
Goodwill at start of period [€102,000/1.8]	(56.667)
Goodwill at end of period [€102,000/1.6]	63.75
	7.083

Answer 2 – Home

Home group: Income statement for the year ended 31 July 2006

	$000
Revenue (3,000 + [650/2.4] − 20.8) (W1)	3,250.0
Cost of sales (2,400 + [550/2.4] − 20.8) (W1)	(2,608.4)
Gross profit	641.6
Distribution costs (32 + [41/2.4])	(49.1)
Administrative expenses (168 + *[87/2.4]*)	(204.3)
Goodwill impairment (W2)	(1.9)
Exchange gain (W3)	1.3
Finance costs (15 + [10/2.4])	(19.2)
Profit before tax	368.4
Income tax (102 − [10/2.4])	(97.8)
Profit for the period	270.6

1. *Workings Intra-group sales*
   Translate at average rate: 50/2.4 = $20.8
   Deduct from both revenue and cost of sales

2. *Goodwill on consolidation and impairment*

	Crowns 000
Cost of investment	204
Acquired:	(181)
Goodwill	23

   Impairment = 23,000 × 20% = 4,600 Crowns
   Translated at average rate = [4,600/2.4] 1.9 (to nearest $100)

3. *Exchange difference on payable*

	$000
Payable recognised on 1 June 2006: [32,000/1.5]	21.3
Payable translated at closing rate: [32,000/1.6]	20.0
Exchange gain	1.3

Long answer questions

Question 1

Little was incorporated over 20 years ago, operating as an independent entity for 15 years until 1998 when it was taken over by Large. Large's directors decided that the local expertise of Little's management should be utilised as far as possible, and since the takeover they have allowed the subsidiary to operate independently, maintaining its existing supplier and customer bases. Large exercises 'arms' length' strategic control, but takes no part in day-to-day operational decisions.

The statements of financial positions of Large and Little at 31 March 2004 are given below. The statement of financial position of Little is prepared in francos (F), its reporting currency.

	Large		Little	
	$000	$000	F000	F000
Non-current assets:				
Property, plant and equipment	63,000		80,000	
Investments	12,000		–	
		75,000		80,000
Current assets:				
Inventories	25,000		30,000	
Trade receivables	20,000		28,000	
Cash	6,000		5,000	
		51,000		63,000
		126,000		143,000
Equity:				
Share capital				
(50 cents/1 Franco shares)		30,000		40,000
Revaluation reserve		–		6,000
Retained earnings		35,000		34,000
		65,000		80,000
Non-current liabilities:				
Long-term borrowings	20,000		25,000	
Deferred tax	6,000		10,000	
		26,000		35,000
Current liabilities:				
Trade payables	25,000		20,000	
Tax	7,000		8,000	
Bank overdraft	3,000		–	
		35,000		28,000
		126,000		143,000

Notes

1. *Investment by Large in Little*

   On 1 April 1998 Large purchased 36,000 shares in Little for 72 million francos. The retained earnings of Little at that date were 26 million francos. It is group policy to carry non-controlling interest as a proportionate share of net asset. At 1 April 2003 goodwill had been fully impaired.

2. *Intra-group trading*

   Little sells goods to Large, charging a mark-up of one-third on production cost. At 31 March 2004, Large held $1 million (at cost to Large) of goods purchased from Little in its inventories. The goods were purchased during March 2004 and were recorded by Large using an exchange rate of $1 = 5 francos. (There were minimal fluctuations between the two currencies during March 2003.) At 31 March 2003, Large's inventories included no goods purchased from Little. On 29 March 2004, Large sent Little a cheque for $1 million to clear the intra-group payable. Little received and recorded this cash on 3 April 2004.

3. *Accounting policies*

   The accounting policies of the two companies are the same, except that the directors of Little have decided to adopt a policy of revaluation of property, whereas Large includes all property in its statement of financial position at depreciated historical cost. Until 1 April 2003, Little operated from rented warehouse premises. On that date, the entity purchased a leasehold building for 25 million francos, taking out a long-term loan to finance the purchase. The building's estimated useful life at 1 April 2003 was 25 years, with an estimated residual value of nil, and the directors decided to adopt a policy of straight line depreciation. The building was professionally revalued at 30 million francos on 31 March 2004, and the directors have included the revalued amount in the statement of financial position. No other property was owned by Little during the year.

4. *Non-controlling interest*
   It is the group's policy to value non-controlling interests at its proportionate share of the fair value of the subsidiary's identifiable net assets.

5. *Exchange rates*

Date	Exchange rate (francos to $1)
1 April 1998	6.0
31 March 2003	5.5
31 March 2004	5.0
Weighted average for the year to 31 March 2004	5.2
Weighted average for the dates of acquisition of closing inventory	5.1

Requirements

(a) Explain (with reference to relevant accounting standards to support your argument) how the financial statements (statement of financial position and income statement) of Little should be translated into $s for the consolidation of Large and Little. **(5 marks)**

(b) Translate the statement of financial position of Little at 31 March 2004 into $s and prepare the consolidated statement of financial position of the Large group at 31 March 2004. **(20 marks)**

Note: Ignore any deferred tax implications of the property revaluation and the intra-group trading. **(Total = 25 marks)**

Question 2 (Nov '08)

On 1 November 2003, DX invested in 100% of the share capital of EY, a new entity incorporated on that date. EY's operations are located in a foreign country where the currency is the Franc. DX has no other subsidiaries. It is the group's policy to value non-controlling interests at its proportionate share of the fair value of the subsidiary's identifiable net assets.

The summary financial statements of the two entities at their 31 October 2008 year end were as follows:

Summary income statements for the year ended 31 October 2008

	DX $000	EY Franc 000
Revenue	3,600	1,200
Cost of sales, other expenses and income tax	(2,800)	(1,000)
Profit for the period	800	200

Summary statements of changes in equity for the year ended 31 October 2008

	DX $000	EY Franc 000
Brought forward at 1 November 2007	5,225	1,500
Profit for the period	800	200
Dividends	(200)	–
Carried forward at 31 October 2008	5,825	1,700

Summary statements of financial position at 31 October 2008

	DX $000	EY Franc 000
Property, plant and equipment	5,000	1,500
Investment in EY	25	–
Current assets	4,400	2,000
	9,425	3,500
Share capital	1,000	50
Retained earnings	4,825	1,650
Current liabilities	3,600	1,800
	9,425	3,500

Relevant exchange rates were as follows:

1 November 2003	1$ = 2.0 francs
31 October 2007	1$ = 2.3 francs
31 October 2008	1$ = 2.7 francs
Average rate for year ended 31 October 2008	1$ = 2.6 francs

Requirements

(a) Explain the meaning of the term "functional currency" as used by IAS 21 *The Effects of Changes in Foreign Exchange Rates,* and identify THREE factors that an entity should consider in determining its functional currency.

(4 marks)

(b) Prepare:
  (i) the summary consolidated income statement for the year ended 31 October 2008;

  (2 marks)

  (ii) the summary consolidated statement of financial position at 31 October 2008.

  (6 marks)

(c) Prepare the summary consolidated statement of changes in equity for the year to 31 October 2008 and a calculation that shows how the exchange gain or loss for the year has arisen.

(13 marks)

(Work to the nearest $)

(Total = 25 marks)

Answers to long answer questions

Answer 1

(a) It is clear from the information contained in the question that, on a day-to-day basis, Little operates as a relatively independent entity, with its own supplier and customer bases. Therefore, the cash flows of Little do not have a day-to-day impact on the cash flows of Large. In these circumstances, IAS 21 – *The effects of changes in foreign exchange rates* – requires that the financial statements be translated using the closing rate (or net investment) method. This involves translating the net assets in the statement of financial position at the spot rate of exchange at the statement of financial position date and the net profit in the income statement at a weighted average rate for the year. Exchange differences are reported as a movement on equity as they do not impact on the cash flows of the group until the relevant investment is disposed of.

(b) **Step 1 – adjust Little's statement of financial position to reflect group accounting policies:**

	F000
DR Revaluation reserve	6,000
CR Property, plant and equipment	6,000

Step 2 – translate the statement of financial position of Little into $ (after incorporating the adjustment in step 1)

	F000	Rate	$000
Non-current assets (80,000 – 6,000)	74,000	5	14,800
Inventories	30,000	5	6,000
Trade receivables	28,000	5	5,600
Cash	5,000	5	1,000
	137,000		27,400
Share capital	40,000	6	6,667
Revaluation reserve (6,000 – 6,000)	–		–
Retained profits:			
Pre-acquisition	26,000	6	4,333
Post-acquisition (34,000 – 26,000)	8,000	Balance	3,800
	74,000		14,800
Interest-bearing borrowings	25,000	5	5,000
Deferred tax	10,000	5	2,000
Trade payables	20,000	5	4,000
Tax	8,000	5	1,600
	137,000		27,400

Step 3 – prepare the consolidated statement of financial position

	$000	$000
Non-current assets:		
Property, plant and equipment (63,000 + 14,800)		77,800
Current assets:		
Inventories (25,000 + 6,000 − 250)	30,750	
Trade receivables (20,000 + 5,600 − 1,000)	24,600	
Cash (6,000 + 1,000 + 1,000)	8,000	
		63,350
		141,150
Capital and reserves:		
Called up share capital		30,000
Accumulated profits (W5)		36,095
Non-controlling interest (W4)		1,455
		67,550
Non-current liabilities:		
Interest-bearing borrowings (20,000 + 5,000)	25,000	
Deferred tax (6,000 + 2,000)	8,000	
		33,000
Current liabilities:		
Trade payables (25,000 + 4,000)	29,000	
Tax (7,000 + 1,600)	8,600	
Overdraft	3,000	
		40,600
		141,150

Workings

1. *Group structure*
   Large owns 36 million of the 40 million Little shares in issue. This is a **90%** subsidiary.

2. *Goodwill on acquisition*

	$000
Investment at cost	12,000
Less share capital acquired (36,000/6)	(6,000)
Less accumulated profits at acquisition ([26,000 × 90%]/6)	(3,900)
Goodwill on acquisition	2,100

   Goodwill was fully impaired by 31 March 2003, five years after acquisition.

3. *Intra-group trading*
   Cost to Large includes 1/3 mark-up on Little's production cost. The unrealised profit in Little is therefore: $1 million × 25% = $250,000. Of this 90% ($225,000) should be adjusted through consolidated reserves and 10% ($25,000) through non-controlling interest. Cash in transit of $1million must be added to consolidated cash and deducted from consolidated receivables.

4. *Non-controlling interest*

Non-controlling interest's share of net assets in Little: (10% × $14,800)	1,480
Less adjustment for intra-group trading (W3)	(25)
	1,455

5. *Accumulated profits*

	$000
Large	35,000
Little (share of post-acquisition: 3,800 × 90%)	3,420
Less goodwill impaired (W2)	(2,100)
Less unrealised profit (W3)	(225)
	36,095

Answer 2 (Nov '08)

(a) An entity's functional currency is the currency of the primary economic environment in which it operates. Entities need to consider the following factors in determining their functional currency:

- Which currency primarily influences selling prices for goods and services?
- Which country's competitive forces and regulations principally determine the selling prices of the entity's goods and services?
- In which currency are funds for financial activities (debt and equity instruments) generated?
- In which currency are receipts from operations generally kept?
- Which currency influences labour, material and other costs of providing goods or services?

(b) (i) **Income statement for the year ended 31 October 2008**

	EY Franc	Rate $	EY $	DX $	Consolidation adjustment	Consolidated
Revenue	1,200,000	2.60	461,538	3,600,000		4,061,538
Expenses	1,000,000	2.60	384,615	2,800,000		3,184,615
Profit	200,000		76,923	800,000		876,923

(ii) **Statement of financial position at 31 October 2008**

	EY Franc	Rate $	EY $	DX $	Consolidation adjustment	Consolidated
PPE	1,500,000	2.70	555,556	5,000,000		5,555,556
Investment				25,000	(25,000)	–
Current assets	2,000,000	2.70	740,741	4,400,000		5,140,741
	3,500,000		1,296,297	9,425,000	(25,000)	10,696,297
Share capital	50,000	2.00	25,000	1,000,000	(25,000)	1,000,000
Retained earnings	1,650,000	Balfig	604,630	4,825,000		5,429,630
Current liabilities	1,800,000	2.70	666,667	3,600,000		4,266,667
	3,500,000		1,296,297	9,425,000	(25,000)	10,696,297

98 Exam Practice Kit: Financial Management

(c) **Statement of changes in equity for the year ended 31 October 2008**

	$
Brought forward at 1 November 2007 (W1)	5,852,174
Profit for the period (from income statement)	876,923
Dividend	(200,000)
Exchange loss (balancing figure)	(99,467)
Closing equity (1,000,000 + 5,429,630)	6,429,630

Working

1. *Equity brought forward at 1 November 2007*

	$
Post-acquisition retained earnings in EY	
Opening equity in EY (1,650,000 + 50,000 − 200,000)	652,174
1,500,000 francs @ 2.30	
Less: share capital in EY (50,000 @ 2.00)	(25,000)
	627,174
DX equity	5,225,000
	5,852,174

Exchange loss for the year

Opening equity in EY (1,500,000 francs as above):

	$	$
Translated at opening rate (1,500,000/2.30)	652,174	
Translated at closing rate (1,500,000/2.70)	555,556	
Exchange loss		96,618
Profit for the year in EY (200,000):		
Translated at average rate (200,000/2.60)	76,923	
Translated at closing rate (200,000/2.70)	74,074	
Exchange loss		2,849
		99,467

8

Complex Group Structures

Complex Group Structures

8

> **LEARNING OUTCOME**
>
> After studying this chapter students should be able to:
> - prepare a consolidated income statement and statement of financial position for a group of entities.

The concept of the sub-subsidiary

- Illustration 1 – Company T is a subsidiary of the group as the control percentage exercised by the parent is 70%; although the effective stake is 56%.

```
      Parent
        |
       80%
        ↓
    Subsidiary
        |
       70%
        ↓
    Company T
```

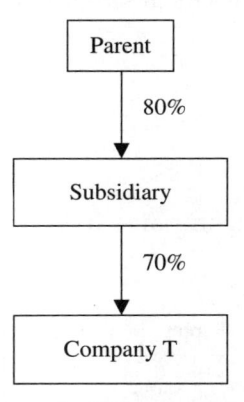

- Illustration 2 – Company T is a subsidiary of the group as the control percentage exercised by the parent is 60%; although the effective stake is 36%.

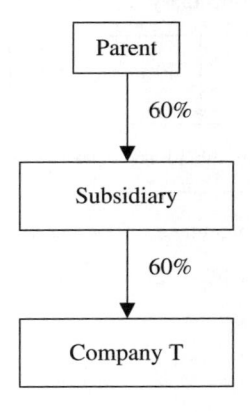

```
      Parent
        |
       60%
        ↓
    Subsidiary
        |
       60%
        ↓
    Company T
```

- When dealing with complex groups it is vital that a distinction is made between
  - Control percentage – used to determine the status of the investment, and hence the consolidation method is used; and
  - Effective percentage – used to actually perform the consolidation.

Key differences for sub-subsidiary

Goodwill on consolidation – sub-subsidiary

	$	$
Consideration		X
Net assets at date of acquisition:		
Share capital ($1 shares)	X	
Retained earnings	X	
	X	
Subsidiary share (%)		X
Subsidiary's goodwill		X
Group share ie parent share of subsidiary		X

Non-controlling interest – proportionate share of net assets approach

	$
NCI share of subsidiary's net assets at statement of financial position date	X
Less NCI share of cost of subsidiary	(X)
NCI share of sub-subsidiary net assets at statement of financial position date	X
(based on effective interest)	X

Mixed group

In these circumstances the parent company has both a direct and indirect stake in the sub-subsidiary.

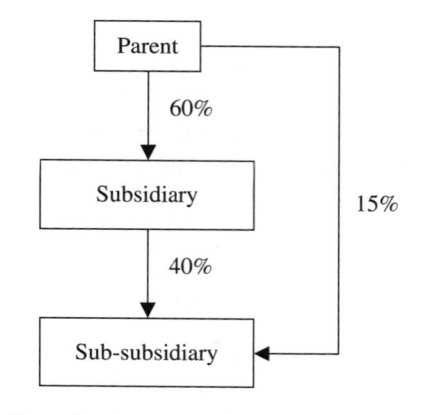

```
        Parent
       /      \
     60%      15%
      ↓        |
   Subsidiary  |
      |        |
     40%       |
      ↓        ↓
    Sub-subsidiary
```

Control percentage = 55% (there a subsidiary)

Effective percentage = 39%

Indirect investment in associates or joint ventures

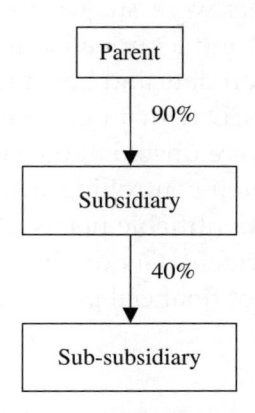

```
        Parent
          │ 90%
          ▼
       Subsidiary
          │ 40%
          ▼
     Sub-subsidiary
```

Control percentage = 40% (hence an associate)

Effective percentage = 36%

- The investment shown above will be consolidated using equity accounting as a 40% associate, and then 4% will be awarded to non-controlling interests to achieve the lower effec percentage.

Medium answer questions

Question 1

AB purchased 40,000 shares in CD on 1 January 2002 for $150,000 when the reserves of CD were $20,000. CD purchased 30,000 shares in EF on 1 January 2001 for $100,000 when the reserves of EF were $10,000. On the 1 January 2002 the reserves of EF were $16,000.

Below are the statements of financial position for three companies for the year ended 30 November 2006.

	AB $000	CD $000	EF $000
Non-current assets			
Investments	150	100	–
Tangibles	160	120	100
Current assets			
Inventory	44	62	34
Receivables	62	48	42
Cash/Bank	20	22	32
	436	352	208
Share Capital $1	80	50	40
Reserves	48	46	36
Non-current liabilities	240	130	60
Current liabilities	68	126	72
	436	352	208

Additional information

1. On 1 January 2002 CD's net assets were subject to a fair value adjustment. CD held plant with a book value of $10,000 and a fair value of $15,000. This land was still owned at the statement of financial position date and had a remaining useful life of five years.
2. During the year AB sold goods to CD with an invoice value of $20,000 and at a mark up on cost of 25%. ¼ of these goods were unsold at the year end.
3. It is the group's policy to value non-controlling interests at its proportionate share of the fair value of the subsidiary's identifiable net assets. Goodwill arising on acquisition of CD has not suffered any impairment. Goodwill arising on acquisition of EF has been impaired by 40% at the statement of financial position date.

Requirement

Prepare the consolidated statement of financial position date for the AB Group as at 30 November 2006.

Question 2

ST purchased 80% of UV on 1 January 2007 for $500m when the balance on the retained earnings was $60m. UV purchased 60% of the share capital of XY on 1 January 2006 for $270m when the retained earnings stood at $80m.

Income statements for the year ended 31 December 2007:

	ST $m	UV $m	XY $m
Revenue	400	340	320
Cost of sales	(88)	(60)	(64)
Gross profit	312	280	256
Operating expenses	(20)	(14)	(14)
Profits before taxation	292	272	242
Income tax	(48)	(30)	(20)
Profit after tax	244	242	222

1. During the year XY sold good to ST for $20m at a mark up on cost of 25%. Half were still in inventory at the end of the year.
2. It is the group's policy to value non-controlling interests at its proportionate sare of the fair value of the subsidiary's identifiable net assets. Goodwill has been impaired in the current year only by 10%. It should be charged to operating expenses.
3. Share capital and retained earnings at 1 January 2007 were:

	SC $m	RE $m
ST	700	100
UV	500	60
XY	300	110

Requirement

Prepare the consolidated income statement for the ST Group for the year ended 31 December 2007. Your answer should be completed to one decimal place.

✓ Answers to medium answer questions

Answer 1

AB Group Consolidated statement of financial position as at 30 November 2006

	$000
Non-current assets	
Goodwill (W3) (86 + 27.8)	113.8
Tangibles (160+120+100+10)	390
Current assets	
Inventory (44 + 62 + 34 − 2 (W6))	138
Receivables (62 + 48 + 42)	152
Cash/Bank (20 + 22 + 32)	74
	867.8
Share capital	80
Reserves (W5)	60.2
Non-controlling interest (W4)	31.6
Non-current liabilities (240 + 130 + 60)	430
Current liabilities (68 + 126 + 72)	266
	867.8

Workings

1. *Goodwill – Goodwill arising on acquisition of CD*

		$m
Cost of investment		150
Less 80% of net assets at acquisition		
OSC	50	
Reserves	20	
Fair value adjustment (30−20)	10	
	×80%	(64)
		80

Goodwill arising on acquisition of EF

		$m
Cost of investment		100
Less 75% of net assets at acquisition		
OSC	40	
Reserves	16	
	×75%	
		(42)
		58
Group share 80%		46.4

106 Exam Practice Kit: Financial Management

2. *Unrealised Profit*

$$\text{Unsold inventory} \times \frac{\text{Mark up}}{100 + \text{Mark up}}$$

$$\tfrac{1}{4} \times \$0m \times \frac{25}{125} = \$2m$$

3. *Non-controlling interest*

	$m
NCI in CD:	
20% net assets at SFP	21.2
20% × (50 + 46 + 10)	
Less 20% COI (100)	(20)
NCI in EF:	
40% net assets at SFP	30.4
40% × (40 + 36)	
	31.6

4. *Group reserves*

	$m
100% Abs	48
80% CD's post acq 80% × (106 − 80)	20.8
60% EF's post acq 60% × (76 − 56)	12
Less PUP (W6)	(2)
Less impairment (W3)	(18.6)
	60.2

Answer 2

Consolidated income statement

	$m
Revenue (400 + 340 + 320) − 20	1040.0
Cost of sales (88 + 60 + 64) − 20 + 2	(194.0)
Gross profit	846.0
Operating expenses (20 + 14 + 14) + 5.2 + 1.9	(55.1)
Profit before tax	790.9
Income tax (48 + 30 + 20)	(98.0)
Profit after tax	692.9
Attributable to NCI (W5)	173.8
Group profit (692.9 − 173.8)	519.1

Workings

1. *Group Structure*

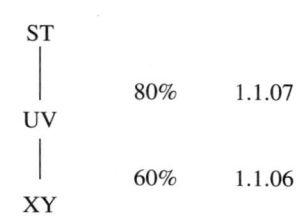

```
        ST
        |
        |  80%   1.1.07
        UV
        |
        |  60%   1.1.06
        XY
```

UV 80% sub from 1.1.07
XY 48% (80% × 60%) sub from 1.1.07

2. *Net assets*

	UV Acq 1.1.07 $m	XY Acq 1.1 07 $m
SC	500	300
RE	60	110
	560	410

3. *Goodwill*

UV

	$m
Cost of investment	500
For 80% NA at acq (80% × 560)	(448)
	52
Less impairment 10%	(5.2)

XY

	$m
Cost of investment	270
For 60% NA at acq (60% × 410)	(246)
UV's goodwill in XY	24
Group share 80% × 24	19.2
Less impairment 10%	(1.9)

4. *Unrealised profit*

$$\text{Unsold inventory} \times \frac{\text{Mark up}}{100 + \text{Mark up}}$$

$$\tfrac{1}{4} \times 20,000 \times \frac{25}{125} = \$1,000$$

5. *Non-controlling interest*

UV 20% post acq PAT (20% × 242)	48.4
XY 52% post acq PAT (52% × 222)	115.4
	173.8

Long answer questions

Question 1 – Big, Small and Tiny

The draft statement of financial position of Big, Small and Tiny at 30 September 20×9 (the accounting date for all three companies) are given below:

	Big $000	Big $000	Small $000	Small $000	Tiny $000	Tiny $000
Non-current assets						
Tangible assets	56,000		66,000		56,000	
Investments (Notes 1–3)	104,000		29,000		-	
		160,000		95,000		56,000
Current assets						
Inventories (Note 4)	45,000		44,000		25,000	
Trade receivables (Note 5)	40,000		30,000		16,000	
Cash	8,000		6,000		3,000	
		93,000		80,000		44,000
		253,000		175,000		100,000
Equity						
Share capital		90,000		80,000		32,000
Reserves		78,000		67,000		22,000
		168,000		147,000		54,000
Non-current liabilities						
Long-term loans		50,000				25,000
Current liabilities						
Trade payables (Note 5)	16,000		12,000		8,000	
Tax payable	7,000		6,000		4,000	
Bank overdraft	12,000		10,000		9,000	
		35,000		28,000		21,000
		253,000		175,000		100,000

Notes

1. On 1 October 20×3, when the reserves of Small showed a balance of $22 million, Big purchased 64 million of Small's $1 equity shares for a consideration of $91.5 million, payable in cash. On 1 October 20×3, a large property owned by Small had a statement of financial position value of $7 million and a fair value to Big of $11 million. With the exception of this property, the fair values of all the identifiable net assets of Small were the same as their carrying values in the statement of financial position of Small. The property that had a fair value of $11 million on 1 October 20×3 was sold by Small on 30 June 20×7.
2. On 1 April 20×9, when the reserves of Tiny stood at $10m, Big purchased 8 million of Tiny's $1 equity shares for a cash consideration of $12.5 million.
   Also on 1 April 20×9, Small purchased 16 million of Tiny's $1 equity shares for a cash consideration of $29 million. A fair-value exercise was carried out but all of the net identifiable assets of Tiny at 1 April 20×9 had a fair value that was the same as their carrying values in the statement of financial position of Tiny.
   A fair-value exercise was carried out but all of the net identifiable assets of Tiny at 1 April 20×9 had a fair value that was the same as their carrying values in the statement of financial position of Tiny.
   During the year ended 30 September 20×9, Tiny made a profit after taxation of $8 million and paid no interim dividends. This profit accrued evenly over the year.

4. A key reason behind the purchases of shares in Tiny by Big and Small was that Tiny supplied a component that was used by both companies. Until 1 April 20×9, the component was supplied by Tiny at cost plus a mark-up of 30 per cent. From 1 April 20×9, the mark-up changed to 20 per cent. On 30 September 20×9, the inventories of components purchased from Tiny (all purchases since 1 April 20×9) were as follows:
   - in Big's books, $9 million;
   - in Small's books, $7.8 million.
5. The trade payables of Big and Small show amounts of $6 million and $5 million respectively as being payable to Tiny, and these balances have been agreed. There was no other inter-group trading.
6. It is the group's policy to value non-controlling interests at its proportionate share of the fair value of the subsidiary's identifiable net assets.

Requirement

Prepare the consolidated statement of financial position of the Big group at 30 September 20×9. **(25 marks)**

☑ Answer to long answer questions

Answer 1

Consolidated Statement of Financial Position at 30 September 20×9

	$000	$000
Non-current assets		
Tangible assets		178,000
Intangible assets (6,700 + 2,000 + 6,400)(W3)		15,100
		193,100
Current assets		
Inventories (45,000 + 44,000 + 25,000 − 2,800)(W4)	111,200	
Receivables (40,000 + 30000 + 16000 − 6000 − 5000)	75,000	
Cash and cash equivalents	17,000	
		203,200
		396,300
Equity attributable to equity holders of the parent		
Share capital		90,000
Retained earnings (W6)		116,780
		206,780
Non-controlling interests (W5)		41,520
		248,300
Non-current liabilities		
Long-term loans (50,000 + 25,000)		75,000
Current liabilities		
Trade payables (16,000 + 12,000 + 8,000 − 6,000 − 5,000)	25,000	
Taxation	17,000	
Bank overdraft	31,000	
		73,000
		396,300

Workings

1. *Group structure*

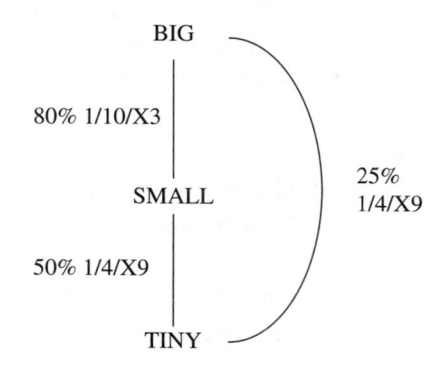

```
            BIG
       /          \
   80% 1/10/X3    25% 1/4/X9
      |            |
    SMALL          |
      |            |
   50% 1/4/X9      |
      |            |
     TINY ---------/
```

2. *Net assets of Small*

	At acquisition $000	At SFP date $000
Share capital	80,000	80,000
Retained earnings	22,000	59,000
Fair value adjustment	4,000	
	106,000	139,000

Net assets of Tiny

	At acq'n 1.4.×9 $000	At statement of financial position date $000
Share capital	32,000	32,000
Retained earnings (W7)	10,000	22,000
	42,000	54,000

3. *Goodwill*

	$000	$000
Big in Small		
Cost of investment		91,500
Less: net assets acquired: (80% × 106,000) (W2)		(84,800)
		6,700
Big in Tiny		
Cost of investment		12,500
Less: net assets acquired: (25% × 42,000) (W3)		(10,500)
		2,000
Big in Tiny (via Small)		
Cost of investment		29,000
Less: net assets acquired: (50% × 42,000) (W3)		(21,000)
Small's goodwill in Tiny		8,000
Group share (80% × 8,000)		6,400

4. *Unrealised profit in inventory*

	$000	$000
Unrealised profit ((9,000 + 7,800) × 20/120)		2,800
Double entry:		
Dr Consolidated retained earnings (65%)	1,820	
Dr Non-controlling interests (35%)	980	
Cr Inventory		2,800

5. *Non-controlling interests*

	$000
Small (20% × 147,000) (W2)	29,400
Less NCI share of cost of Tiny (20% × 29,000)	(5,800)
Tiny (35% × 54,000) (W2)	18,900
Less PUP W4	(980)
	41,520

6. *Retained earnings*

	$000	$000
Big		78,000
Small: At 30 September 20×9	147,000	
At acquisition (W2)	(106,000)	
	41,000	
Group share (80%)		32,800
Tiny: Indirect		
At 30 September 20×9	54,000	
At acquisition (W2)	(42,000)	
	12,000	
Group share (40%)		4,800
Tiny: Direct		
At 30 September 20×9	54,000	
At acquisition (W2)	(42,000)	
	12,000	
Group share (25%)		3,000
Less PUP W4		(1,820)
		116,780

9

Substance Over Form

Substance Over Form 9

> **LEARNING OUTCOMES**
>
> After studying this chapter students should be able to:
> - discuss the principle of substance over form applied to a range of transactions; including:
>   - Sale and repurchase agreements
>   - Consignment stock
>   - Debt factoring
>   - Securitised assets and loan transfers.

The concept of substance over form and off-statement of financial position financing

There is no stand alone IAS on substance over form, but useful sources of reference include:
- IAS 1 *Presentation of financial statements*
- IAS 18 *Revenue*
- IAS 39 *Financial instruments: recognition and measurement.*

Incentives for taking liabilities off the statement of financial position include:
- lowering gearing
- increasing the apparent scope for further borrowing
- cost maybe lower thereby increasing profit and triggering management incentives.

IAS 18 – *Revenue*

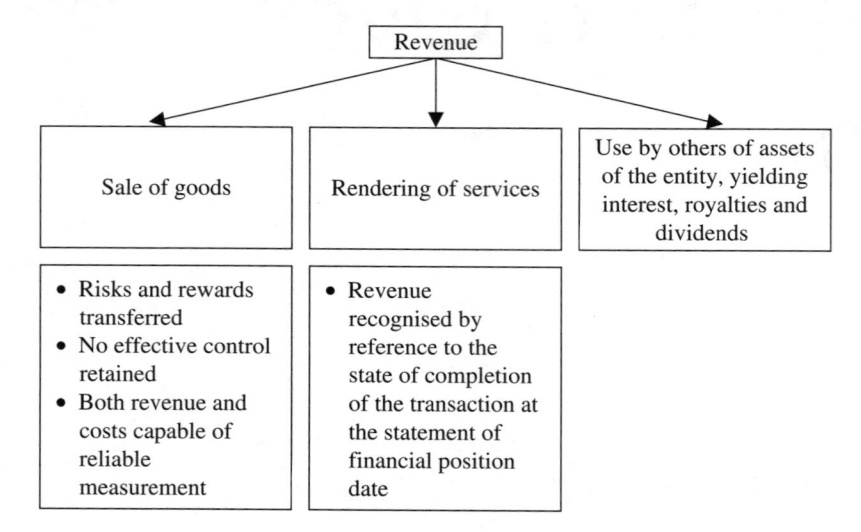

```
                    Revenue
         ┌─────────────┼─────────────┐
   Sale of goods   Rendering    Use by others of assets
                   of services  of the entity, yielding
                                interest, royalties and
                                dividends
```

- Risks and rewards transferred
- No effective control retained
- Both revenue and costs capable of reliable measurement

- Revenue recognised by reference to the state of completion of the transaction at the statement of financial position date

Recognition and derecognition of assets and liabilities

- The *Framework for the Preparation and Presentation of Financial Statements* indicates that an asset or liability should be recognised if:
    - there is sufficient evidence of existence of the item
    - the item can be measured at a monetary amount with sufficient reliability.
- IAS 39 specifies that derecognition occurs when an asset or liability is transferred together with the rights and rewards that attach to it.

Specific examples of substance over form

Sale and repurchase agreements

It is important to consider the terms of the arrangement and whether or not a sale has actually taken place. An assessment of the main risks and rewards will normally focus on the value and ultimate use of the asset being 'sold'. Consider the commercial sense of the transaction – would a financing company use the asset itself or is it just lending using it as security?

Consignment stock

Consignment stock is held by one party but owned by another. For example, motor dealers commonly hold inventory in the form of cars on their premises which will be either sold to customers or returned unsold to the manufacturer. There are benefits to both manufacturer and dealer in this type of arrangement. The dealer has access to a wider range of stock than would be possible if he or she were required to make a commitment to purchase, and the manufacturer avoids the costs of holding large quantities of inventory.

Which party, manufacturer or dealer, receives the benefits and is exposed to the risks associated with the inventory? The substance of the commercial arrangement must be examined carefully.

The table below shows the risks and benefits that may arise, depending upon the nature of the contractual arrangements, for the dealer:

Benefits	Risks
1. The cash flow arising from sales	1. The risk of having to retain obsolete inventory
2. The right to retain items of inventory to assist in making sales	2. The risk of slow movement of inventory, increasing finance costs and the risk of obsolescence
3. Insulation from price changes after the inventory has been consigned	
4. The right to use the inventory for demonstration purposes	

Factoring of receivables

Factoring of receivables can be a very useful way of raising cash quickly. However, where such transactions take place it is important to establish their substance. Factoring can be a financing transaction in substance, where cash is advanced against the security of receivables. Or, the transaction may be more in the nature of a working capital shift, where receivables are simply sold on in order to be able to receive cash more quickly.

Factors provide a range of services, and it can be difficult to establish the substance of the transaction. Essentially, the key to understanding lies in the ownership of the receivable. If the provider of the cash has any opportunity of recourse to the seller (i.e. being able to pass receivables back) the deal probably constitutes a financing arrangement.

Securitised assets and loan transfers

These are similar in nature to factoring of receivables, where a loan asset is transferred to a third party as a way of securitising finance. The benefits associated with the asset are the future cash flows from the repayments and associated interest. The risks would include the risks of slow and non payment or reduction in future cash flows as a result of early repayment.

Special purpose entities (SPEs)

The purpose of SPEs is very often to remove part of a group's activities from the requirement to consolidate. They are often set up using complex legal structures. However, the SIC's guidance on this point is quite straightforward:

> An SPE should be consolidated when the substance of the relationship between an entity and the SPE indicates that the SPE is controlled by that entity (para 8).

The true substance of the relationship can be determined by examining where the decision-making powers lie, and which parties benefit from the rewards and bear the risks related to the SPE.

Medium answer questions

Question 1 – Juncus plc

Juncus plc heads a diversified group of companies that provide a range of goods and services to more than 35 countries. The year end audit has been completed, and a clean audit report issued, but the auditors have submitted a long management letter highlighting some serious concerns about the recognition of revenues. There is a clear suggestion in the letter that as the group continues to grow the issues raised could ultimately prove sufficient to lead to a qualified opinion in future years unless resolved.

An extract from the letter is shown below:

Areas of particular concern brought to our attention during our audit of your systems and year-end position are:

(i) When new industrial gas cookers are delivered to customers from your French manufacturing plant the sale is recognised upon delivery at the clients' premises.
(ii) To improve group cash flows you have wisely convinced two of your largest customers in the USA to make a 30% advance payment when they place orders irrespective of whether or not the inventory is currently held in the warehouse. This cash is recognised within your statement of financial position and revenues on the payment date.
(iii) As part of the contract to deliver and install new textiles processing equipment in Malaysia you undertake a six month training programming for the employees of your customers in the use of the equipment. This involves a trainer visiting the clients' premises for one day a month over the training period. You currently recognise the full value of the sale on the date the plant is brought into operation.

Requirements

(a) Briefly comment on the rules for the recognition of revenues on the sale of goods and services. **(4 marks)**

(b) Comment on the appropriateness of revenue recognition procedures adopted by Juncus plc in each of the cases raised by the auditor's management letter. **(6 marks)**
(Total = 10 marks)

Question 2 – LMN (May '06)

LMN trades in motor vehicles, which are manufactured and supplied by their manufacturer, IJK. Trading between the two entities is subject to a contractual agreement, the principal terms of which are as follows:

- LMN is entitled to hold on its premises at any one time up to 80 vehicles supplied by IJK. LMN is free to specify the ranges and models of vehicle supplied to it. IJK retains legal title to the vehicles until such time as they are sold to a third party by LMN.

- While the vehicles remain on its premises, LMN is required to insure them against loss or damage.
- The price at which vehicles are supplied is determined at the time of delivery; it is not subject to any subsequent alteration.
- When LMN sells a vehicle to a third party, it is required to inform IJK within three working days. IJK submits an invoice to LMN at the originally agreed price; the invoice is payable by LMN within 30 days.
- LMN is entitled to use any of the vehicles supplied to it for demonstration purposes and road testing. However, if more than a specified number of kilometres are driven in a vehicle, LMN is required to pay IJK a rental charge.
- LMN has the right to return any vehicle to IJK at any time without incurring a penalty, except for any rental charge incurred in respect of excess kilometres driven.

Requirement

Discuss the economic substance of the contractual arrangement between the two entities in respect of the recognition of inventory and of sales. Refer, where appropriate, to IAS 18 *Revenue*. **(Total = 10 marks)**

Long answer questions

Question 3 – Ned (Nov '08)

Ned is a recently appointed non-executive director of ABC Corp, a listed entity. ABC's corporate governance arrangements permit non-executives to seek independent advice on accounting and legal matters affecting the entity, where they have any grounds for concern. Ned has asked you, an independent accountant, for advice because he is worried about certain aspects of the draft financial statements for ABC's year ended 30 September 2008.

The ownership of most of ABC's ordinary share capital is widely dispersed, but the three largest institutional shareholders each own around 10% of the entity's ordinary shares. In meetings with management, these shareholders have made it clear that they expect improvements in the entity's performance and position. ABC appointed a new Chief Financial Officer (CFO) at the start of the 2007/08 financial year, and the board has set ambitious financial targets for the next five years.

The 2007/08 targets were expressed in the form of three key accounting ratios, as follows:

- Return on capital employed (profit before interest as a percentage of debt + equity): 7%
- Net profit margin (profit before tax as a percentage of revenue): 5%
- Gearing (long-term and short-term debt as a percentage of the total of debt + equity): below 48%

The draft financial statements include the following figures:

	$
Revenue	31,850,000
Profit before interest	2,972,000
Interest	1,241,000
Equity	22,450,800
Debt	18,253,500

The key ratios, based on the draft financial statements, are as follows:

Return on capital employed	7.3%
Net profit margin	5.4%
Gearing	44.8%

Ned's copies of the minutes of board meetings provide the following relevant information:

1. On 1 October 2007 ABC sold an item of plant for $1,000,000 to XB, an entity that provides financial services to businesses. The carrying value of the plant at the date of sale was $1,000,000. XB has the option to require ABC to repurchase the plant on 1 October 2008 for $1,100,000. If the option is not exercised at that date, ABC will be required under the terms of the agreement between the entities to repurchase the plant on 1 October 2009 for $1,210,000. ABC has continued to insure the plant and to store it on its business premises. The sale to XB was recognised as revenue in the draft financial statements and the asset was derecognised.

2. A few days before the 30 September 2008 year end, ABC entered into a debt factoring agreement with LM, a factoring business. The terms of the agreement are that ABC is permitted to draw down cash up to a maximum of 75% of the receivables that are covered under the factoring arrangement. However, LM is able to require repayment of any part of the receivables that are uncollectible. In addition, ABC is obliged to pay interest at an annual rate of 10% on any amounts it draws down in advance of cash being received from customers by LM. As soon as the agreement was finalised, ABC drew down the maximum cash available in respect of the $2,000,000 receivables it had transferred to LM as part of the agreement. This amount was accounted for by debiting cash and crediting receivables.

3. In October 2007, ABC issued 2,000,000 $1 preference shares at par. The full year's dividend of 8% was paid before the 30 September 2008 year end, and was recognised in the statement of changes in equity. The preference shares are redeemable in 2015, and the entity is obliged to pay the dividend on a fixed date each year. The full $2,000,000 proceeds of the issue were credited to equity capital.

Requirements

(a) Discuss the accounting treatment of the three transactions, identifying any errors that you think have been made in applying accounting principles with references, where appropriate, to IFRS. Prepare the adjustments that are required to correct those errors and identify any areas where you would require further information. **(15 marks)**

(b) Calculate the effect of your adjustments on ABC's key accounting ratios for the year ended 30 September 2008. **(7 marks)**

(c) Explain, briefly, the results and the implications of your analysis to the non-executive director. **(3 marks)**

(Total = 25 marks)

Question 4 (May '07)

You are the accounting adviser to a committee of bank lending officers. Each loan application is subject to an initial vetting procedure, which involves the examination of the application, recent financial statements, and a set of key financial ratios.

The key ratios are as follows:

- Gearing (calculated as debt/debt + equity, where debt includes both long- and short-term borrowings)
- Current ratio
- Quick ratio
- Profit margin (using profit before tax).

Existing levels of gearing are especially significant to the decision, and the committee usually rejects any application from an entity with gearing of over 45%.

The committee will shortly meet to conduct the initial vetting of a commercial loan application made by TYD, an unlisted entity. As permitted by national accounting law in its country of registration, TYD does not comply in all respects with International Financial Reporting Standards. The committee has asked you to interview TYD's finance director to determine areas of non-compliance. As a result of the interview, you have identified two significant areas for examination in respect of TYD's financial statements for the year ended 30 September 2006.

1. Revenue for the period includes a sale of inventories at cost to HPS, a banking institution, for $85,000, which took place on 30 September 2006. HPS has an option under the contract of sale to require TYD to repurchase the inventories on 30 September 2008, for $95,000. TYD has derecognised the inventories at their cost of $85,000, with a charge to cost of sales of this amount. The inventories concerned in this transaction, are, however, stored on TYD's premises, and TYD bears the cost of insuring them.

2. Some categories of TYD's inventories are sold on a sale or return basis. The entity's accounting policy in this respect is to recognise the sale at the point of despatch of goods. The standard margin on sales of this type is 20%. During the year ended 30 September 2006, $100,000 (in sales value) has been despatched in this way. The finance director estimates that approximately 60% of this value represents sales that have been accepted by customers; the remainder is potentially subject to return.

The financial statements of TYD for the year ended 30 September 2006 are as presented below. (Note: at this stage of the analysis only one year's figures are considered).

TYD: Income statement for the year ended 30 September 2006

	$000
Revenue	600
Cost of sales	450
Gross profit	150
Expenses	63
Finance costs	17
Profit before tax	70
Income tax expense	25
Profit for the period	45

TYD: Statement of changes in equity for the year ended 30 September 2006

	Share capital $000	Retained earnings $000	Total $000
Balances at 1 October 2005	100	200	300
Profit for the period		45	45
Balances at 30 September 2006	100	245	345

TYD: Statement of financial position at 30 September 2006

	$000	$000
ASSETS		
Non-current assets:		
Property, plant and equipment		527
Current assets:		
Inventories	95	
Trade receivables	72	
Cash	6	
		173
		700
EQUITY AND LIABILITIES		
Equity:		
Called up share capital		100
Retained earnings		245
		345
Non-current liabilities:		
Long-term borrowings		180
Current liabilities:		
Trade and other payables	95	
Bank overdraft	80	
		175
		700

Requirements

Prepare a report to the committee of lending officers that

(i) discusses the accounting treatment of the two significant areas identified in the interview with the FD, with reference to the requirements of International Financial Reporting Standards (IFRS) and to fundamental accounting principles; **(8 marks)**

(ii) calculates any adjustments to the financial statements that are required in order to bring them into compliance with IFRS (ignore tax); **(5 marks)**

(iii) analyses and interprets the financial statements, calculating the key ratios before and after adjustments, and making a recommendation to the lending committee on whether or not to grant TYD's application for a commercial loan. **(12 marks)**

(Total = 25 marks)

✓ Answer to medium answer questions

Answer 1 – Juncus plc

(a) IAS 18 *Revenue* recognition criteria

Revenue is the gross inflow of economic benefits during the period arising in the ordinary course of business, when those inflows result in increases in equity, other than increase relating to contributions from equity participants. Revenue should be measured at the fair value of the consideration received.

Sale of goods: The recognition of revenue from the sale of goods should only occur when the following conditions have been met:

- The entity has transferred the significant risks and rewards of ownership of the goods.
- The entity retains neither managerial involvement to the degree usually associated with ownership nor effective control over the goods sold.
- The amount of revenue can be measured reliably.
- It is probable that the economic benefits associated with the transaction will flow to the entity.
- The cost incurred or to be incurred in respect of the transaction can be measured reliably.

Although the most usual point of recognition will be the transfer of possession or the transfer of legal title. It is important to look at the substance of the transaction in each case.

Sale of services: Revenue should only be recognised when the outcome of the transaction can be estimated reliably. This will be indicated by the following criteria:

- The amount of revenue must be measured reliably.
- It is probable that the economic benefits associated with the transaction will flow to the entity.
- The stage of completion of the transaction at the statement of financial position date can be measured reliably.
- The costs incurred for the transaction and the costs to complete the transaction can be measured reliably.

(b) Specific scenarios
Gas cookers

It is normal for revenue to be recognised when a buyer accepts delivery, and both installation and inspection are complete. It is unlikely that the customers in France will install the new gas cookers delivered by Juncus plc, and hence the revenue should not be recognised when the goods are delivered to the premises.

Recognition on delivery would only be appropriate if:

- the installation process is simple and requires minimal resource, this seems unlikely in this case
- another supplier will complete the installation and Juncus plc only has responsibility to manufacture the cookers and get them to the premises of the customer.

(c) Advance payments

The payment of a cash advance will have to be recognised in the statement of financial position of Juncus plc on the date of receipt, but it is inappropriate to recognise revenues in the income statement as the inventory has not yet been delivered to the buyer.

Consequently when the cash arrives it should be shown as a liability in the statement of financial position. It is reasonable to assume that if the goods are not delivered by Juncus plc they will be liable to repay the cash advance.

(d) Customer training

To be certain of the most appropriate pattern of revenue recognition in this case it would be necessary to know more about the contract. If the training is a separately identified component with a known cost then this element should not be recognised upon the delivery of the machines. It would be more appropriate to recognise it over the period of instruction. Effectively this is matching the cost and benefit.

However if the contract shows a single price and it is estimated that the tuition element is minor in comparison to the overall price it would be appropriate to recognise the full fee on delivery. If Juncus adopts this approach it must do so consistently.

Answer 2 – LMN (May '06)

(a) The economic substance of the arrangement between the two entities is determined by analysing the risks and benefits of the transaction. The entity that receives the benefits and bears the risks of ownership should recognise the vehicles as inventory. LMN, the motor vehicle dealer, appears to derive the following benefits:

- It is free to determine the nature of the inventorystock it holds, in terms of ranges and models.
- It is protected against price increases between the date of delivery to it and the date of sale because the price is determined at the point of delivery.
- It has access to the inventory for demonstration purposes.

LMN incurs the following costs and risks:

- IJK retains legal title to the goods, so in the case of dispute IJK would probably be entitled to recover its legal property.
- LMN is required to bear the cost of insuring the vehicles against loss or damage.
- Although LMN obtains the benefit of using vehicles for demonstration purposes a rental charge may become payable.
- If price reductions occur between the date of delivery and the date of sale, LMN will lose out because it will be required to pay the higher price specified upon delivery.

The analysis of the risks and benefits of the transaction does not produce a clear decision as to the economic substance of the arrangement between the two parties. IJK bears the substantial risk of incurring costs related to slow-moving or obsolete vehicles because LMN can return any vehicle to it, without incurring a penalty. This point alone is highly significant and may be sufficient to ensure that IJK, the manufacturer, should continue to recognise the vehicles in its own inventory. A further relevant point is that IJK is not paid until the point of sale to a third party, and thus it bears the significant financial risk involved in financing the inventory.

(b) In respect of the sale of goods, IAS 18 *Revenue* requires that a sale should be recognised when the selling entity transfers to the buyer the significant risks and rewards of ownership of the goods. As noted in part (a) above, significant risks and some of the rewards of ownership remain with the manufacturer, IJK, until such time as the goods are sold by the dealer to a third party. Therefore, revenue should be recognised by IJK only when a sale to a third party takes place.

Answer to long answer questions

Answer 3 – Ned (Nov '08)

(a) *Transaction 1*

The relevant accounting principle that should be applied in this case is that of substance over form, which, according to the *Framework for the Preparation and Presentation of Financial Statements*, is an important aspect of the qualitative characteristic of financial statement reliability. While this transaction apparently has some of the characteristics of a sale, in substance it is a financing arrangement. The substance of the transaction is that ABC has borrowed $1,000,000 at an interest rate of 10%. IAS 18 *Revenue* permits the recognition of revenue only where the selling entity has transferred the risks and rewards of ownership to the buyer. This is clearly not the case in respect of this transaction as ABC continues to insure and to store the plant.

Correcting accounting entries should be made to remove $1,000,000 from sales and cost of sales and the asset should be reinstated as part of plant and machinery. A charge to depreciation should be made for the year ended 30 September 2008, but there is insufficient information available in the facts presented to estimate the amount and impact of this charge. The amount of $1,000,000 should be recognised as borrowings, either long term if the liability is to be settled on 1 October 2009, or short term if it is settled on 1 October 2008. Interest of $100,000 should be charged to profit or loss for the year, with a corresponding credit entry to borrowings.

The correcting journal entries to correspond with the above description would be:

DR	Revenue	1,000,000	
CR	Cost of sales		1,000,000
DR	Plant	1,000,000	
DR	Interest payable	100,000	
CR	Borrowings		1,100,000

Transaction 2

Like the first transaction, this one should be reflected in the financial statements according to the principle of substance over form. ABC continues to bear the risks relating to all the receivables covered by the factoring arrangement; this is indicated by the fact that LM can require repayment in respect of any uncollectible element. The substance of the transaction is that ABC has borrowed $1,500,000 (75% of the total of $2,000,000 transferred to LM), against the security of its receivables. Interest is chargeable on these amounts at a rate of 10%.

Insufficient information is available to calculate the charge for interest, but because the agreement was made only a few days before the year end the interest would not be a very significant amount. The amount of $1,500,000 should, however, be reinstated as part of receivables and a short-term payable of the same amount should be recognised.

The correcting journal entry would be:

DR	Receivables	1,500,000	
CR	Borrowings		1,500,000

Transaction 3

The relevant accounting standard in this case is IAS 32 *Financial Instruments: Presentation*. One of the objectives of this standard is to establish principles for presenting financial instruments as liabilities or equity. The classification as equity or liability must be made in accordance with the substance of the contract, so this transaction provides another instance where substance over form must be considered. The preference shares in this case are redeemable on a specific date, and this fact, together with the unavoidable obligation to pay annual interest, points towards the instrument being a liability rather than equity. The preference shares should therefore be reclassified as a long-term liability. The 'dividend' (8% × $2,000,000 = $160,000) in respect of the shares appears in the statement of changes in equity in the draft financial statements, but this should be reclassified as interest in the income statement.

(b) Effects of the adjustments on ABC's key ratios

	Before adjustment $	Transaction 1 $	Transaction 2 $	Transaction 3 $	After adjustment $
Revenue	31,850,000	−1,000,000			30,850,000
Profit before interest	2,972,000				2,972,000
Interest	1,241,000	+100,000		+160,000	1,501,000
Equity	22,450,800	−100,000		−2,000,000	20,350,800
Debt	18,253,500	+1,000,000	+1,500,000	+2,000,000	22,753,500

Key ratios recalculated:

Return on capital employed

$$\frac{2,972,000}{20,350,800 + 22,753,500} = 6.9\%$$

Net profit margin

$$\frac{1,471,000}{30,850,800} = 4.8\%$$

Gearing

$$\frac{22,753,000}{20,350,800 + 22,753,500} = 52.8\%$$

(c)

To: Ned

From: Independent accountant

After making the adjustments in respect of the three transactions that you have identified as questionable, all three of the key ratios fail to meet the targets set by the directors, although the shortfall is not great in respect of any of the three. A greater cause for concern is the fact that the transactions have not been accounted for in accordance with IFRS. This suggests a willingness on the part of the CFO to engage in creative accounting. You have identified three instances, but there may be others that are less obvious. In future years, performance and position may continue to be misstated in order to meet budgets and targets, and the ways in which the misstatements are achieved may be more subtle.

Answer 4

To: Members of the Lending Committee
From: Accounting Adviser
Subject: TYD's financial statements for the year ended 30 September 2006

(i) *Treatment of two significant items in TYD's financial statements*

The principle at issue in the case of the first transaction is that of 'substance over form'. While there is currently no IFRS that deals specifically with substance over form, the principle is recognised as contributing to the reliability of financial statements in the IASB's *Framework* statement. Transactions and other events should be accounted for and presented in accordance with their substance and economic reality, and not merely their legal form. The legal form of this transaction, a sale and repurchase agreement, is that of a contract for sale of inventories. However, the 'sale' does not meet the criteria for treatment as a sale set out in IAS 18 *Revenue*. In substance, the transaction is a secured loan of $85,000 from HPS to TYD. The difference between the amount advanced at 30 September 2006 ($85,000) and the amount for which the inventories will be repurchased after two years ($95,000) represents, effectively, the interest payable on the loan. The existence of the option, exercisable by the bank, to ensure repurchase after two years by TYD is a persuasive indicator of the true substance of the transaction. The facts that the inventories remain on TYD's premises, and that TYD bears the cost of insuring them, provide further supporting evidence that TYD continues to bear the risks and rewards of ownership of the inventories. The correct accounting treatment of this transaction is to treat it as a long-term loan.

The question of the transfer of the risks and rewards of ownership is also an issue in determining the true nature of the disposals of inventories on a sale or return basis. As noted above IAS 18 *Revenue* states that revenue can be recognised provided that a set of conditions have been satisfied. One of those conditions is that the risks and rewards of ownership have been transferred to the buyer. Another is that the selling entity should retain no effective control over the goods. Where the option is open to buyers to return the goods, it is likely that neither of these important conditions has been fulfilled, and that the sales cannot be recognised until and unless there is no possibility of the goods being returned.

(ii) *Adjustment of TYD's financial statements*

Both of these transactions are examples of creative accounting techniques that would not be permissible under IFRS regulation. In order to be able to fairly assess the loan application, it is necessary to adjust the financial statements, as follows:

TYD: Income statement for the year ended 30 September 2006

		Adjustment	Trans ref	Adjusted
		$000	$000	$000
Revenue	600	−85	1	475
		(W1) − 40	2	
Cost of sales	450	(W1) − 32	2	333
		− 85	1	
Gross profit	150			142
Expenses	63			63
Finance costs	17			17
Profit before tax	70			62
Income tax expense	25			25
Profit for the period	45	(W1) − 8	2	37

TYD: Statement of financial position at 30 September 2006

	$000	$000	Adjustment $000	Trans ref	Adjusted $000
ASSETS					
Non-current assets:					
Property, plant and equipment		527			527
Current assets:					
Inventories	95		(W1) + 32	2	212
			+ 85	1	
Trade receivables	72		(W1) − 40	2	32
Cash	6				6
		173			
		700			777
EQUITY AND LIABILITIES					
Equity:					
Called up share capital	100				100
Retained earnings	245		(W1) − 8	2	237
		345			
Non-current liabilities:					
Long-term borrowings		180	+ 85	1	265
Current liabilities:					
Trade and other payables	95				95
Bank overdraft	80				80
		175			
		700			777

Working

1. *Sale or return items*

    40% of the sales cannot be recognised: 40% × $100,000. Remove from trade receivables and from sales.

    The related cost of sales figure is $40,000 × 80% (i.e., deducting profit margin) = $32,000.

    Remove from cost of sales and add to inventories in the statement of financial position.

    The net effect on profit is to remove $8,000.

Examiner's note:

The income statement and statement of financial position have been adjusted to show the impact of the adjustments; however, there are many other valid ways of setting out the adjustments, for example, using journal entries, that might be quicker under exam conditions. Credit will be given for correct understanding of the adjustments, and not for a particular way of setting them out.

(iii) *Key ratio calculations and analysis*
The key ratio calculations are shown in the following table:

	Before adjustment	After adjustment
Gearing	$\dfrac{80 + 80}{(180 + 80 + 345)} \times 100 = 43.0\%$	$\dfrac{265 + 80}{(265 + 80 + 337)} \times 100 = 50.6\%$
Current ratio	$\dfrac{173}{175} = 0.99:1$	$\dfrac{(212 + 32 + 6)}{175} = 1.43:1$
Quick ratio	$\dfrac{(72 + 6)}{175} = 0.45:1$	$\dfrac{(32 + 6)}{175} = 0.22:1$
Profit margin	$\dfrac{70}{600} \times 100 = 11.7\%$	$\dfrac{62}{475} \times 100 = 13.1\%$

It is clear from a very quick examination of the financial statements that TYD is quite highly geared. The gearing ratio before making any adjustments is 43%, close to the point where the application is likely to be rejected without discussion. After adjustment, gearing is at the unacceptably high level (for us) of 50.6%.

Although the current ratio improves substantially after adjustment, the already low quick ratio worsens. Also, it should be noted that the uplift in current assets relates to inventories which, after adjusting the financial statements, amount to 63% of cost of sales. It is quite likely that the inventories could not be rapidly realised in case of default, and so for our purposes, the quick ratio is likely to be a more useful guide.

The profit margin improves after adjustment. However, all other things being equal, it would be due to deteriorate in 2007 and 2008 because of the additional interest charge arising from the sale and repurchase agreement.

Taking these various points into consideration, the appropriate course of action is likely to be to reject TYD's application for loan finance.

10

Accounting for Financial Instruments

Accounting for Financial Instruments

10

LEARNING OUTCOMES

After studying this chapter students should be able to:

▶ discuss the possible treatments of financial instruments in the issuer's accounts, including the classification of liabilities and equity, and the implications for the associated finance costs;

▶ identify circumstances in which amortised cost, fair value and hedge accounting are appropriate for financial instruments, and explain the principles of these accounting methods.

Core definitions

- Financial instrument – any contract that gives rise to both a financial asset of one entity and a financial liability or equity instrument of another entity.

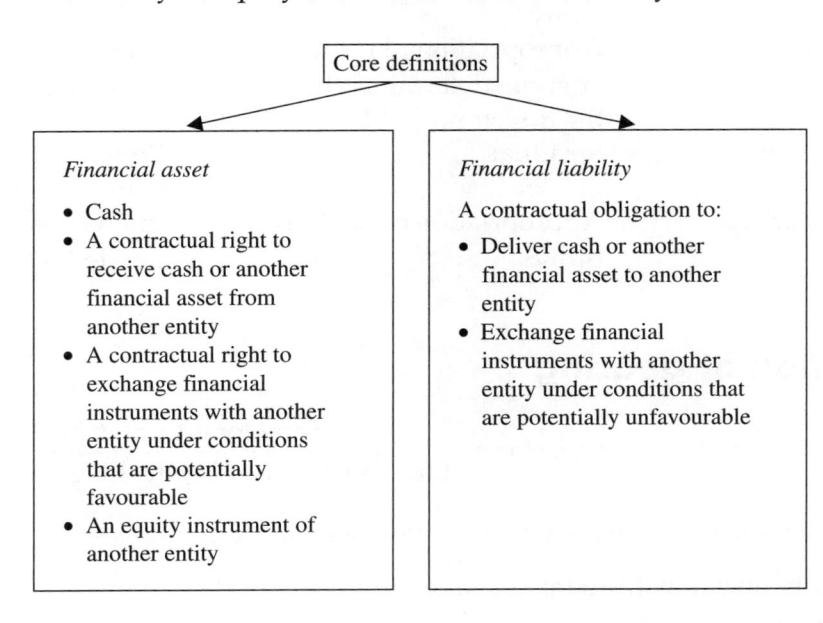

Core definitions

Financial asset
- Cash
- A contractual right to receive cash or another financial asset from another entity
- A contractual right to exchange financial instruments with another entity under conditions that are potentially favourable
- An equity instrument of another entity

Financial liability
A contractual obligation to:
- Deliver cash or another financial asset to another entity
- Exchange financial instruments with another entity under conditions that are potentially unfavourable

- Equity instrument – any contract that evidences a residual interest in the assets of an entity after deducting all of its liabilities.
- Financial instruments not captured under the remit of IAS 32 are:
  - interests in subsidiaries
  - interests in associates and joint ventures
  - employee benefit plans
  - obligations arising under insurance contracts.

IAS 32 *Classification rules*

- When a financial instrument is issued the issuer must designate its classification as either a liability or equity.
- The classification principles are:
  - Substance prevails over legal form.
  - Where there is a contractual obligation, potentially unfavourable to the issue of the instrument, to deliver either cash or another financial asset to the holder of the instrument, the instrument meets the definition of a financial liability.
  - Where a financial instrument does not give rise to a contractual obligation under potentially unfavourable conditions, then the instrument is classified as equity.
  - Where there is a requirement for mandatory redemption of the instrument by the issuer at a fixed or determinable future date, the instrument meets the definition of a financial liability.

Debt or equity?

Some of the basic characteristics of debt and equity are set out in the table below:

	Equity	*Debt*
Return	Dividend	Interest
Rights	Legal ownership of the entity	Repayment of capital
Effect on income statement	Appropriation of profit after tax determined by the directors	Charge against profits before tax
Interest on winding up of the entity	Residual	Preferential, ranking before equity holders
Taxation implications	Appropriation of post-tax profits	Interest payments are tax-deductible

Manipulation of gearing

$$\text{Manipulation of gearing} = \frac{\text{Total long-term debt}}{\text{Shareholders funds plus long-term debt}}$$

Gearing is a key indicator of the risk levels within a business.

Many complex financial instruments have features of both debt and equity and hence can be used for creative accounting.

There are many potentially dubious strategies available to the management of a business to reduce debt or increase equity, for example,
- Special purpose entities
- Revaluation of assets
- Inclusion of intangibles within non-current assets
- Sale and leaseback.

Specific examples of financial instruments and their treatment

Warrants and options	equity;
Redeemable preferred shares	debt unless redemption is solely at the option of the issuer when they are closer to equity;
Non-redeemable preferred shares	distributions are at the discretion of the issuer then these are likely to be classified as equity, but when the distribution is mandatory the instrument is more akin to debt;
Convertible securities with options	these often contain a put option that allows the holders of the debt to require redemption at a premium, and consequently they often carry a low rate of interest to balance the high premium;
Financial instruments with contingent settlement	as redemption is dependent on the occurrence of an uncertain future event the instrument should be classified as debt;
Zero coupon bonds	debt;

Hybrid instruments

IAS 32 recognises certain categories of financial instrument as having characteristics of both debt and equity. These are known as hybrid financial instruments, and the most common example is that of convertible debt securities. The view taken by IAS 32 is that this type of single financial instrument creates both debt and equity interests. The standard requires that the component parts of the instrument should be classified separately.

	$
Present value of the capital element of the bond issue	X
Interest at present value	X
Value of liability element	X
Equity element (balancing figure)	X
Total value of instrument	X

Initial recognition

The initial measurement of all financial instruments should be at fair value. Transactions costs should be included in the initial measurement, except for assets and liabilities held at fair value through profit or loss..

Fair value is the amount for which an asset could be exchanged, or a liability settled, between knowledgeable, willing parties in an arm's-length transaction.

IAS 39 provides the following guidance for establishing fair values:

1. Quoted market prices
2. Where there is no active market, fair value should be established using a valuation technique that refers, where possible, to market conditions.
3. Where there is no active market and if no reliable estimate of fair value can be made, the entity must measure the financial instrument at cost less any impairment.

Financial assets

Fair value through profit or loss
Financial assets categorised as 'fair value through profit or loss' are those that fall into one of these categories:

1. Those that are classified as 'held-for-trading'. This classification is appropriate where financial assets are acquired principally for the purpose of short-term resale, or where the asset is acquired as part of a portfolio where short-term profit taking is the norm.
2. Those that are held as part of a group of financial assets that are managed on a fair value basis in accordance with a documented risk management or investment strategy.

Loans and receivables
These financial assets include non-derivative assets with fixed or determinable payments that are not quoted in an active market, and that are not held as fair value through profit or loss, or as available-for-sale assets. Examples would include loans made to other entities that may be sold on or exchanged at some point before they mature.

Held-to-maturity investments
These are non-derivative financial assets with fixed or determinable payments that an entity intends to hold until they mature. The intention to hold until maturity must be demonstrable. For example, if an entity sells a 'held-to-maturity' investment of a significant amount before its maturity date, the validity of its intentions in respect of other 'held-to-maturity' investments is called into question. The standard requires that in such cases the investments must be reclassified as available-for sale. (Note that this point is important because of differences in approach to measurement of financial assets, which will be discussed in the next section of this chapter.)

Available-for-sale financial assets
A financial asset that is not classified as fair value through profit or loss, or as loans and receivables or as held-to-maturity, will be classified as available-for-sale. Available-for-sale financial assets are held at fair value, with subsequent gains or losses recognised in equity until disposal.

Financial liabilities

Financial liabilities is not specifically mentioned as a category in IAS 39, however it is obviously a very important category as it includes loans, payables, preference shares, debentures, etc.

Financial liabilities can be designated as 'fair value through profit or loss', provided that it is either held for trading, or is designated by the entity as such.

Note that derivatives would normally fall into the 'fair value through profit or loss' category and depending on whether the terms are favourable or unfavourable will determine whether it is shown as a financial asset or liability.

Subsequent measurement of financial instruments

Financial assets

The regulations in IAS 39 in respect of financial asset categories are as follows:

- *fair value through profit or loss*: fair value;
- *loans and receivables*: amortised cost, using the effective interest rate method;
- *held-to-maturity investments*: amortised cost, using the effective interest rate method;
- *available-for-sale financial assets*: fair value.

Treatment of gains and losses

Where financial assets are accounted for at fair value, gains and losses on periodic remeasurement (e.g. at the year end date) should be taken straight to the income statement. The exception to this is where financial assets are classified as available-for-sale. Gains and losses arising on these assets should be taken to the statement of changes in equity and included in other comprehensive income. Upon their disposal, gains and losses previously taken to equity should be recognised in the income statement.

Financial liabilities

There are two categories of financial liabilities – those held at fair value through profit or loss; and all other financial liabilities.

The general rule is that financial liabilities should be measured at amortised cost, using the effective interest rate method. The associated finance cost is charged to the income statement.

Derivatives not designated for hedging purposes, however, should be measured at fair value as should those financial liabilities that have been designated at fair value through profit or loss. Profits and losses on subsequent measurement are recognised in the income statement.

Derivatives

The definition of a derivative is as follows:

A derivative is a financial instrument with all three of the following characteristics:

1. its value changes in response to the change in a specified interest rate, security price, commodity price, foreign exchange rate, index of prices or rates, a credit rating or credit index or other variable;
2. it requires no initial net investment;
3. it is settled at a future date.

Examples of derivatives include:

- Forward contracts: contracts to purchase or sell specific quantities of commodities of foreign currencies at a specified price determined at the inception of the contract, with delivery or settlement to take place at a specified future date.
- Options: these are contracts that give a purchaser the right to buy (call option) or to sell (put option) a specified quantity of, for example, a financial instrument, commodity or currency at a specified price.

Impairment

- Reassess carrying value at each statement of financial position date.
- If indicators of impairment exist then a full review must be undertaken.
- Impairment losses recognised in the income statement.

Hedging

- A management strategy to reduce risk.

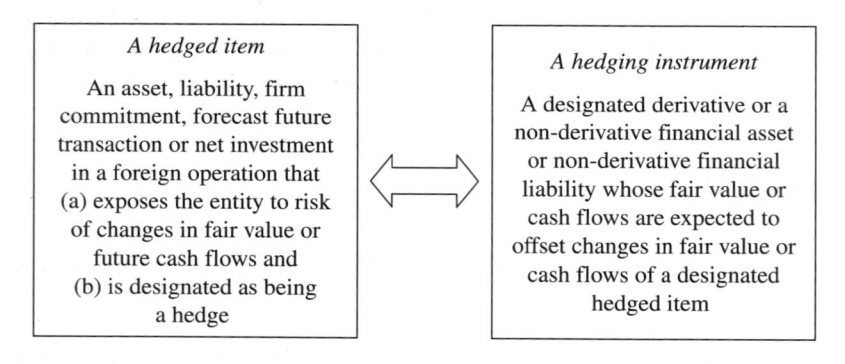

A hedged item	*A hedging instrument*
An asset, liability, firm commitment, forecast future transaction or net investment in a foreign operation that (a) exposes the entity to risk of changes in fair value or future cash flows and (b) is designated as being a hedge	A designated derivative or a non-derivative financial asset or non-derivative financial liability whose fair value or cash flows are expected to offset changes in fair value or cash flows of a designated hedged item

A hedge must be formally designated and documented. There must be an expectation that it will be effective. Examples include:

Fair value hedge	The value of the item being hedged changes as market price changes
Hedge Cash	The cash flows of the item being hedged change as market price changes

A retrospective measure of hedge effectiveness is that an effective hedge falls within the 80–125% window from the bench mark value.

IFRS 7 Financial Instruments: Disclosures

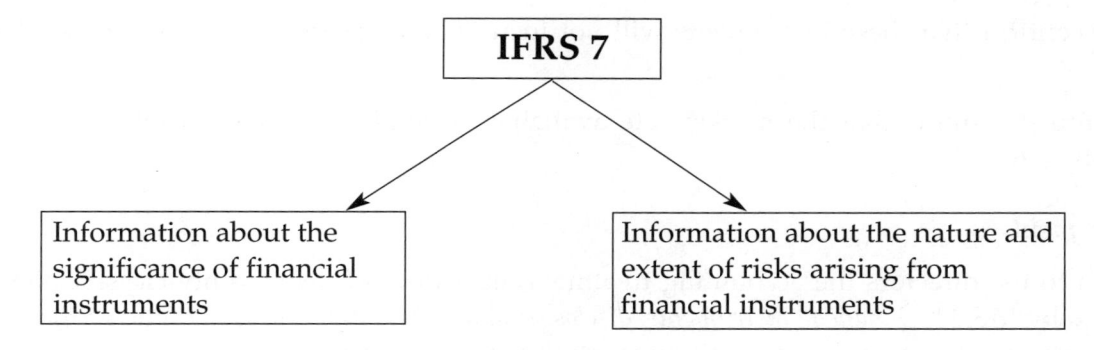

```
                    IFRS 7
                   /      \
    Information about the   Information about the nature and
    significance of         extent of risks arising from
    financial instruments   financial instruments
```

- Disclosure of significance to position and performance of each major financial instrument category (e.g. loans & receivables)
  - Reclassifications
  - Derecognition
  - Fee income and expense
- Impairment
- Accounting policies
- Details of hedge accounting and risk management

- Qualitative disclosures
  - Management objectives & policies
  - Changes from prior period
- Qualitative disclosures
  - Credit risk
  - Liquidty risk
  - Market risk

Medium answer questions

Question 1

The directors of QRS, a listed entity, have met to discuss the business's medium to long-term financing requirements. Several possibilities were discussed, including the issue of more shares using a rights issue. In many respects this would be the most desirable option because the entity is already quite highly geared. However, the directors are aware of several recent cases where rights issues have not been successful because share prices are currently quite low and many investors are averse to any kind of investment in shares.

Therefore, the directors have turned their attention to other options. The finance director is on sick leave, and so you, her assistant, have been given the task of responding to the following note from the Chief Executive:

'Now that we've had a chance to discuss possible financing arrangements, the directors are in agreement that we should structure our issue of financial instruments in order to be able to classify them as equity rather than debt. Any increase in the gearing ratio would be unacceptable. Therefore, we have provisionally decided to make two issues of financial instruments as follows:

1. An issue of non-redeemable preferred shares to raise $4 million. These shares will carry a fixed interest rate of 6%, and because they are shares they can be classified as equity.
2. An issue of 6% convertible bonds, issued at par value, to raise $6 million. These bonds will carry a fixed date for conversion in four years' time. Each $100 of debt will be convertible at the holder's option into 120 $1 shares. In our opinion, these bonds can

actually be classified as equity immediately, because they are convertible within five years on terms that are favourable to the holder.

Please confirm that these instruments will not increase our gearing ratio should they be issued.'

Note: You determine that the market rate available for similar non-convertible bonds is currently 8%.

Requirement

Explain to the directors the accounting treatment, in respect of debt/equity classification, required by *IAS 32 – Financial instruments: disclosure and presentation* for each of the proposed issues, advising them on the acceptability of classifying the instruments as equity.

Your explanation should be accompanied by calculations where appropriate.

(Total = 10 marks)

Question 2 – PX plc (May '05)

During its financial year ended 31 December 2004, an entity, PX, entered into the transactions described below:

In November 2004, having surplus cash available, PX made an investment in the securities of a listed entity. The directors intend to realise the investment in March or April 2005, in order to fund the planned expansion of PX's principal warehouse.

PX lent one of its customers, DB, $3,000,000 at a variable interest rate pegged to average bank lending rates. The loan is scheduled for repayment in 2009, and PX has provided an undertaking to DB that it will not assign the loan to a third party.

PX added to its portfolio of relatively small investments in the securities of listed entities. PX does not plan to dispose of these investments in the short term.

Requirements
In accordance with IAS 39 *Financial Instruments: Recognition and Measurement*

(a) Identify the appropriate classification of these three categories of financial asset and briefly explain the reason for each classification.

(6 marks)

(b) Explain how the financial assets should be measured in the financial statements of PX at 31 December 2004.

(4 marks)
(Total = 10 marks)

Question 3 (May '08)

On 1 February 2007, the directors of AZG decided to enter into a forward foreign exchange contract to buy 6 million florins at a rate of $1 = 3 florins, on 31 January 2010. AZG's year end is 31 March.

Relevant exchange rates were as follows:

1 February 2007 $1 = 3 florins
31 March 2007 $1 = 2.9 florins
31 March 2008 $1 = 2.8 florins

Requirements
(a) Identify the three characteristics of a derivative financial instrument as defined in IAS 39 *Financial Instruments: Recognition and Measurement*. **(3 marks)**

(b) Describe the requirements of IAS 39 in respect of the recognition and measurement of derivative financial instruments. **(2 marks)**

(c) Prepare relevant extracts from AZG's income statement and statement of financial position to reflect the forward foreign exchange contract at 31 March 2008, with comparatives.
(Note: ignore discounting when measuring the derivative). **(5 marks)**
(Total = 10 marks)

Question 4

Hedging establishes a relationship between a hedging instrument and a hedged item or items. It is essentially all about making exceptions to accounting rules in respect of where gains and losses on subsequent measurement.

ABC purchases a $1 million bond that has a fixed interest rate of 6% per year. The instrument is classed as an available-for-sale financial asset. The fair value of the instrument is $1 million.

The company enters into an interest rate swap (fair value zero) to offset the risk of a decline in fair value. The company designates and documents the swap as a hedging instrument.

Market interest rates increase to 7% and the fair value of the bond decreases to $960,000.

Requirements
(a) Explain the distinction between a hedging instrument and hedged item. **(2 marks)**
(b) Explain how ABC's hedging arrangement should be dealt with. **(8 marks)**
(Total = 10 marks)

Answers to medium answer questions

Answer 1

In general, under the requirements of *IAS 32 – Financial instruments: disclosure and presentation –* financial instruments that fulfil the characteristics of a liability should be classified as such. Although preferred shares carry the description of 'shares' this does not mean that they can necessarily be classified as equity. In cases where the payment of the 'dividend' is a fixed sum that is normally paid in respect of each accounting period, the instrument is really a long-term liability and must be classified as such.

The convertible bonds would be classified as a compound, or hybrid, instrument by IAS 32; that is, they have characteristics of both debt and equity, and would therefore be presented partly as debt and partly as equity in the statement of financial position. Valuation of the equity element is often difficult. One method permitted by IAS 32 involves valuation of the liability element using an equivalent market rate of interest for non-convertible bonds, with equity as a residual figure.

Tutorial note: IAS 32 also permits the use of a pricing model to value the equity element, but the question does not contain sufficient information to use this approach.

Applying this approach to the proposed instrument, the following debt/equity split results:

	$
Present value of the capital element of the bond issue:	
$6 million $\times 1/(1.08^4)$	4,410,000
Interest at present value:	
($6,000,000 $\times$ 6%) $\times$ (1/(1.08) + 1/(1.08^2) + 1/(1.08^3) + 1/(1.08^4)) = $360,000 $\times$ 3.312 (from tables)	1,192,320
Value of liability element	5,602,320
Equity element (balancing figure)	397,680
Total value of instrument	6,000,000

Apart from the relatively small element of the hybrid instrument that can be classified as equity, the two proposed issues will be classified as debt under the provisions of IAS 32. If the directors wish to obtain finance through an issue of financial instruments that can be properly classified as equity, they should reconsider the rights issue proposal.

Answer 2 – PX plc (May '05)

(a) Classification
1. This is classified as a financial asset at fair value through profit or loss. IAS 39 requires this classification for financial assets held for trading. Because the directors acquired the securities with the intention of selling them in the short term, the securities are regarded as held for trading.
2. The loan is classified as a held-to-maturity financial asset. The loan is an unlisted security with determinable payments. The intention to hold the asset until maturity is demonstrated by the undertaking not to assign the loan to a third party.
3. There is no plan to sell these investments in the short term; they do not fall into the category of held-for-trading financial assets. Financial assets that do not fall into the three other classifications identified by IAS 39 are classified as available-for-sale.

(b) Measurement
IAS 39 permits entities the option of initially designating virtually any financial asset at fair value through profit or loss. Otherwise, it includes the following requirements relevant to the measurement of PX's financial assets:

1. Financial assets at fair value through profit or loss are, as the designation implies, measured at fair value.
2. Held-to-maturity financial assets are measured at amortised cost.
3. Available-for-sale financial assets are measured at fair value.

Answer 3 (May '08)

(a)
According to IAS 39, a derivative financial instrument must have all three of the following characteristics:

(i) Its value changes in response to the change in a specified interest or exchange rate, or in response to the change in a price, rating, index or other variable;
(ii) It requires no initial net investment;
(iii) It is settled at a future date.

(b)
IAS 39 requires that derivative financial instruments should be recognised as either assets or liabilities. They should be measured at fair value both upon initial recognition and subsequently.

(c)
AZG: extract from income statement for the year ended 31 March 2008

	2008 $	2007 $
Gain on derivative	73,891	68,966

AZG: extract from statement of financial position at 31 March 2008

	2008 $	2007 $
Derivative asset	142,857	68,966

Working:

	$
Value of forward foreign exchange contract: Fl 6,000,000/3 =	2,000,000
31 March 2007: fair value = Fl 6,000,000/2.9 =	2,068,966
31 March 2008: fair value = Fl 6,000,000/2.8 =	2,142,857
Gain recognised in year ended 31 March 2007: 2,068,966 − 2,000,000 =	68,966
Gain recognised in year ended 31 March 2008: 2,142,857 − 2,068,966 =	73,891
Derivative asset at fair value at 31 March 2008:	142,857

Answer 4

(a)
A hedged item is an asset, liability, firm commitment, forecast future transaction or net investment in a foreign operation that

(a) exposes the entity to risk of changes in fair value or future cash flows and
(b) is designated as being hedged.

A hedging instrument is a designated derivative or (in limited circumstances) a non-derivative financial asset or non-derivative financial liability whose fair value or cash flows are expected to offset changes in the fair value or cash flows of a designated hedged item.

(b)

If the derivative hedging instrument is effective, any decline in the fair value of the bond should offset by opposite increases in the fair value of the derivative instrument.

Because the instrument is classified as 'available for sale', the decrease in fair value would normally be recorded directly in reserves.

However, since the instrument is a hedged item in a fair value hedge, this change in fair value of the instrument is recognised in profit or loss, as follows:

Dr Income statement $40,000
Cr Bond $40,000

The fair value of the swap has increased by $40,000. Since the swap is a derivative, it is measured at fair value with changes in fair value recognised in profit or loss.

Dr Derivative $40,000
Cr Income statement $40,000

The changes in fair value of the hedged item and the hedging instrument exactly offset, the hedge is 100% effective and, the net effect on profit or loss is zero.

11

Employee Benefits

Employee Benefits 11

LEARNING OUTCOMES

After studying this chapter students should be able to:
- discuss the recognition and valuation issues concerned with pension schemes and the treatment of actuarial deficits and surpluses;
- discuss the recognition and valuation issues concerned with share-based payments.

IAS 19 – *Accounting for employee benefits*

The basics

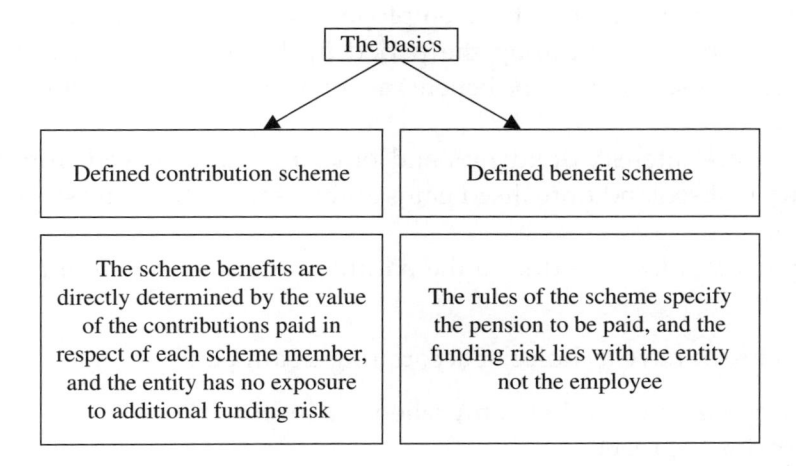

```
                    The basics
                   /         \
    Defined contribution    Defined benefit scheme
    scheme

    The scheme benefits are      The rules of the scheme specify
    directly determined by       the pension to be paid, and the
    the value of the             funding risk lies with the entity
    contributions paid in        not the employee
    respect of each scheme
    member, and the entity
    has no exposure to
    additional funding risk
```

- The valuation of pension funds is a complex process as it requires anticipation of numerous future events (e.g. inflation, interest rates, life expectancy), and this work will be undertaken by actuaries who specialise in this field.
- A funded pension plan is one in which the assets are held externally to the employer company's business.

Accounting for pensions

- Defined contribution scheme – the fixed pension costs are expensed against operating profits for the period against the receipt of service from the employee.
- Defined benefit scheme:

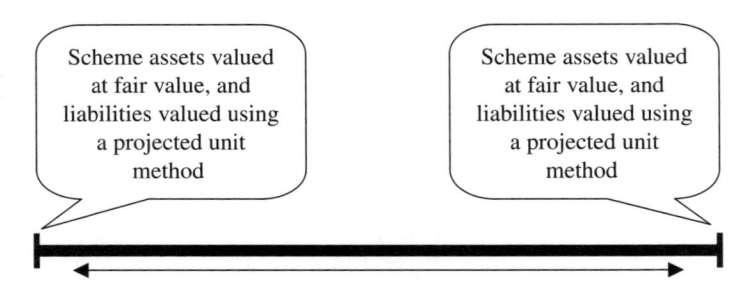

> Scheme assets valued at fair value, and liabilities valued using a projected unit method

> Scheme assets valued at fair value, and liabilities valued using a projected unit method

- Current service cost, interest expense and expected return taken to income statement
- Actuarial gains and losses not recognised in income statement immediately unless 10% corridor exceeded

Income statement

The income statement is charged/credited with a number of actuarial assumptions:

- Current service cost – increase in the present value of expected future payments required to settle the obligation resulting from employee service in the current and prior periods.
- Interest cost – the increase during the period in the present value of a defined benefit obligation which arises because the benefits are one period closer to settlement – unwinding the discount.
- Expected return – interest, dividends and other revenue derived from the plan assets, together with realised and unrealised gains and losses on the plan assets, less any administration costs.
- Actuarial gains and losses – due to the nature of the actuarial assumptions differences will arise.

These gains and losses have a choice of accounting treatment:

- Recognise immediately in other comprehensive income
- Apply a corridor approach

10% Corridor
The greater of:

- 10% of the present value of the obligation
- 10% of the fair value of any plan assets

is compared to the net cumulative unrecognised actuarial gains and losses. The excess is spread over the average remaining working lives of employees participating in the scheme.

Statement of financial position

Scheme assets are valued at fair value, scheme liabilities are valued at fair value (present value) using a projected unit method.

Inevitably there will be a difference between the value of the scheme assets and liabilities – a surplus or deficit.

Only the surplus or deficit meets the definition of asset or liability per the IASB's Framework and as such will be recognised on the entity's statement of financial position.

The statement of financial position shows the following:

Pension scheme surplus/deficit	X/(X)
Unrecognised actuarial gains/losses	(X)/X
	X/(X)

Accounting for share-based payments

Types of share-based payments

The IASB intends that the IFRS should be applied to all share-based payment transactions, and it identifies three principal types:

1. Equity-settled share-based payment transactions.
2. Cash-settled share-based payment transactions. This is where the provider of services or goods (i.e. in most cases the employee) is rewarded in cash, but the cash value is based upon the price of the entity's shares or other equity instruments.
3. Transactions where one of the parties involved can choose whether the provider of services or goods is rewarded in cash (value based on equity prices) or in shares.

The underlying assumption of the IFRS is that the issue of share options and grants of shares to employees and others creates a financial instrument which must be accounted for.

Medium answer questions

Question – BGA (Nov '07)

The following information relates to the defined benefits pension scheme of BGA, a listed entity:

The present value of the scheme obligations at 1 November 2006 was $18,360,000, while the fair value of the scheme assets at that date was $17,770,000. During the financial year ended 31 October 2007, a total of $997,000 was paid into the scheme in contributions. Current service cost for the year was calculated at $1,655,000, and actual benefits paid were $1,860,300. The applicable interest cost for the year was 6.5% and the expected return on plan assets was 9.4%.

The present value of the scheme obligations at 31 October 2007 was calculated as $18,655,500, and the fair value of scheme assets at that date was $18,417,180.

BGA adopts the '10% corridor' criterion in IAS 19 *Employee Benefits* for determining the extent of recognition of actuarial gains and losses. The average remaining service life of the employees was 10 years. Net unrecognised actuarial losses on 1 November 2006 were $802,000.

Requirement

(a) Calculate the actuarial gain or loss on BGA's pension scheme assets and liabilities for the year ended 31 October 2007. **(8 marks)**

(b) Calculate the extent to which, if at all, actuarial gains or losses should be recognised in BGA's income statement for the year ended 31 October 2007, using the '10% corridor' criterion. **(2 marks)**
(Total = 10 marks)

Question 2 – CBA (Nov '06)

CBA is a listed entity that runs a defined benefit pension scheme on behalf of its employees. In the financial year ended 30 September 2006, the scheme suffered an actuarial loss of $7.2 million. The entity's directors are aware that the relevant Accounting Standard, IAS 19 *Employee Benefits*, was amended recently. They have asked you, the financial controller, to write a short briefing paper, setting out an outline of the options for accounting for the actuarial loss in accordance with the amended version of the Standard.

Requirement

Prepare the briefing paper explaining the options and identifying, as far as possible from the information given, the potential impact on the financial statements of CBA of the two alternative accounting treatments. **(10 marks)**

Question 3

During the year ended 30 November 2008 the directors of EFG decided to form a defined benefit pension scheme for the employees of the company. At the end of that year the present value of the obligation was $30 million and the fair value of the plan assets was $28 million. During the year ended 30 November 2009 EFG made contributions $60 million to the scheme. The following details relate to the scheme at 30 November 2009:

	$ million
Present value of obligation	78
Fair value of plan assets	75
Current service cost	36
Past service cost	10
Interest cost	5%
Expected return on pension scheme assets	6%

The past service cost relates to an increase in the benefit paid to employees and vests immediately.

Requirements

(a) Calculate the charge/credit to other comprehensive income for the actuarial gain or loss for the year ended 30 November 2009. **(8 marks)**

(b) Give one reason for the inclusion of actuarial gains and losses in other comprehensive income rather than the income statement itself. **(2 marks)**
(Total = 10 marks)

Employee Benefits 151

Question 4

CFA grants share options to its directors in the year ended 31 December 2008. Each of the ten directors is granted 500 options if they remained employed by CFA for three years. The fair value of the options at the date they were granted was $3.

During the year ended 31 December 2008 one of the Directors left CFA but no further leavers were expected. During the year ended 31 December 2009 two directors left but the remainder reassured CFA that they would see out their three year commitment.

Requirements

Explain the different types of share option schemes and what they are intended to do.

(4 marks)

Calculate the charge to the income statement for the year ended 31 December 2009 briefly explaining the accounting entries.

(6 marks)
(Total = 10 marks)

✓ Answer to medium answer questions

Answer 1 – BGA (Nov '07)

(a) BGA: Calculation of actuarial gains or losses on pension scheme assets and liabilities for the year ended 31 October 2007

	$
PV of obligation at 1 November 2006	18,360,000
Interest cost ($18,360,000 × 6.5%)	1,193,400
Current service cost	1,655,000
Benefits paid	(1,860,300)
Actuarial gain (balancing figure)	(692,600)
PV of obligation at 31 October 2007	18,655,500
Fair value of plan assets at 1 November 2006	17,770,000
Expected return on plan assets (17,770,000 × 9.4%)	1,670,380
Contributions to scheme	997,000
Benefits paid	(1,860,300)
Actuarial loss on scheme assets	(159,900)
FV of scheme assets at 31 October 2007	18,417,180

(b)
10% corridor limits: higher of:
10% × PV of scheme obligations at start of year: 10% × $18,360,000 = $1,836,000
10% × fair value of scheme assets at start of year: 10% × $17,770,000 = $1,777,000

The corridor limit of $1,836,000 is greatly in excess of the net actuarial loss of $802,000 brought forward and so no loss is recognised in the income statement for the year ended 31 October 2007.

Answer 2 – CBA (Nov '06)

The amended version of IAS 19 permits two possible approaches in accounting for actuarial gains and losses:

1. The first option is the accounting treatment that was required by the original IAS 19.

   Actuarial gains and losses are not recognised immediately in the income statement except where they exceed certain parameters. Where the parameters in the Standard are met, the gain or loss is recognised over the average remaining service lives of the employees. This may be a fairly lengthy period (e.g. 10 or 15 years would not be unusual), so, even if the actuarial loss of $7.2 million were to exceed the parameters, the impact on the financial statements is likely to be very small.

   Where this option requires part of the loss to be recognised, it is recognised in the income statement, and so has a direct effect upon reported profit.

2. The Standard permits entities to adopt any systematic method that results in faster recognition of actuarial gains and loss than stipulated in the first approach, provided that the same basis is applied to both gains and losses, and that this is applied consistently. Thus, entities are able to opt for a policy of recognising the whole of any actuarial gains or losses in the accounting period in which they occur. In CBA's case, this would mean recognising the full amount of the $7.2 million loss in the financial year ended 30 September 2006. In such cases (where actuarial gains and losses are recognised in full as they are incurred) there would be no direct impact on the income statement. The standard requires that gains and losses should be recognised in a 'Statement of Recognised Income and Expense'.

Answer 3

(a)

	Plan assets $ million	Plan liabilities $ million
Bfwd 1 December 2008	28	30
Contributions	60	
Current service cost		36
Past service cost		10
Interest cost (5% × 30)		1.5
Expected return (6% × 28)	1.7	
Actuarial loss	(14.7)	0.5
Cfwd 30 November 2009	75	78

	$m
Other comprehensive income	
Actuarial loss (14.7 − 0.5)	(14.2)

(b) The purpose of recognising and reporting such gains and losses outside the income statement is to protect reported profits from the potentially volatile effects of some very significant items.

Answer 4

Share option schemes are frequently used as a means of rewarding employees. They may also be used as a means of buying-in goods or services from parties outside the entity. They may or may not be dependent on performance conditions. There are three main types of share-based payments according to IFRS2 *Share-Based Payments*.

1. Equity-settled share-based payment transactions. This involves the issue of equity instruments rather than payment of cash.
2. Cash-settled share-based payment transactions. This is where the provider of services or goods (i.e. in most cases the employee) is rewarded in cash, but the cash value is based upon the price of the entity's shares or other equity instruments.
3. Transactions where one of the parties involved can choose whether the provider of services or goods is rewarded in cash (value based on equity prices) or in shares.

The granting of share options to the directors is an example of an equity-settled transaction where the cost of rewarding the directors for their continued service needs to be recognised over the vesting period. A charge is made to staff costs in the income statement with a corresponding entry to reserves.

2008 – estimated eligible directors = 9 (10 − 1)

Total equivalent cost of issuing options = ($3 × 9 directors × 500 options) = $13,500

Allocated over the vesting period of 3 years gives a charge of $4,500 ($13,500/3)

Recorded as:
  Dr Staff costs $4,500
      Cr Other reserves $4,500

2009 – estimated eligible directors = 7 (10 − 1−2)

Total equivalent cost of issuing options = ($3 × 7 directors × 500 options) = $10,500.

We want to have recognised two-thirds of this by the end of 2009 = 7,000

Less the amount recognised in 2008 = $2,500 ($7,000 − $4,500)

Recorded as:
  Dr Staff costs $2,500
      Cr Other reserves $2,500

The balance on other reserves is now $7,000

12

Financial Reporting in an Environment of Price Changes

Financial Reporting in an Environment of Price Changes

12

LEARNING OUTCOMES

After studying this chapter students should be able to:
- discuss the problems of profit measurement and alternative approaches to asset valuations;
- discuss measures to reduce distortion in financial statements when price levels change.

Defects of historical cost accounting

- In a time of changing prices reported results in the income statement may be distorted as revenues at current values are matched with costs incurred at an earlier date.
- Cost of sales is likely to be understated in a time of price inflation.
- The valuation of assets in the statement of financial position is at cost *less* accumulated depreciation. The resultant net book values may bear no relationship to the current value of the asset.
- The three points listed above are likely to give rise to faulty estimates of return on capital employed (ROCE). Typically, in a time of rising prices, profits are likely to be overstated and assets understated, relative to current values, thus giving rise to unrealistically rosy measurements of ROCE.
- The results of comparison of performance and position statements over time will be unreliable, because amounts are not valued in terms of common units.
- Borrowings are shown in monetary terms, but in a time of rising prices a gain is actually made (or a loss in times of falling prices) at the expense of the lender as, in real terms, the value of the loan has decreased (in a time of rising prices) or increased (in a time of falling prices).
- Conversely, gains arising from holding assets are not recognised.
- Depreciation writes off the historical cost over time, but, where asset values are low (because based on outdated historical costs), depreciation will be correspondingly lower, so that a realistic charge for asset consumption is not matched against revenue in the performance statements.

Capital

- There are two concepts of capital maintenance:

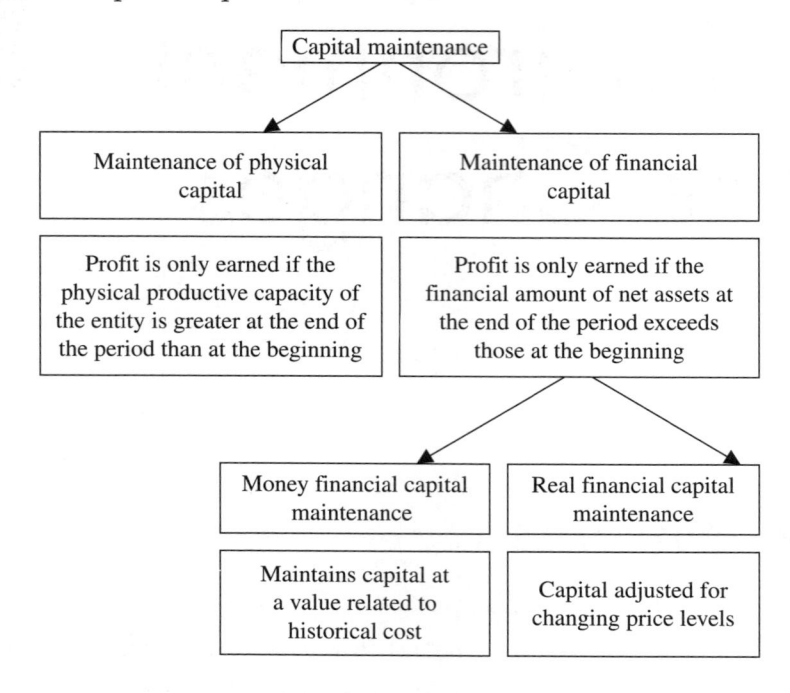

```
                        Capital maintenance
                       /                    \
        Maintenance of physical      Maintenance of financial
               capital                       capital
        
        Profit is only earned if the   Profit is only earned if the
        physical productive capacity of  financial amount of net assets at
        the entity is greater at the end of  the end of the period exceeds
        the period than at the beginning   those at the beginning
                                            /              \
                                Money financial capital   Real financial capital
                                     maintenance              maintenance
                                
                                Maintains capital at      Capital adjusted for
                                a value related to         changing price levels
                                  historical cost
```

Replacement cost accounting

- Replacement cost – the price at which identical goods or capital equipment could be purchased at the date of valuation.
- In times of rising prices leads to higher statement of financial position values and hence revaluation surpluses.
- Net current replacement cost is more appropriate for non-current assets as it reflects their existing state of consumption.
- Pros and cons include:

For	*Against*
Separates holding and operating gains	Some values subjective
Statement of financial position more relevant	Focus on operating capital rather than financial capital and hence less relevant to investors

Exit values

- Value in the statement of financial position on the basis of the selling values of the assets.

Current cost accounting

In valuing assets, current cost accounting (CCA) adopts the principle of *value to the business*.

The preparation of the financial statements based on value to the business would involve identifying each individual asset and deciding what action would be taken, given the three values available: replacement cost, realisable value and economic value.

Statement of financial position assets valuations under CCA may, therefore, be a mix of net realisable values, replacement cost and value in use (economic value).

In the income statement CCA requires the disclosure of a set of four adjustments to historical cost profit:

1. *The cost of sales adjustment (COSA)*. This adjustment shows the value to the business of the inventories consumed during the year by updating the cost of sales; in practice, this adjustment is usually computed by reference to replacement cost. Usually, entities would use price indices prepared by national statistical services.
2. *The depreciation adjustment*. The CCA depreciation charge is the value to the business of the assets consumed during the year. In practice, again, the value is usually computed by reference to replacement cost. The depreciation adjustment is the difference between the CCA depreciation charge and the historical cost depreciation charge.
3. *The monetary working capital adjustment (MWCA)*. This adjustment takes account of the additional investment required to maintain the monetary working capital of business, recognising that, in a time of rising prices, there may be gains arising from holding trade payables, and losses from holding monetary assets. Monetary working capital comprises trade receivables and trade payables, and the adjustment charges (or credits) the income statement with the increase (or decrease) in the real value of monetary working capital which has arisen between the beginning and the end of the financial year.
4. *The gearing adjustment*. Where an entity is financed by a mixture of debt and equity capital, it may be argued that only part of the three adjustments listed above is attributable to equity holders, with the rest attributable to borrowings. The gearing adjustment apportions the total of COSA, depreciation adjustment and MWCA between equity holders and lenders in proportion to their holdings.

Advantages of CCA
- CCA incorporates valuable information into the financial statements which allows users to make informed economic decisions.
- It embodies a concept of capital maintenance which is particularly relevant to industries which are capital intensive in terms of physical assets.
- Appropriate indices are easily obtainable.
- CCA-adjusted statements could provide the basis for a more rational assessment of corporation tax.
- It provides a more prudent statement of profit in times of rising prices than that provided by historical cost accounting.

Disadvantages of CCA
- CCA has been tested in practice and found to be very unpopular with the majority of preparers.
- It is time-consuming and costly to prepare and audit, and it is difficult to assess whether or not these costs are outweighed by the benefits offered by the additional information.
- It is an inappropriate system for service businesses that do not have significant investments in physical capital.
- The selection of appropriate indices introduces an element of subjectivity and judgement.
- It is questionable whether the majority of users would be able to understand CCA statements.
- Essentially CCA is not an inflation accounting system.

Current purchasing power (CPP) accounting

A method of accounting for inflation in which the values of the non-monetary items in the historical cost accounts are adjusted using a general price index to show the change in the general purchasing power of money. The CPP statement of financial position shows the effect of financial capital maintenance.

Advantages of CPP
- Preparation and audit of CPP statements is not especially costly or time-consuming.
- The method has inherent appeal in that it uses easily obtainable and widely recognised measures of inflation.
- The conceptual basis of CPP is probably easier than that of CCA for the non-specialist user of financial statements to understand.
- In times of rising prices the use of CPP allows for a reasonable measure of capital maintenance.
- The use of the RPI is objective; there is no scope for judgement in the selection of indices as in CCA.

Disadvantages of CPP
- The RPI is based upon average price inflation across the economy. It may bear little relationship to the specific price inflation that affects a particular entity or industry.
- The CPP model is particularly weak as a realistic measure of asset valuation, because it values money rather than assets. This is a very significant objection to its use, especially in the case of entities which employ large amounts of physical capital.
- The application of the CPP model for some entities is as unsatisfactory as historical cost accounting.

The 'real terms' system

The 'real terms' system of accounting for changing price levels is a hybrid system which combines the best features of CPP and CCA. One of the key drawbacks to the CPP system is that assets are presented in terms related to general purchasing power and the resultant 'values' may bear little relationship to the real movement in the value of the asset. The 'real terms' system therefore avoids the problem by retaining CCA valuations for assets. The assets side of the statement of financial position, therefore adopts entirely the CCA system.

The 'real terms' system serves the useful purpose of clearly comparing the effects of general and specific price inflation. Gains calculated using specific price indices (holding gains) can be compared to the general effects of moving prices.

Financial reporting in hyperinflationary economies

IAS 29 *Financial reporting in hyperinflationary economies* identifies the following characteristics of the economic environment of a country which would indicate that hyperinflation is a problem:

- The general population prefers to keep its wealth in non-monetary assets or in a relatively stable foreign currency. Amounts of local currency held are immediately invested to maintain purchasing power.
- The general population regards monetary amounts not in terms of the local currency but in terms of a relatively stable foreign currency. Prices may be quoted in that currency.

- Sales and purchases on credit take place at prices that compensate for the expected loss of purchasing power during the credit period, even if the period is short.
- Interest rates, wages and prices are linked to a price index.
- The cumulative inflation rate over 3 years is approaching, or exceeds, 100 per cent.

Dealing with hyperinflation

The IAS requires that the primary accounting statements of entities reporting in the currency of a hyperinflationary economy should be restated in current terms at the year end date. Corresponding figures for previous periods should also be restated so that all reported figures are expressed in common terms.

The restatement required by the IAS involves the application of a general price index to most non-monetary items and all items in the income statement and is very similar to the CPP system explained earlier in the chapter. The IAS specifically notes, however, that where items in the statement of financial position are stated at current cost they do not need to be further adjusted.

Medium answer questions

Question 1 – DCB (Nov '05)

DCB is a manufacturing and trading entity with several overseas operations. One of its subsidiaries, GFE, operates in a country which experiences relatively high rates of inflation in its currency, the crown. Most entities operating in that country voluntarily present two versions of their financial statements: one at historical cost, and the other incorporating current cost adjustments. GFE complies with this accepted practice.

Extracts from the income statement adjusted for current costs for the year ended 30 September 2005 are as follows:

	Crowns 000	Crowns 000
Historical cost operating profit		750
Current cost adjustments:		
Cost of sales adjustment	65	
Depreciation adjustment	43	
Loss on net monetary position	16	
		124
Current cost operating profit		626

Requirements

(a) Explain the defects of historical cost accounting in times of increasing prices.
(4 marks)

(b) Explain how EACH of the three current cost accounting adjustments in GFE's financial statements contributes to the maintenance of capital. **(6 marks)**
(Total = 10 marks)

Question 2

The current cost accounting (CCA) method of accounting for changing price levels requires a series of adjustments to historical cost operating profit.

Requirements

(a) Describe the purpose and nature of the cost of sales adjustment (CoSA) and depreciation adjustment. **(4 marks)**

(b) Give three advantages and three disadvantages of current cost accounting. **(6 marks)**

(Total = 10 marks)

✓ Answer to medium answer questions

Answer 1 – DCB (Nov '05)

(a) In times of increasing prices, historical cost accounting displays the following defects:

   (i) Revenues are stated at current values, but they tend to be matched with costs incurred at an earlier date. Therefore, profit is overstated.
   (ii) Where historical cost accounting is applied consistently, asset values are stated at cost less accumulated depreciation. Current values of the assets may be considerably in excess of net book value, with the result that the historical cost depreciation charge does not constitute a realistic estimate of the value of the asset consumed.
   (iii) By the time monetary liabilities are repayable, the amount of the outflow in current value terms is less than the original inflow. An entity can therefore gain by holding liabilities, but historical cost accounting does not recognise these gains. The opposite effect is experienced in respect of monetary assets.
   (iv) Typically, in a time of rising prices, profits are likely to be overstated, and capital to be understated, thus giving rise to unrealistic measurements of return on capital employed.

(b) The cost of sales adjustment comprises the additional amount of value over and above value at historical cost that is consumed at current cost. It represents an additional charge against profits, thus tending to reduce distributable earnings and ensuring that the business conserves the resources that allow it to continue to trade at current levels.

The depreciation adjustment is the difference between the historical cost accounting and current cost depreciation charges. Current cost depreciation is the value of the non-current asset consumption that has taken place during the year. In a time of rising prices it is a more realistic representation of the asset consumption. It tends to reduce distributable profits thus contributing to capital maintenance.

In the case of GFE, there is a loss on net monetary position. As noted earlier in part (a) holding monetary liabilities in times of rising prices tends to give rise to gains, whereas holding monetary assets produces losses. GFE appears, therefore, to have an excess of monetary assets over monetary liabilities, as the net effect is a loss. The recognition of this loss produces a more realistic estimation of distributable profit, and thus contributes to capital maintenance.

Answer 2

(a) *The cost of sales adjustment (COSA).* The purpose of the cost of sales adjustment is to recognise the value to the business of the inventories consumed during the accounting period. In a time of rising prices historical cost of sales reflects only part of the total value, and so an adjustment must be made that, effectively, increases cost of sales and reduces current cost profit.

The depreciation adjustment. The CCA depreciation charge is the value to the business of the assets consumed during the year. In practice, again, the value is usually computed by reference to replacement cost. The depreciation adjustment is the difference between the CCA depreciation charge and the historical cost depreciation charge.

(b) Any two of the following:

Advantages of CCA
- CCA incorporates valuable information into the financial statements which allows users to make informed economic decisions.
- It embodies a concept of capital maintenance which is particularly relevant to industries which are capital intensive in terms of physical assets.
- Appropriate indices are easily obtainable.
- CCA-adjusted statements could provide the basis for a more rational assessment of corporation tax.
- It provides a more prudent statement of profit in times of rising prices than that provided by historical cost accounting.

Disadvantages of CCA
- CCA has been tested in practice and found to be very unpopular with the majority of preparers.
- It is time-consuming and costly to prepare and audit, and it is difficult to assess whether or not these costs are outweighed by the benefits offered by the additional information.
- It is an inappropriate system for service businesses that do not have significant investments in physical capital.
- The selection of appropriate indices introduces an element of subjectivity and judgement.
- It is questionable whether the majority of users would be able to understand CCA statements.
- Essentially CCA is not an inflation accounting system.

13

Interpretation of Accounting Ratios

Interpretation of Accounting Ratios 13

> **CALCULATE LEARNING OUTCOME**
>
> After studying this chapter students should be able to:
> ▸ interpret a full range of accounting ratios.

The stakeholders

- Different user groups refer to financial statements to achieve different objectives:
  - Present and potential investors
  - Lenders and potential lenders
  - Suppliers and creditors
  - Employees
  - Customers
  - Government
  - The general public.

The basis of effective analysis

- Calculating financial ratios alone will not give a complete picture and must be complemented with other attributes:
  - History of the business
  - Knowledge of the risks to which the business is exposed
  - Capabilities of the management team
  - Awareness of broader economic factors such as trends in interest rates.
- Sources of data should not be restricted to the statement of financial position, income statement, etc., but should have regard to the range of voluntary disclosures made by many companies (e.g. environmental review) plus external sources such as specialist business research agencies.

Ratios

Performance ratios

$$\text{Gross profit margin} = \frac{(\text{Sales} - \text{Cost of sales})}{\text{Sales of the period}} \times 100$$

$$\text{Operating profit margin} = \frac{\text{Operating profit}}{\text{Revenue}} \times 100$$

$$\text{Net profit margin} = \frac{\text{Net profit}}{\text{Revenue}} \times 100$$

- EBITDA – earnings before interest, taxation, depreciation and amortisation. This figure is often used as an approximation of operating cash flows, but care is required as no adjustments have been made for changes in working capital.

Activity ratios

$$\text{Asset turnover} = \frac{\text{Revenue}}{\text{Total assets}}$$

$$\text{Inventory turnover} = \frac{\text{Cost of sales}}{\text{Average inventory}}$$

or

$$= \frac{\text{Average inventory}}{\text{Cost of sales}} \times 365$$

Return on capital ratios

$$\text{Return on capital employed} = \frac{\text{Profit}}{\text{Capital employed}} \times 100$$

$$\text{Return on assets} = \frac{\text{Operating profit}}{\text{Total assets}} \times 100$$

$$\text{Return on shareholders funds} = \frac{\text{Profits attributable to shareholders}}{\text{Shareholders funds}} \times 100$$

For the purposes of the ROCE measurement, capital employed includes the following:

- Issued share capital
- Reserves
- Preference shares
- Non-controlling interests
- Loan capital
- Provisions (including provisions for tax)
- Bank overdraft
- Investments

Liquidity ratios

$$\text{Current ratio} = \frac{\text{Current assets}}{\text{Current liabilities}}$$

$$\text{Quick ratio} = \frac{\text{Current assets less inventory}}{\text{Current liabilities}}$$

$$\text{Receivable days} = \frac{\text{Average receivables}}{\text{Credit sales}} \times 365$$

$$\text{Payables days} = \frac{\text{Average payables}}{\text{Credit purchases}} \times 365$$

- The working capital cycle – The length of the cycle is calculated by adding the inventory turnover days and receivable days and deducting the payables days.

Valuation and investor ratios

$$\text{Price/Earning ratio} = \frac{\text{Current market price per share}}{\text{Earnings per share}}$$

$$\text{Profit retention ratio} = \frac{\text{Profit after dividends}}{\text{Profit before dividends}} \times 100$$

$$\text{Dividend payout rate} = \frac{\text{Dividend per share}}{\text{Earnings per share}} \times 100$$

$$\text{Dividend yield} = \frac{\text{Dividend per share}}{\text{Market price per share}} \times 100$$

$$\text{Dividend cover} = \frac{\text{Earnings per share}}{\text{Dividends per share}}$$

Cash flow ratios

$$\text{Return on capital employed to cash} = \frac{\text{Cash generated from operations}}{\text{Capital employed}} \times 100$$

$$\text{Cash generated from operations to total debt} = \frac{\text{Cash generatd from operations}}{\text{Total long-term borrowings}}$$

$$\text{Net cash from operating activities to capital expenditure} = \frac{\text{Net cash from operating activities}}{\text{Net capital expenditure}} \times 100$$

Capital structure ratios

$$\text{Interest cover ratio} = \frac{\text{Profit before interest and tax}}{\text{Interest expense}}$$

$$\text{Gearing} = \frac{\text{Total long-term debt}}{\text{Shareholder funds}} \times 100$$

Or:

$$= \frac{\text{Total long-term debt}}{\text{Shareholders funds } + \text{ long-term debt}} \times 100$$

Long-term debt includes debentures, mortgages and other long-term debt, including preference shares. Any bank overdraft would be included to the extent that it is actually a source of long-term finance. Shareholders' funds comprises equity share capital and reserves.

Service industries

- Some ratios do not provide a meaningful assessment tool for service industries for which a large proportion of their value is represented by intangibles not reflected on the statement of financial position (e.g. employees).

Long answer questions

Question 1 – BZJ (May '06)

You advise a private investor who holds a portfolio of investments in smaller listed companies. Recently, she has received the annual report of the BZJ Group for the financial year ended 31 December 2005. In accordance with her usual practice, the investor has read the chairman's statement, but has not looked in detail at the figures. Relevant extracts from the chairman's statement are as follows:

'Following the replacement of many of the directors, which took place in early March 2005, your new board has worked to expand the group's manufacturing facilities and to replace non-current assets that have reached the end of their useful lives. A new line of storage solutions was designed during the second quarter and was put into production at the beginning of September. Sales efforts have been concentrated on increasing our market share in respect of storage products, and in leading the expansion into Middle Eastern markets.

The growth in the business has been financed by a combination of loan capital and the issue of additional shares. The issue of 300,000 new $1 shares was fully taken up on 1 November 2005, reflecting, we believe, market confidence in the group's new management. Dividends have been reduced in 2005 in order to increase profit retention to fund the further growth planned for 2006. The directors believe that the implementation of their medium- to long-term strategies will result in increased returns to investors within the next two to three years.'

The group's principal activity is the manufacture and sale of domestic and office furniture. Approximately 40% of the product range is bought in from manufacturers in other countries.

Extracts from the annual report of the BZJ Group are as follows:

BZJ Group: Consolidated income statement for the year ended 31 December 2005

	2005 $000	2004 $000
Revenue	120,366	121,351
Cost of sales	(103,024)	(102,286)
Gross profit	17,342	19,065
Operating expenses	(11,965)	(12,448)
Profit from operations	5,377	6,617
Interest payable	(1,469)	(906)
Profit before tax	3,908	5,711
Income tax expense	(1,125)	(1,594)
Profit for the period	2,783	4,117
Attributable to:		
Equity holders of the parent	2,460	3,676
Non-controlling interest	323	441
	2,783	4,117

BZJ Group: Summarised consolidated statement of changes in equity for the year ended 31 December 2005 (attributable to equity holders of the parent)

	Accum. profit $000	Share capital $000	Share premium $000	Reval. reserve $000	Total 2005 $000	Total 2004 $000
Opening balance	18,823	2,800	3,000		24,623	21,311
Surplus on revaluation of properties				2,000	2,000	–
Profit for the period	2,460				2,460	3,676
Issue of share capital		300	1,200		1,500	–
Dividends paid 31/12	(155)				(155)	(364)
Closing balance	21,128	3,100	4,200	2,000	30,428	24,623

BZJ Group: Consolidated statement of financial position at 31 December 2005

	2005 $000	2005 $000	2004 $000	2004 $000
Non-current assets:				
Property, plant and equipment	40,643		21,322	
Goodwill	1,928		1,928	
Trademarks and patents	1,004		1,070	
		43,575		24,320
Current assets:				
Inventories	37,108		27,260	
Trade receivables	14,922		17,521	
Cash	–		170	
		52,030		44,951
		95,605		69,271
Equity:				
Share capital ($1 shares)	3,100		2,800	
Share premium	4,200		3,000	
Revaluation reserve	2,000		–	
Accumulated profits	21,128		18,823	
		30,428		24,623
Non-controlling interest		2,270		1,947
Non-current liabilities				
Interest bearing borrowings		26,700		16,700
Current liabilities:				
Trade and other payables	31,420		24,407	
Income tax	1,125		1,594	
Short-term borrowings	3,662		–	
		36,207		26,001
		95,605		69,271

Requirements

(a) Calculate the earnings per share figure for the BZJ Group for the years ended 31 December 2005 and 2004, assuming that there was no change in the number of ordinary shares in issue during 2004. **(3 marks)**

(b) Produce a report for the investor that

    (i) analyses and interprets the financial statements of the BZJ Group, commenting upon the group's performance and position; and **(17 marks)**

    (ii) discusses the extent to which the chairman's comments about the potential for improved future performance are supported by the financial statement information for the year ended 31 December 2005. **(5 marks)**

(Total = 25 marks)

Question 2 – AXZ (Nov '06)

AXZ is a rapidly expanding entity that manufactures and distributes hair care and other beauty products. Its directors are currently considering expansion into foreign countries by means of acquisitions of similar entities. Two acquisition possibilities are to be considered at the next board meeting: DCB, an entity operating in Lowland, and GFE which operates in Highland. The target acquisitions are of similar size, and operate within similar economic parameters and the same currency, although their tax regimes differ substantially. Neither entity is listed. Neither Lowland nor Highland requires unlisted entities to comply with IFRS, and consequently both entities comply with local GAAP. Local GAAP in both countries is, in most respects, similar to IFRS but there are some differences that must be taken into account when making comparisons between financial statements produced in the two countries. AXZ is listed, and complies with IFRS.

The directors of both DCB and GFE have co-operated fully in providing detailed information about their businesses. Provided that a reasonable price is offered for the shares, takeover is unlikely to be resisted by either entity. AXZ can afford to fund one acquisition but not both.

The most recent income statements of the three entities are provided below, together with some relevant statement of financial position totals.

Income statements for the year ended 30 September 2006

	AXZ $000	DCB $000	GFE $000
Revenue	8,300	1,900	2,200
Cost of sales	(5,600)	(1,300)	(1,400)
Gross profit	2,700	600	800
Distribution costs	(252)	(60)	(65)
Administrative expenses	(882)	(180)	(250)
Finance costs	(105)	(25)	(65)
Profit before tax	1,461	335	420
Income tax expense	(366)	(134)	(105)
Profit for the period	1,095	201	315

Extracts from statement of financial positions at 30 September 2006

	AXZ	DCB	GFE
Total equity	4,820	1,350	1,931
Non-current liabilities (borrowings)	1,500	500	650
Non-current assets	9,950	1,680	2,400

Notes

1. It is customary for entities complying with local GAAP in Lowland to adopt the rates of depreciation used by the tax authorities. Tax depreciation is calculated on the straight-line basis in all cases, at a rate of 12.5% each year on all non-current assets. DCB's noncurrent assets have been held, on average, for three years, and none are fully depreciated. The age profile of non-current assets held by AXZ and GFE is very similar to that of DCB, but both entities charge an average of 10% straight line depreciation each year.

   All depreciation in all three entities has been charged to cost of sales.

2. Accounting for financial instruments is similar under Lowland GAAP and IFRS. However, Highland's GAAP takes a less prescriptive approach. GFE has $100,000 of 5% nonparticipating shares included in equity. Under IFRS, these shares would be classified as non-current liabilities. The 5% fixed charge on these shares has been reflected in the statement of changes in equity; under IFRS it would be shown as part of finance costs. This charge would not, however, be allowable against income tax in Highland.

3. The directors of AXZ plan to finance the acquisition through a combination of equity and debt that will be similar, proportionately, to the existing capital structure. When assessing possible takeover targets the following key accounting ratios are of especial interest:
   - Gross profit margin
   - Profit before tax as a percentage of sales
   - Return on equity
   - Return on total capital employed
   - Non-current asset turnover
   - Gearing (long-term debt as a percentage of equity)

   Their policy is to consider targets for takeover only if the above ratios for the combined group would not be adversely affected to any material extent.

Requirements

(a) Calculate and tabulate for each entity the key ratios listed in note 3. both before **and** after taking the information in notes 1. and 2. above into account. **(15 marks)**

(b) Write a concise report for the directors of AXZ, which analyses the financial statement information and interprets the ratios calculated in your answer to part (a). You should also include in your analysis any additional ratios that are likely to be useful to the directors of AXZ in making their decision. **(10 marks)**

(Total = 25 marks)

Question 3 – DPC (Nov '07)

The directors of DPC, a listed entity, have been approached by three out of the five shareholders of PPS, an unlisted competitor. The PPS shareholders are nearing retirement age, and would like to realise their investment in the business. The two remaining shareholders do not object, but would like to retain between them at least a significant influence over the business.

The directors of DPC are currently concerned about the threat of a takeover bid for DPC itself. Although they would like to acquire an interest in PPS as it would help them to increase DPC's market share, they do not want to take any action that would adversely affect their financial statements and certain key accounting ratios (EPS, gearing [calculated as debt/equity], and non-current asset turnover).

There are two possibilities for consideration:

1. DPC could purchase 40% of the ordinary shares of PPS, giving it significant influence, but not control. The cost of this would be $3.5 million, to be settled in cash. DPC would pay $1 million out of its cash resources and would increase its existing long-term borrowings for the balance.
2. DPC could purchase 60% of the ordinary shares of PPS, giving it control. The cost of this would be $6 million, to be settled in cash. DPC would pay $3 million out of its cash resources, and would increase its existing long-term borrowings for the balance.

The purchase would take place on the first day of the new financial year, 1 January 2008. Projected summary income statements for the 2008 financial year, and projected summary statement of financial positions at 31 December 2008 are shown below. The DPC figures are consolidated to include its existing 100% held subsidiaries (it currently holds no interests in associates). The projected financial statements for PPS are for that entity alone.

Summary projected income statements for the year ended 31 December 2008

	DPC consolidated Projected: 2008 $000	PPS entity Projected: 2008 $000
Revenue	60,300	10,200
All expenses including income tax	(55,300)	(9,500)
Profit for the period attributable to equity holders	5,000	700

Summary projected statement of financial positions at 31 December 2008

	DPC consolidated Projected: 2008 $000	PPS entity Projected: 2008 $000	Notes
Non-current assets	50,400	9,800	2
Current assets	82,000	16,000	
	132,400	25,800	
Equity	31,400	4,000	3 & 4
Long-term liabilities	10,000	9,300	
Current liabilities	91,000	12,500	
	132,400	25,800	

Notes:

1. DPC's consolidated projected financial statements at 31 December 2008 do not take into account the proposed acquisition of PPS.
2. DPC's non-current asset figure includes goodwill on acquisition of various subsidiaries.
3. PPS's equity comprises 100,000 ordinary shares of $1 each, $3,200,000 of retained earnings brought forward on 1 January 2008 and $700,000 profit for the period.
4. DPC will have 10 million ordinary shares of $1 each on 1 January 2008. No issues of shares will be made during 2008.

Requirements

(a) Prepare draft projected financial statements for the DPC group for the year ending 31 December 2008 under each of the following assumptions:
   (i) DPC acquires 40% of the ordinary shares of PPS on 1 January 2008;
   (ii) DPC acquires 60% of the ordinary shares of PPS on 1 January 2008.

   It can be assumed that no impairment of either investment would have taken place by 31 December 2008. **(14 marks)**

(b) Calculate EPS, gearing and non-current asset turnover ratios based on the draft projected 31 December 2008 financial statements for:
   (i) DPC and its existing subsidiaries;
   (ii) DPC including the acquisition of an associate interest in PPS;
   (iii) DPC including the acquisition of a subsidiary interest in PPS. **(6 marks)**

(c) Discuss the differences in the accounting ratios under the different scenarios, identifying reasons for the most significant differences. **(5 marks)**

(Total = 25 marks)

Question 4 – BHG (May '08)

BHG is a successful listed entity that designs and markets specialist business software. BHG's directors have decided to adopt a policy of expansion into overseas territories through the acquisition of similar software businesses possessing established shares of their domestic markets. BHG's aim is to obtain control, or at the minimum, significant influence (represented by at least 40% of issued share capital) of investee entities. Target investee entities are likely to be listed entities in their own countries, but the acquisition of unlisted entities is not ruled out.

You are a senior accountant in BHG, and you have been asked by the Chief Financial Officer (CFO) to establish a set of key accounting ratios for use in:

1. the initial appraisal of potential acquisitions;
2. on-going appraisal following acquisitions.

The ratios will be used as part of a suite of quantitative and non-quantitative measurements to compare businesses with each other. The CFO has suggested that it would be appropriate to identify no more than 5–7 key financial ratios.

One of your assistants has suggested a list of 5 key accounting ratios as suitable for both initial and on-going appraisal and comparison. She has provided reasons to support the case for their inclusion as key ratios.

1. Earnings per share: 'one of the most important investor ratios, widely used by all classes of investor to assess business performance'.
2. Dividend yield: 'this ratio provides a very useful measurement that allows comparison with yields from other equity and non-equity investments'.
3. Gearing: 'this is of critical importance in determining the level of risk of an equity investment'.
4. Gross profit margin: 'allows investors to assess business performance, and is of particular use over several accounting periods within the same organisation. It is also very useful for comparing performances between businesses'.

5. Asset turnover ratios: 'allow the investor to compare the intensity of asset usage between businesses, and over time'.

Requirements

(a) Discuss the extent to which each of the 5 suggested accounting ratios is likely to be useful to BHG for both initial and on-going appraisal and comparison, and the extent to which your assistant's assessments of the value of the ratios are justified. **(15 marks)**

(b) Explain the problems and limitations of accounting ratio analysis in making interfirm and international comparisons. **(10 marks)**
(Total = 25 marks)

Question 5 – BSP (May '07)

BSP, a listed entity, supplies, installs and maintains burglar alarm systems for business clients. As a response to increased competition and falling margins in the burglar alarm market, the entity's directors decided, towards the end of 2005, to extend its operations into the provision of fire alarm and sprinkler systems. A training programme for staff was undertaken in the early months of 2006 at a cost of around $200,000. An aggressive marketing campaign, costing $250,000, was launched at the same time. Both costs were incurred and settled before the 31 March 2006 year end. BSP commenced its new operations with effect from the beginning of its financial year on 1 April 2006.

BSP's cash resources were at a low level in early 2006, so, in order to finance the costs of the new operation and the necessary increase in working capital to fund the new operations, BSP made a new issue of shares. The issue took place in May 2006. During March 2007, BSP disposed of its two overseas subsidiaries in order to concentrate on operations in its home market. Both were profitable businesses and therefore sold for an amount substantially in excess of carrying value. These subsidiaries accounted for almost 10% of group sales during the 2006/2007 financial year.

As the finance director's assistant you have been responsible for the preparation of the draft financial statements, which have been circulated to the directors in advance of a board meeting to be held later this week.

The marketing director, who was appointed in June 2006, has sent you the following e-mail:

'When I did my university course in marketing I studied a module in finance and accounting, which covered the analysis of financial statements. Unfortunately, it was a long time ago, and I've forgotten quite a lot about it.

I'm puzzled by the cash flow statement, in particular. The income statement shows a loss, which is obviously bad news, especially as the budget showed a profit for the year. However, the cash resources of the business have actually increased by quite a large amount between March 2006 and March 2007. It is said that "cash is king", so I'm assuming that the poor profitability is a short-term problem while the new operation settles down.

As you know, we almost managed to achieve our sales targets in both the fire and burglar alarm sectors for the year, (although of course we did have to offer some customers special discounts and extended credit as inducements). I'm assuming, therefore, that the lack of profitability is a problem of cost control.

It would be really helpful if you could provide me with a brief report, in advance of this week's meeting, which tells me what this cash flow statement means. You could include ratios, provided that you show how they are calculated.'

The consolidated cash flow statement for the year ended 31 March 2007 (with comparative figures for 2006) is as follows:

BSP: Consolidated cash flow statement for the year ended 31 March 2007

	2007 $000	2007 $000	2006 $000	2006 $000
Cash flows from operating activities				
(Loss)/profit before tax		(453)		306
Adjustments for:				
Depreciation	98		75	
Foreign exchange loss	22		37	
Profit on sale of investments	(667)		–	
Interest expense	161		45	
		(839)		463
Increase in inventories		(227)		(65)
Increase in receivables		(242)		(36)
Increase in payables		62		12
Cash (outflow)/inflow from operations		(1,246)		374
Interest paid		(157)		(42)
Tax paid		(38)		(38)
Net cash (outflow)/inflow from operating Activities		(1,441)		277
Cash flows from investing activities				
Proceeds from sale of investments	2,320		–	
Purchase of property, plant and equipment	(661)		(425)	
Income from associates	23		26	
Net cash inflow/(outflow) from investing Activities		1,682		(399)
Cash flows from financing activities				
Proceeds from issue of share capital	850		–	
Dividends paid	–		(200)	
Net cash inflow/(outflow) from financing Activities		850		(200)
Net increase/(decrease) in cash		1,091		(322)
Cash at start of period		27		349
Cash at end of period		1,118		27

Additional information:

Revenue in the 2005/06 financial year was $12.11 million. In the 2006/07 financial year, total revenue was $12.32 million, $10.93 million of which arose in respect of the sale of burglar alarms.

Inventories at the start of the 2005/06 financial year were $591,000, and receivables were $1,578,000. There was no increase in long-term borrowings throughout the two-year period covered by the cash flow statement above.

Requirement

Analyse and interpret the information given, and produce a report to the marketing director. The report should explain the difference between cash and profit, and should discuss the business's profitability and working capital position. It should also discuss, to the extent possible from the information given, the prospects for BSP's future.

(Total = 25 marks)

Answers to long answer questions

Answer 1 – BZJ (May '06)

(a) Earnings per share for the year ended 31 December 2004:

$$\frac{2,800,000}{\$3,676,000} = 131.3\text{c per share} \quad \$3,676,000 = 131.3¢ \text{ per share}$$

Earnings per share for the year ended 31 December 2005:

$$\frac{2,850,000}{\$2,460,000} = 86.3\text{c per share}$$

(W1) Weighted average number of shares in issue

10/12 × 2,800,000	2,333,333
2/12 × 3,100,000	516,667
	2,850,000

(b) **Report**
To: Investor
From: Adviser
The financial statements of the BZJ Group for the year ended 31 December 2005
Financial performance

The performance of the group has declined sharply. Revenue has fallen by 0.8% between 2004 and 2005. Gross, operating and pre-tax profit margins are all substantially lower in 2005 than in the previous year: gross profit has fallen from 15.7% to 14.4%; operating profit has fallen from 5.5% to 4.5%; pre-tax profit margin has fallen from 4.7% to 3.2%. The fall in revenue is particularly striking, given the large amount of investment in non-current assets that has taken place. Margins may have been adversely affected by additional depreciation charges arising because of the increase in non-current assets. It is also possible that the expansion into new markets and the new storage products will result in permanently lower margins. Return on equity (ROE) and return on total capital employed (ROTCE) have both dropped by significant margins: ROE has fallen from 21.5% to 12.0%, and ROTCE has fallen from 15.3% to 89.51%.

Investors will be disappointed with the significant drop in the amount of dividend received. The dividend payout ratio is also substantially lower.

The amount of interest payable has increased by over $500,000 during the year, because of the large increase in borrowings intended, according to the chairman's statement, to fund business growth. Interest cover has halved, but the group's current levels of earnings cover the charge 3.7 times, which provides a reasonable margin of safety. However, it is worth noting that the average interest charge (taking interest payable as a percentage of long- and short-term borrowings) is less than 5% in 2005. This may suggest that borrowings have reached their current level quite recently, and that the interest charge in the 2006 financial statements will be significantly higher.

The analysis of financial performance suggests that, with falling margins and rising interest, potential returns from the business are likely to be more volatile in future.

Financial position

A very large increase in non-current assets has taken place. The increase of nearly $20 million appears to be mostly accounted for by purchases of new assets, although a revaluation of $2 million has taken place during the financial year. The investment in non-current assets has been financed in part by an increase in long-term borrowings of $10 million, and also by an issue of share capital at a premium which raised $1.5 million in funds. Current liabilities have increased by around $7 million and the business has moved from a position of holding cash at the end of 2004 to quite substantial short-term borrowings at the end of 2005.

Inventories have increased by almost $10 million, and the turnover period is much greater at 131.5 days than at the end of 2004. It could be that the business is building up stocks of its new products; alternatively, it is possible that the new ranges have not sold as well as expected, in which case the build-up of inventories is a worrying sign. Receivables turnover has improved; this is the only element of working capital management that shows any sign of improvement. The current ratio is probably adequate at its present level, but it, too, shows a significant decline over from the previous year.

Even before the current year's expansion programme, gearing was at a high level. It has increased still further to the point where borrowings represent over 80% of equity. The business has no cash at the year end, and it may find that it becomes difficult and expensive to obtain further loan capital. There is an urgent need to improve working capital management and, especially, to start turning over inventories.

Chairman's comments

The chairman refers to 'growth in the business'. However, closer examination of the financial statements shows that the growth is all in statement of financial position items, especially inventories, trade and other payables and non-current assets. The increased investment in fixed and working capital has not, by the 2005 year end, started to yield any benefits in terms of improved performance; the non-current asset turnover ratio has declined sharply from 4.99 in 2004 to 2.76 in 2005. All the performance indicators derived from the income statement are in decline. It is possible that the expansion into new markets and products had not begun to yield benefits by the end of 2005, but investors and other stakeholders will expect the promised improvements to start to pay off in 2006.

The chairman also refers to the successful issue of further ordinary shares only two months before the year end. This is, indeed, reassuring, as it suggests that investors are prepared to accept the high level of gearing, and that they are prepared to place confidence in the directors' strategies.

In summary, the business is in no immediate danger of failing, but the position could become critical if management's current expansionary policies do not succeed.

Appendix

	2005	2004
Gross profit margin	$\dfrac{17,342}{120,366} \times 100 = 14.4\%$	$\dfrac{19,065}{121,351} \times 100 = 15.7\%$
Operating profit margin	$\dfrac{5,377}{120,366} \times 100 = 4.5\%$	$\dfrac{6,617}{121,351} \times 100 = 5.5\%$
Pre-tax profit margin	$\dfrac{3,908 \times 100}{120,366} = 3.2\%$	$\dfrac{5,711}{121,351} \times 100 = 4.7\%$
Interest cover	$\dfrac{5,377}{1,469} = 3.7\%$	$\dfrac{6,617}{906} = 7.3$
Debt/equity	$\dfrac{26,700 \times 100}{(30,428 + 2,270)} = 81.7\%$	$\dfrac{16,700 \times 100}{(24,623 + 1,947)} = 62.9\%$
Return on equity	$\dfrac{3,908 \times 100}{(30,428 + 2,270)} = 12.0\%$	$\dfrac{5,711 \times 100}{(24,623 + 1,947)} = 21.5\%$
Return on total capital Employed	$\dfrac{5.377 \times 100}{(30,428 + 2,270 + 26,700 + 3,662)} = 8.5\%$	$\dfrac{6,617 \times 100}{(24,623 + 1,947 + 16,700)} = 15.3\%$
Non-current asset Turnover	$\dfrac{120,366}{43,575} = 2.76$	$\dfrac{12,351}{24,320} = 4.99$
Inventory turnover	$\dfrac{37.108}{103,024} \times 365 = 131.5$ days	$\dfrac{27,260}{102,286} \times 365 = 97.3$ days
Receivables turnover	$\dfrac{14,922}{120,366} \times 365 = 45.2$ days	$\dfrac{17,521}{121,351} \times 365 = 52.7$ days

Answer 2 – AXZ (Nov '06)

(a)
Table: key ratios before and after adjustment for GAAP differences

	AXZ	DCB		GFE	
		Before adjusting	After adjusting	Before adjusting	After adjusting
Gross profit margin	32.5%	31.6%	35.1%	36.4%	Unchanged
PBT/Sales %	17.6%	17.6%	21.2%	19.1%	18.9%
Return on equity	30.3%	24.8%	25.9%	21.8%	22.7%
ROTCE	24.8%	19.5%	20.8%	18.8%	18.8%
NCA turnover	0.83	1.13	1.01	0.92	Unchanged
Gearing	31.1%	37.0%	32.2%	33.7%	41.0%

Workings:

1. *Ratios before adjustment*

	AXZ	DCB	GFE
Gross profit margin	2,700/8,300 × 100 = 32.5%	600/1,900 × 100 = 31.6%	800/2,200 × 100 = 36.4%
PBT/Sales %	1,461/8,300 × 100 = 17.6%	335/1,900 × 100 = 17.6%	420/2,200 × 100 = 19.1%
ROE	1,461/4,820 × 100 = 30.3%	335/1,350 × 100 = 24.8%	420/1,931 × 100 = 21.8%
ROTCE	$\frac{(1,461 + 105)}{(4,820 + 1,500)} \times 100 = 24.8\%$	$\frac{(335 + 25)}{(1,350 + 500)} \times 100 = 19.5\%$	$\frac{(420 + 65)}{(1,931 + 650)} \times 100 = 18.8\%$
NCA turnover	8,300/9,950 = 0.83	1,900/1,680 = 1.13	2,200/2,400 = 0.92
Gearing	1,500/4,820 × 100 = 31.1%	500/1,350 × 100 = 37.0%	650/1,931 × 100 = 33.7%

2. *Adjustments to DCB's depreciation and non-current assets*

Non-current assets at net book value = $1,680,000, after an average 3 years' depreciation out of an 8 year estimated life. NBV = 5/8 × cost, so cost = $1,680,000 × 8/5 = $2,688,000

Annual depreciation charges on this basis = $2,688,000 × 12.5% = $336,000

If a rate of 10% SL depreciation is applied, net book value would be as follows:

$2,688,000 × 7/10 = $1,881,600

Annual depreciation charges on this basis = $2,688,000 × 10% = $268,800

NBV would increase by $1,881,600 − $1,680,000 = $201,600

Equity would increase to $1,551,600 ($1,350,000 + $201,600)

Cost of sales would decrease by the difference in depreciation charges:

$1,300,000 − $336,000 + $268,800 = $1,232,800.

Gross profit would be: $1,900,000 − $1,232,800 = $667,200.

Profit before tax would be $667,200 − $60,000 − $180,000 − $25,000 = $402,200

3. *Revised ratio calculations for DCB*

DCB	
Gross profit margin	667.2/1,900 × 100 = 35.1%
PBT/Sales %	402.2/1,900 × 100 = 21.2%
ROE	402.2/1,551.6 × 100 = 25.9%
ROTCE	(402.2 + 25)/(1,551.6 + 500) × 100 = 20.8%
NCA turnover	1,900/1,881.6 = 1.01
Gearing	500/1,551.6 × 100 = 32.2%

(W4) *Adjustments in respect of reclassification of GFE's financial instrument*

Equity reduces from	$1,931,000	to	$1,831,000
Non-current liabilities increase from	$650,000	to	$750,000
Finance costs increase from	$65,000	to	$70,000
Profit before tax decreases from	$420,000	to	$415,000

(W5) Revised ratio calculations for GFE

GFE	
Gross profit margin	Remains the same
PBT/Sales %	415/2,200 × 100 = 18.9%
ROE	415/1,831 × 100 = 22.7%
ROTCE	(415 + 70)/(1,831 + 750) × 100 = 18.8%
NCA turnover	Remains the same
Gearing	750/1,831 = 41.0%

(b) **Report on financial statement information for AXZ, DCB and GFE: financial year ended 30 September 2006**

Before any adjustment is made in respect of depreciation, DCB's ratios indicate a poorer performance and position than GFE in several important respects: gross margin, profit before tax as a percentage of sales and gearing are all worse than GFE's, and all ratios, with the exceptions of non-current asset turnover and profit before tax as a percentage of sales are worse than AXZ's.

After adjustment, however, DCB's ratios are much improved, especially once adjustments in respect of GFE's financial instruments are made. The adjusted figures show that both DCB and GFE produce significantly better profit margins than AXZ. DCB's profit before tax as a percentage of sales is superior to those of the other entities. Non-current asset turnover in DCB has reduced following the increase in net book value because of the depreciation adjustment. However, it is still better than the equivalent for the other entities. DCB's gearing percentage is similar to that of AXZ; both are lower than GFE's which is significantly higher following the reclassification of some of the equity to debt. Interest cover (see appendix) would not give cause for concern in any of the entities, but GFE's is significantly lower than in the other two entities.

On most of the key ratios, DCB appears to be the preferable acquisition target of the two under review. Return on equity and return on total capital employed are both lower, and gearing is slightly higher, than in AXZ. However, the effect overall on the new group's ratios might not be regarded as material. On the other hand, even where the ratios are more advantageous, the overall effect on group ratios might not make much of a difference. For example, if AXZ and DCB were to combine, total profit before tax would be $1,461,000 + 402,200 = $1,863,200, all other things being equal. Total sales would be $8,300,000 + $1,900,000 = $10,200,000. The group profit as a percentage of sales figure would be $1,863.2/10,200 × 100 = 18.3%. This is only 0.7% higher than AXZ's existing figure.

Further investigation would be needed before making a final decision. DCB has followed the tax treatment in depreciating its non-current assets; however, it is possible that an average asset life of 8 years actually represents a better assessment of DCB's own asset base. Also, it is worth noting that DCB does appear to be subject to a significantly higher rate of income tax than the other two entities (see appendix). This perception requires further investigation, and detailed tax advice should be obtained before the directors of AXZ make their decision.

Appendix:

Additional ratio calculations

	AXZ	DCB	GFE
Income tax expense as a percentage of profit before tax	366/1,461 × 100 = 25.1%	134/335 × 100 = 40%	105/420 × 100 = 25%
Interest cover	(2,700 − 252 − 822)/105 = 15.5	(667.2 − 50 − 180)/25 = 17.5	(800 − 65 − 250)/70 = 6.9

Answer 3 – DPC (Nov '07)

(a)

(i) DPC's summary projected financial statements to include the acquisition of an associate interest in PPS:

Summary projected income statement for the year ended 31 December 2008

	Projected: 2008 $000
Revenue	60,300
All expenses including income tax	(55,300)
Share of profit of associate (W1)	280
Profit for the period attributable to equity holders	5,280

Summary projected statement of financial position at 31 December 2008

	Projected: 2008 $000
Non-current assets	50,400
Investment in associate (W2)	3,780
Current assets (82,000 − 1,000)	81,000
	135,180
Equity (W3)	31,680
Long-term liabilities (10,000 + 2,500)	12,500
Current liabilities	91,000
	135,180

(ii) DPC's summary projected financial statements to include the acquisition of a subsidiary interest in PPS:

Summary projected income statement for the year ended 31 December 2008

	Projected: 2008 $000
Revenue (60,300 + 10,200)	70,500
All expenses including income tax (55,300 + 9,500)	(64,800)
Non-controlling interest in PPS (700 × 40%)	(280)
Profit for the period attributable to equity holders	5,420

Summary projected statement of financial position at 31 December 2008

	Projected: 2008 $000
Non-current assets (50,400 + 9,800 + 4,020 (W4))	64,220
Current assets (82,000 + 16,000 − 3,000)	95,000
	159,220
Equity (W5)	31,820
Non-controlling interest in PPS (4,000 × 40%)	1,600
Long-term liabilities (10,000 + 9,300 + 3,000))	22,300
Current liabilities (91,000 + 12,500)	103,500
	159,220

Workings

1. *Share of profits of associate:* $700,000 × 40% = $280,000

2. *Investment in associate:*

	$000
Investment at cost	3,500
Share of post-acquisition profits	280
	3,780

3. *Equity*

	$000
As given in the question	31,400
Share of post-acquisition profits in associate	280
	31,680

4. *Goodwill on acquisition*

	$000
Investment at cost	6,000
Share of net assets acquired:	
([100 + 3,200] × 60%)	1,980
Goodwill on acquisition	4,020

5. *Equity*

	$000
As given in the question	31,400
Share of post-acquisition profits in subsidiary	420
	31,820

(b)

		DPC existing		DPC + PPS associate		DPC + PPS subsidiary	
EPS	5,000/10,000	50¢	5,280/10,000	52.8¢	5,420/10,000		54.2¢
Gearing	10,000/31,400 × 100	31.8%	12,500/31,680 × 100	39.5%	22,300/33,420 × 100		66.7%
NCA turnover	60,300/50,400	1.20	Same	1.20	70,500/64,220		1.10

(c) Earnings per share would be improved under either acquisition scenario. Net current asset turnover would be reduced if the investment in a subsidiary interest were to be acquired in PPS. However, it is the gearing ratio that shows the biggest potential differences. The gearing ratio if PPS were acquired as an associate worsens because of the additional borrowing of $2.5 million required to acquire the shareholding. If a subsidiary interest were to be purchased not only is there additional borrowing of $3 million to take into account in the gearing calculation, but, much more significantly, PPS's own borrowings have to be included in long-term liabilities. PPS is highly geared and so the impact on consolidation is very substantial. If an associate interest were acquired PPS's borrowing would be kept off statement of financial position.

Answer 4 – BHG (May '08)

(a) 1. *Earnings per share*

Earnings per share (EPS) is calculated by dividing the earnings attributable to ordinary shareholders by the weighted average of the number of ordinary shares in issue. Its disclosure by listed businesses is required by IFRS, and it is, as the assistant says, a very important ratio for investors in assessing business performance. However, it is of only limited use in comparison between entities: for one thing, the number of shares in issue almost always differs between entities. Even at the single business entity level, it is of most interest to investors who hold a relatively small number of shares for a relatively lengthy time period (to allow comparison over several time periods). EPS forms part of the calculation of the price/earnings ratio, and used in that way, it could be of assistance in the initial appraisal and comparison of potential investments in listed businesses. However, once control or significant influence had been acquired it would be of little use for the purposes of on-going appraisal.

2. *Dividend yield*

Dividend yield is the ratio of the dividend, and the market value, of one share. The assistant is correct in saying that it allows for comparison with the yields from other investments. However, it can be calculated only in cases where a market value is obtainable, and so would be useless in the appraisal of unlisted businesses. Dividend yield is likely to be of most use to investors in relatively small numbers of shares in listed businesses, where it is quite feasible to liquidate the investment rapidly and to put the cash released to other uses that produce higher yields. Where investments are held for the longer term, dividend yield is less relevant. It is not relevant at all where the investment gives control, or a high level of significant influence over an investee's activities, as dividend policy is controlled or heavily influenced by the investor. Dividend yield might be of minor interest upon initial appraisal, but it would be of no relevance to BHG post-acquisition.

3. *Gearing*

    Gearing expresses the relationship between equity and debt finance of a business. A high level of debt compared to equity is generally regarded as increasing the risk to ordinary shareholders, and so the ratio is often useful for investors. When initially appraising businesses as potential investments, BHG will be interested in their gearing ratio, compared to its own. A level of gearing that BHG regards as too high may provide a disincentive to investment, where repayment of debt would have to be undertaken on disadvantageous terms. However, once a business becomes part of the BHG group, BHG management will be in a position to control or influence gearing levels, and so the gearing ratio is likely to be relatively unimportant once the investee's gearing is brought into equilibrium with that of the group.

4. *Gross profit margin*

    This ratio is, as suggested by the assistant, very important for investors (and others) in assessing business performance, especially when compared over several accounting periods. However, when using it to make comparisons between businesses, it is important to be sure that revenue and cost of sales are recognised on comparable bases. There can be significant differences between revenue recognition policies, for example, in respect of the sale of software, and as always when using ratios, it is important to ensure that the comparison is valid. Some businesses may recognise particular elements of cost as part of cost of sales whereas others would recognise similar costs in, say, administrative expenses. For these reasons, gross profit margin is likely to be the most useful as an indicator of performance of potential acquisitions where the takeover is welcomed by the target entity management so that detailed information about cost classification is available. Following acquisition, when policies and practices can be brought into line with other group entities, gross profit margin is likely to be a very useful indicator.

5. *Asset turnover ratios*

    These ratios are calculated by dividing revenue by asset values. Often, a total asset turnover figure is calculated, but this may be further broken down into, for example, non-current and current asset turnover. The assistant is correct in asserting that these ratios allow investors to compare the intensity of asset usage both within and between businesses. However, as is usually the case with accounting ratios, the measurements must be treated with some caution. Where the comparison is between entities it is important to ensure that policies in respect of revenue recognition and asset valuation are consistent; if they are not the comparison likely to be misleading. Therefore, asset turnover may not be a valid measurement for use in initial appraisal. Post-acquisition, when accounting policies have been brought into line or where sufficient information is available to make adjustments for comparability, the ratio may well be helpful in making comparisons over time. Even so, it should be treated with some caution in cases where there is a significant level of unrecorded assets, such as intellectual capital and other intangibles.

(b) Accounting ratios must be treated with care in any inter-firm and/or international comparison, for the following reasons:

Variations in accounting regulation

Many of BHG's proposed acquisitions are likely to be listed entities. In many countries, for example, all countries within the European Union, listed entities are required to comply with IFRS in preparing their financial statements. Where this is the case, a reasonable level of comparability could be expected. However, in some jurisdictions unlisted entities are entitled to prepare their financial statements under local GAAP which may differ significantly from IFRS. Financial statements may also, in certain circumstances, be prepared under US GAAP. It is important to ensure that comparisons are valid by ensuring that like is compared with like.

Accounting policies

Even where financial statements are prepared using a common set of accounting standards there may still be significant variations in accounting policies. IFRS, for example, permits the adoption of either the cost or revaluation models for property, plant and equipment.

Deprecation charges are likely to vary significantly, depending upon which model is adopted, and so the policy difference affects not only the statement of financial position but also the income statement.

Size of entities

If BHG compares a much smaller entity with its own financial statements, the comparison may not be truly valid because of the effects of, for example, economies of scale.

International economic variations

It is often the case that national economies experience cycles of economic growth and decline that differ from the patterns experienced in other economies. An entity that appears to be performing badly in a particular national context may, compared to others, be performing relatively well.

Comparability of activities

It is difficult to find truly comparable entities. BHG designs and markets specialist business software, and there may be many entities that claim to do the same. However, the balance of their activities compared to BHG's may be subtly different. One entity may supply a different set of business sectors than BHG and the margins achievable on its sales may differ accordingly, for example. It is important to be aware, when comparing businesses, that no two are exactly alike, and that similarities may be superficial.

Answer 5

To: Marketing Director of BSP
From: Assistant to Finance Director
Report on draft cash flow statement for the financial year ended 31 March 2007
Note: The appendix to this report contains some ratio and other relevant calculations.

1. *The difference between cash and profit*

   Because of the use of the accruals basis in financial accounting, it is often the case that profit or loss differs significantly from the cash flows arising during an accounting period. This is not necessarily a problem, unless significant cash shortages affect the viability of the business, but it does mean that the cash flow statement should be interpreted with some caution. An apparently healthy cash balance can disguise underlying problems.

   In the case of BSP's cash flow statement, there is, indeed, a significant amount of cash at 31 March 2007. However, upon closer examination, it can be seen that the cash inflows have arisen from investing and financing activities, rather than from operating activities which produced negative cash flows. A total of $3,170,000 (that is $2,320,000 from the sale of the subsidiaries and $850,000 from the issue of share capital) was received in cash during the year.

   While some of this (approximately one-third) remained in the statement of financial position at 31 March 2007, most of it had been absorbed by the major cash outflow from operations and the acquisition of property, plant and equipment.

2. *Profit and loss*

   BSP's profit before tax has declined sharply between 2006 and 2007. The decline is even more marked if unusual items are taken into account. Towards the end of the 2006 financial year, the business incurred $450,000 in costs of training and marketing associated with the new product line. Profit before these items was $756,000. The loss before tax in the year ended 31 March 2007 was mitigated substantially by the profit on disposal of the foreign subsidiaries. If this profit is excluded, the loss from operations is $1,120,000. Using these adjusted figures, net profitability (measured on a pre-tax basis) was 6.2% in the 2006 financial year, whereas the loss in 2007 represented 9.1% of revenue.

3. *Working capital*

   The operating section of the cash flow statement includes adjustments for increases and decreases in working capital. Both inventories and receivables increased by a substantial amount in the year ended 31 March 2007. Inventories increased by 11% in 2006 and by 34.6% in 2007. Some increase in inventories is consistent with the move into a new area of operations, but the increase of 34.6% does appear very high.

   Receivables have also increased substantially, by 15% between 2006 and 2007. The overall revenue figure has increased very little. The receivables figure at 31 March 2007 does not include any amounts relating to the two subsidiaries disposed of. The revenue figure for the year has therefore been reduced to 90% of the total, to exclude the revenues relating to these subsidiaries. Using these two figures, receivables days at the year end is approximately 61 days. Receivables days at the previous year end was about 49 days. (It should be noted that these two figures are not directly comparable because the 2006 revenue and receivables figures include the two subsidiaries). The policy of offering extended credit as an inducement to customers may very well have paid off in terms of additional sales, but there are some drawbacks.

   Compared to inventories and receivables, the movements in the two years in payables are relatively minor. In both 2006 and 2007 there are increases which partly offset the outflows on other working capital items.

4. *Prospects for the future*

   Although sales targets for the 2007 financial year were almost met, the decline in profitability does, as you suggest, indicate that there is a problem in controlling costs. However, it cannot necessarily be assumed that this is a short-term problem while the new operation settles down; careful cost control will be required if the business, overall, is to return to profitability. Offering discounts in order to attract new business may be effective in increasing revenue, but this practice tends to reduce profitability.

Because the sale of the subsidiaries took place so recently, the revenue figures for 2007 are not affected. However, these two subsidiaries have accounted for around 10% of the sales, and have been consistently profitable. Therefore, unless there is an improvement in sales and profitability in the remaining group businesses, the 2008 performance is likely to be even worse than in 2007. The effect may be mitigated to some extent by lower interest charges. These rose substantially in 2007, compared to 2006, but the large cash balance in hand at the beginning of the new financial year should ensure that, for some months at least, there will be no short-term borrowings and hence, no interest payments.

The breakdown of the revenue figure shows that there has been a sharp decline in the sales relating to burglar alarms; sales in 2007 were only 90.3% of sales in 2006. The shortfall has been made up by sales of fire alarm systems, which tends to justify the change in business strategy. However, if tough conditions continue in the burglar alarm market, revenues from this source may continue to fall.

A final point relates to dividend. A dividend of $200,000 was paid in the 2006 financial year, but there was no dividend in 2007. Shareholders made a substantial contribution in the form of new capital in 2007; while they may be content to wait for a return while the new line of business is getting established, they may become impatient if no dividend is forthcoming in 2008.

5. *Conclusion*

   In conclusion, the cash flow statement serves to emphasise some worrying trends in the business. The cash balance available at 31 March 2007 will rapidly disappear unless the losses can be reversed. Working capital management and cost control must be improved. This cash flow statement shows the more positive side of disposing of two profitable subsidiaries; the negative aspects are likely to make an impact on the 2008 and subsequent cash flow statements.

Appendix: Calculations

1. *(Loss)/profit before tax as a percentage of revenue*

2007	2006
(453)/12,320 × 100 = (3.7%)	306/12,110 × 100 = 2.5%

2. *(Loss)/profit before tax as a percentage of revenue – after adjustment for unusual items*
   2006: calculate profit before deduction of unusual items:
   $306 + 200 + 250 = $756
   2007: calculate loss before setting off profit on disposal of subsidiaries:
   $(453) + (667) = (1,120)

2007	2006
(1,120)/12,320 × 100 = (9.1%)	756/12,110 × 100 = 6.2%

3. *Inventory movement*

	$	*Increase year on year %*
At 1 April 2005	591,000	
At 31 March 2006 (591 + 65)	656,000	11.0%
At 31 March 2007 (656 + 227)	883,000	34.6%

4. *Receivables movement*

	$	*Increase year on year %*
At 1 April 2005	1,578,000	
At 31 March 2006 (1,578 + 36)	1,614,000	2.3%
At 31 March 2007 (1,614 + 242)	1,856,000	15%

Receivables days (using year end figures):

2007	2006
$1,856/(12,320 \times 90\%) \times 365 = 61.1$ days	$1,614/12,110 \times 365 = 48.6$ days

14

Analysis of Financial Statements: Earnings per Share

Analysis of Financial Statements: Earnings per Share

14

LEARNING OUTCOME

After studying this chapter students should be able to:
- interpret a full range of accounting ratios.

Basic EPS

$$\text{EPS} = \frac{\text{Net profit attributable to ordinary shareholders}}{\text{Weighted average number of ordinary shares}}$$

- Consolidated profit after tax, non-controlling interests, preference dividends
- Weighted on a time basis this reflects the issues and repurchases of ordinary shares in the year

- Special attention needs to be given to:

Issues at full market price in the period	These generate new earning potential from their issue date, and hence are factored into the weighted average from this date

Bonus issues	These generate no new earnings and are assumed to be in issue throughout the accounting period irrespective of their issue date ie issued on the first day of the year It is also necessary to adjust the corresponding EPS to reflect these issues
Rights issues	These effectively constitute an issue of shares at full market price and an additional bonus issue To identify the bonus element the theoretical ex-rights price (TERPs) must be calculated and compared to the fair value of the shares prior to the issue

Diluted EPS

- This reflects that an entity has financial instruments in issue that carry rights to become ordinary shares in the future

    - Convertible debt or equity instruments
    - Share warrants and options
    - Rights granted under employee share schemes.

- Convertible financial instruments

Earnings	Will increase by the saving in interest or preference dividends Remember that interest is a tax deductible expense, and hence part of the interest saving will be lost in the form of a higher tax charge
Number of shares	Assume conversion on the most advantageous terms to the holder of the financial instrument thereby recording the maximum dilution

- Share warrants and options

Earnings	No effect on basic earnings
Number of shares	The holder of an option or warrant will only exercise their conversion rights if the price is favourable compared to that of the market Hence increase the number of shares by the difference between the number of shares that would have been issued at fair value, for the proceeds obtained from the options, and the actual number of new shares

- When there are several potentially diluting factors each must be considered individually (starting with the most dilutive), and only those that have a genuinely dilutive effect should be included in the diluted EPS calculation.

EPS disclosure

- The basic and diluted EPS should be shown on the face of the income statement.

Analysis of Financial Statements: Earnings per Share **197**

Medium answer questions

Question 1 – JKL plc

JKL is a listed entity preparing financial statements to 31 August. At 1 September 2003, JKL had 6,000,000 50¢ shares in issue. On 1 February 2004, the entity made a rights issue of 1 for 4 at 125¢ per share; the issue was successful and all rights were taken up. The market price of one share immediately prior to the issue was 145¢ per share. Earnings after tax for the year ended 31 August 2004 were $2,763,000.

Several years ago, JKL issued a convertible loan of $2,000,000. The loan carries an interest rate of 7% and its terms of conversion (which are at the option of the stockholder) are as follows:

For each $100 of loan inventory:

        Conversion at 31 August 2008   105 shares
        Conversion at 31 August 2009   103 shares JKL

is subject to an income tax rate of 32%.

Requirements

(a) Calculate basic earnings per share and diluted earnings per share for the year ended 31 August 2004.

(7 marks)

(b) The IASC *Framework for the preparation and presentation of financial statements* states that the objective of financial statements is to provide information that is useful to a wide range of users in making economic decisions.

Explain to a holder of ordinary shares in JKL both the usefulness and limitations of the diluted earnings per share figure.

(3 marks)
(Total = 10 marks)

Question 2 (Nov '07)

Earnings per share (EPS) is generally regarded as a key accounting ratio for use by investors and others. Like all accounting ratios, however, it has its limitations. You have been asked to make a brief presentation to CIMA students on the topic.

Requirements

(a) Explain why EPS is regarded as so important that the IASB has issued an accounting standard on its calculation;

(2 marks)

(b) Explain the general limitations of the EPS accounting ratio and its specific limitations for investors who are comparing the performance of different entities.

(8 marks)
(Total = 10 marks)

Question 3 – AGZ (Nov '08)

AGZ is a listed entity. You are a member of the team drafting its financial statements for the year ended 31 August 2008.

Extracts from the draft income statement, including comparative figures, are shown below:

	2008 $ million	2007 $ million
Profit before tax	276.4	262.7
Income tax expense	85.0	80.0
Profit for the period	191.4	182.7

At the beginning of the financial year, on 1 September 2007, AGZ had 750 million ordinary shares of 50¢ in issue. At that date the market price of one ordinary share was 87.6¢.

On 1 December 2007, AGZ made a bonus issue of one new ordinary 50¢ share for every three held.

In 2006, AGZ issued $75 million convertible bonds. Each unit of $100 of bonds in issue will be convertible at the holder's option into 200 ordinary 50¢ shares on 31 August 2012. The interest expense relating to the liability element of the bonds for the year ended 31 August 2008 was $6.3 million (2007 – $6.2 million). The tax effect related to the interest expense was $2.0 million (2007 – $1.8 million).

There were no other changes affecting or potentially affecting the number of ordinary shares in issue in either the 2008 or 2007 financial years.

Requirements

(a) Calculate earnings per share and diluted earnings per share for the year ended 31 August 2008, including the comparative figures.

(8 marks)

(b) Explain the reason for the treatment of the bonus shares as required by IAS 33 *Earnings per Share*.

(2 marks)
(Total = 10 marks)

Question 4 – CB (May '05)

On 1 February 2004, CB, a listed entity, had 3,000,000 ordinary shares in issue.

On 1 March 2004, CB made a rights issue of 1 for 4 at $650 per share. The issue was completely taken up by the shareholders.

Extracts from CB's financial statements for the year ended 31 January 2005 are presented below:

CB: Extracts from income statement for the year ended 31 January 2005

	$000
Operating profit	1,380
Finance cost	(400)
Profit before tax	980
Income tax expense	(255)
Profit for the period	725

CB: Extracts from summarised statement of changes in equity for the year ended 31 January 2005

	$000
Balance at 1 February 2004	7,860
Issue of share capital	4,875
Surplus on revaluation of properties	900
Profit for the period	725
Equity dividends	(300)
Balance at 31 January 2005	14,060

Just before the rights issue, CB's share price was $750, rising to $825 immediately afterwards. The share price at close of business on 31 January 2005 was $625.

At the beginning of February 2005, the average price earnings (P/E) ratio in CB's business sector was 284, and the P/E of its principal competitor was 425.

Requirements

(a) Calculate the earnings per share for CB for the year ended 31 January 2005, and its P/E ratio at that date.

(6 marks)

(b) Discuss the significance of P/E ratios to investors and CB's P/E ratio relative to those of its competitor and business sector.

(4 marks)
(Total = 10 marks)

Question 5 – BAQ (May '07)

BAQ is a listed entity with a financial year end of 31 March. At 31 March 2007, it had 8,000,000 ordinary shares in issue.

The directors of BAQ wish to expand the business's operations by acquiring competitor entities.

They intend to make no more than one acquisition in any financial year.

The directors are about to meet to discuss two possible acquisitions. Their principal criterion for the decision is the likely effect of the acquisition on group earnings per share.

Details of the possible acquisitions are as follows:

1. *Acquisition of CBR*
    - 100% of the share capital of CBR could be acquired on 1 October 2007 for a new issue of shares in BAQ;
    - CBR has 400,000 ordinary shares in issue;
    - Four CBR shares would be exchanged for three new shares in BAQ;
    - CBR's profit after tax for the year ended 31 March 2007 was $625,000 and the entity's directors are projecting a 10% increase in this figure for the year ending 31 March 2008.

2. *Acquisition of DCS*
    - 80% of the share capital of DCS could be acquired on 1 October 2007 for a cash payment of $10.00 per share;
    - DCS has 1,000,000 ordinary shares in issue;
    - The cash would be raised by a rights issue to BAQ's existing shareholders. For the purposes of evaluation it can be assumed that the rights issue would take place on 1 October 2007, that it would be fully taken up, that the market value of one share in BAQ on that date would be $5.36, and that the terms of the rights issue would be one new share for every five BAQ shares held at a rights price of $5.00;
    - DCS's projected profit after tax for the year ending 31 March 2008 is $860,000.

BAQ's profit after tax for the year ended 31 March 2008 is projected to be $4.2 million. No changes in BAQ's share capital are likely to take place, except in respect of the possible acquisitions described above.

Requirements

Calculate the group earnings per share that could be expected for the year ending 31 March 2008 in respect of each of the acquisition scenarios outlined above.

(10 marks)

Answers to medium answer questions

Answer 1 – JKL plc

(a) **Workings**

1. *Calculate the theoretical ex-rights price after the rights issue*

	¢
4 shares × 145¢	580
1 share × 125¢	125
Theoretical value of holding of 5 shares	705
Theoretical ex-rights price of 1 share after rights issue: 705/5	141

2. *Calculate bonus fraction*

$$\frac{\text{Fair value of one share before rights issue}}{\text{Theoretical ex-rights price of one share}} [W1] = \frac{145}{141}$$

3. *Weighted average number of shares in issue in the year to 31 August 2004*

	Number of shares
1 September 2003–1 February 2004 (6,000,000 × 145/141 × 5/12)	2,570,922
1 February 2004–31 August 2004 (7,500,000 × 7/12)	4,375,000
	6,945,922

Basic earnings per share: 2,763,000/6,945,922 = 39.8¢

4. *Adjustment to earnings for calculation of diluted EPS*

	$
Earnings	2,763,000
Add: Interest after tax	95,200
(2,000,000 × 7%) × (1 − 0.32)	
Diluted earnings	2,858,200

5. *Adjustment to number of shares for calculation of diluted EPS*

Note: Use the most advantageous (for loan stockholders) conversion rate.

	Number of shares
Weighted average shares in issue in year to 31 August 2004 [W3]	6,945,922
Add: Dilutive effect (2,000,000/100 × 105)	2,100,000
Diluted shares	9,045,922

(b) Much of the information contained in financial statements refers to events that have occurred in the past, and so it is of relatively restricted usefulness in making decisions. Diluted earnings per share, however, can be quite useful to investors and potential investors in that it incorporates some information about likely future events. Where potentially dilutive financial instruments have been issued, it is helpful to investors to be able to appreciate the impact full dilution would have upon the earnings of the business. However, it should be appreciated that only some elements of the calculation relate to the future. One of the key elements of the calculation, the basic earnings for the period, relates to events that have already taken place, and that may not be replicated in the future.

Answer 2 (Nov '07)

Notes on earnings per share

(a) EPS is of particular importance because it is one of the component parts of the Price/Earnings (P/E) ratio. P/E is used by investors to help them identify the relative riskiness of investments, and investments that are over-valued or under-valued by the stock market. Also, EPS is accorded great importance by investors, analysts and others as a key measurement of performance and as a basis for making decisions. It is principally for these reasons that some accounting standard setters, amongst them the IASB, have produced accounting standards regulating its calculation.

(b) The principal general limitations of EPS include the following:
- EPS is based on accounting figures, and can only be as reliable as those figures. Accounting figures may be subject to manipulation by using creative accounting techniques. Even where no malicious manipulation is intended, the figures are often imprecise because they involve the use of estimation.
- EPS is essentially a backward looking measure because it is based on accounting figures reporting on transactions and events that have already taken place. It is of limited use for predictive purposes, although, perhaps inevitably, it is used as an indicator of future performance.
- EPS, like all other accounting information published in the annual report of a business, is soon out of date. The P/E ratio calculation uses an up to date price figure, but where the price has been affected significantly by events after the statement of financial position date, the mixing of a current price with an old earnings figure may be, essentially, meaningless.

The specific limitations of EPS for the purposes of making comparisons include the following:
- In some instances, accounting standards permit a choice of accounting treatments. It is quite likely, therefore, that entities being compared with each other use different policies and/or bases for preparation of the financial statements. Where such policies and bases impact upon the profit figure, as will usually be the case, EPS figures are not strictly comparable.
- The problem of comparability is made worse where the entities being compared are subject to different sets of accounting standards.
- EPS is calculated on the basis of after tax figures. Where entities are subject to significantly differing rates of tax because they are based in different countries, the comparison is unrealistic.

Answer 3 – AGZ (Nov '08)

(a)

	2008		2007	
Earnings per share:	191.4/1,000 (W1)	19.1¢	182.7/1,000 (W1)	18.3¢
Diluted earnings per share	$\dfrac{195.7 \text{ (W2)}}{1,150 \text{ (W3)}}$	17.0¢	$\dfrac{187.1 \text{ (W2)}}{1,150 \text{ (W3)}}$	16.3¢

Workings

1. *Bonus issue of shares:* 1 new share for every 3 already in issue = 750 million/3 × 4 = 1,000 million.

2. *Diluted earnings adjustments*

	2008		2007	
Profit for the period		191.4		182.7
Add back interest	6.3		6.2	
Less: tax effects	(2.0)		(1.8)	
		4.3		4.4
		195.7		187.1

3. *Fully diluted shares*

If all conversion options are taken up:

$$\frac{\$75 \text{ m}}{100} \times 200 = 150 \text{ m}$$

Added to the existing shares this gives a fully diluted number of shares of 1,150 m (1,000 m + 150 m).

(b) Bonus shares are issued for no consideration, and so there is no increase in resources associated with them. All other things being equal, no increase in earnings can be expected following a bonus issue; the effect is that the same amount of earnings is divided by a greater number of shares. In order to ensure continuing comparability, the bonus issue is adjusted for as if it had taken place at the beginning of the earliest period presented.

Answer 4 – CB (May '05)

(a) **Earnings per share and price earnings ratio**

Earnings per share $\dfrac{725,000}{3,694,349} = 19.6c$

Price earnings ratio $\dfrac{625}{19.6} = 31.9$

Workings

1. *Theoretical ex-rights price and bonus fraction*

	$
4 shares @ $7.50	30.00
1 share @ 6.50	6.50
5 shares	36.50

Theoretical ex-rights price $\dfrac{36.50}{5} = 7.30$

Bonus fraction: $\dfrac{7.50}{7.30}$

2. *Weighted average number of shares in issue for the year ended 31 January 2005*

	Number
1 February 2004 – 1 March 2004 3,000,000 × 7.50/7.30 × 1/12	256,849
1 March 2004 – 31 January 2005 3,750,000 × 11/12	3,437,500
	3,694,349

(b) **Significance of the price earnings ratio**

The price earnings ratio (P/E ratio) shows how many current year's earnings investors are prepared to pay to acquire shares. A high P/E ratio normally suggests a safe investment, or one where there is expected to be significant future earnings growth. A low P/E ratio is normally a sign that the market views the investment as a poor or risky prospect. It should be remembered that the P/E ratio is based on market prices, which are to some extent subjective. Some companies (such as those in the information technology sector) can become fashionable and therefore have high P/E ratios, while remaining highly risky investments.

CB's P/E ratio is slightly higher than the sector average, but considerably lower than that of its main competitor. This suggests that it is viewed as a reasonably sound investment within its sector, but that the market currently regards its main competitor as a much better investment.

Answer 5 – BAQ (May '07)

1. *CBR acquisition*

	$
BAQ's projected earnings	4,200,000
CBR's projected earnings – 6 months	
$625,000 × 110% × $\tfrac{6}{12}$	343,750
Projected group earnings for year ending 31 March 2008	4,543,750
Weighted average of shares in issue:	
1 April 2007 – 30 September 2007 $\tfrac{6}{12}$ × 8,000,000	4,000,000
1 October 2007 – 31 March 2008 {[¾ × 400,000] + 8,000,000} × $\tfrac{6}{12}$	4,150,000
	8,150,000

Projected group earnings per share if CBR acquisition takes place:

$$\frac{8,150,000}{\$4,543,750} = 55.8c$$

2. *DCS acquisition*

   Working 1: theoretical ex-rights price

5 × $5.36	26.80
1 × $5.00	5.00
	31.80

   TERP = $31.80/6 = $5.30
   Bonus fraction = $5.36/5.30

   Working 2: number of BAQ shares in issue after 1 October 2007

   (1/5 × 8,000,000) + 8,000,000 = 9,600,000

	$
BAQ's projected earnings	4,200,000
DCS's projected earnings – group share for 6 months $860,000 × 80% × $\frac{6}{12}$	344,000
Projected group earnings for year ending 31 March 2008	4,544,000

   Weighted average of shares in issue:

1 April 2007 – 30 September 2007 $\frac{6}{12}$ × 8,000,000 × 5.36/5.30 (W1)	4,045,283
1 October 2007 – 31 March 2008 $\frac{6}{12}$ × 9,600,000 (W2)	4,800,000
	8,845,283

   Projected group earnings per share if DCS acquisition takes place:

   $$\frac{8,845,283}{\$4,544,000} = 51.4c$$

15

Interpretation of Financial Statements

Interpretation of Financial Statements

15

LEARNING OUTCOMES

After studying this chapter students should be able to:

- interpret a full range of accounting ratios;
- analyse financial statements in the context of information provided in the accounts and corporate report;
- evaluate performance and position based on analysis of financial statements;
- discuss segmental analysis, with inter-firm and international comparisons taking account of possible aggressive or unusual accounting policies and pressures on ethical behaviour;
- discuss the results of an analysis of financial statements and its limitations.

Basic ground rules

```
                    Basic ground rules
         ┌─────────────────┼─────────────────┐
         ▼                 ▼                 ▼
  Horizontal analysis  Vertical analysis  Common size
                                           analysis

  Comparing equivalent  Expressing each figure  Involves setting one
  figures across        in a primary financial  figure as the
  accounting periods    statement as a          benchmark in each
  to identify trends    percentage of one       year and comparing all
                        key figure              other figures against
                                                this as a percentage
```

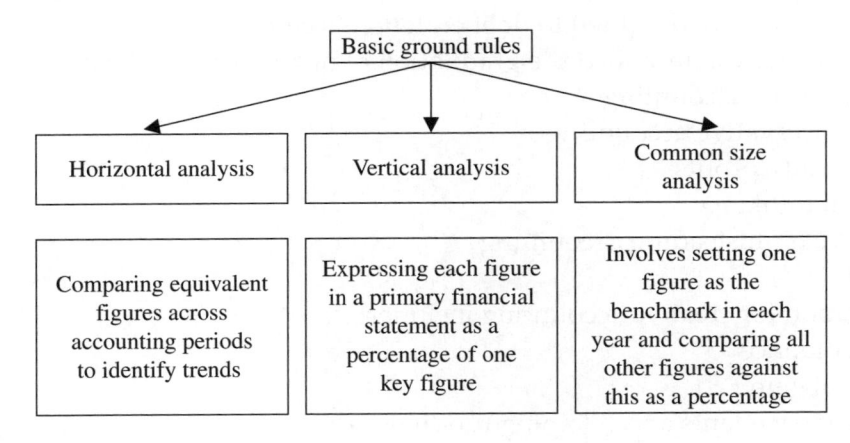

Limitations of financial reporting information

- The IASB's own Framework for the preparation and presentation of financial statements concedes that financial information cannot be 'all things to all men'.
- Timeliness – the historic information in financial statements is not guaranteed to be an indicator of future performance.
- Comparability can be undermined by a variety of factors:
    - Businesses evolve over time moving into or withdrawing from markets
    - The effects of inflation make chronological comparison difficult
    - Changes in accounting policy
    - Some businesses have unique attributes that make them different from apparently similar entities
    - Different entities have different year ends which can impact significantly on their closing statement of financial position particularly if they have seasonal products
    - Large and small companies in the same sector are subject to different constraints and advantages such as economies of scale
    - Overseas entities will be subject to different regulatory and tax regimes.

Limitations of ratio analysis

- With the exception of EPS there is no mandatory guidance as to the basis of calculation leading to variability between entities; particularly with ratios such as ROCE and gearing.
- Several ratios, such as payables days, use averaged figures based on the position at the beginning and end of the financial period but this may not be representative of the true position.
- For some ratios a 'norm' is often quoted, such as the current ratio should not fall below 2, but these may bear no relationship to the figures seen in specific industries.

Creative accounting

- Creative accounting covers a wide range of practices some of which are totally legitimate whilst others are designed to deliberately mislead the user.
- One financial analyst described the graduation of outcomes as follows:
    - Conservative accounting
    - Less conservative accounting
    - Low quality profits
    - Wishful thinking
    - Creative or misleading accounting
    - Fraud.
- The motivation for creative accounting includes:
    - Tax avoidance
    - Personal gain
    - Meeting covenants and retaining funding.
- Methods of creative accounting.
- The treatment of contingencies will remain prominent due to the judgement required in evaluating the probability attached to their final resolution.

Methods of creative accounting (diagram)

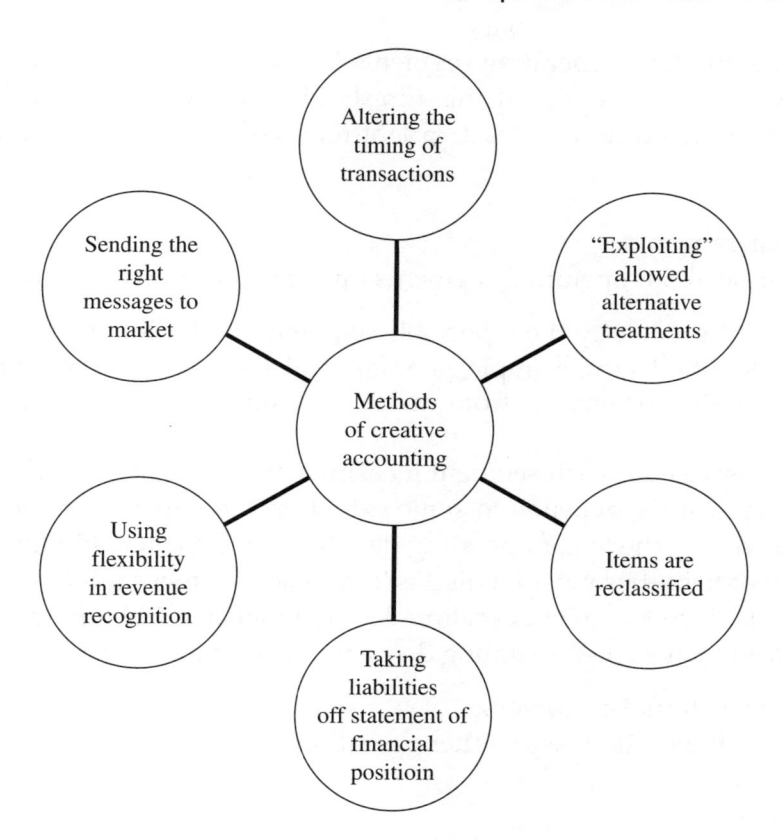

- Altering the timing of transactions
- "Exploiting" allowed alternative treatments
- Items are reclassified
- Taking liabilities off statement of financial positioin
- Using flexibility in revenue recognition
- Sending the right messages to market

IFRS 8 *Operating Segments*

Definition of an operating segment
Quoting directly from the standard:

'An operating segment is a component of an entity:

(a) that engages in business activities from which it may earn revenues and incur expenses (including revenue and expenses relating to transactions with other components of the same entity),
(b) whose operating results are regularly reviewed by the entity's chief operating decision-maker to make decisions about resources to be allocated to the segment and assess its performance, and
(c) for which discrete financial information is available.'

This description therefore excludes those parts of a business that do not engage directly in business activities, such as head office functions. However, it does include business segments whose activities are principally concerned with trading intra-group.

Criteria for reporting segment results
IFRS 8 sets quantitative thresholds for reporting. Entities should report information about an operating segment that meets any one of three quantitative thresholds:

1. Segment reported revenue (including both intra-group and external sales) exceeds 10% of the combined revenue of all operating segments.
2. Segment profit or loss is 10% of the greater of (i) the combined reported profit of all operating segments that did not report a loss; and (ii) the combined reported loss of all operating segments that reported a loss.
3. Segment assets exceed 10% of the combined assets of all operating segments.

The revenue of the disclosed operating segments that meet the criteria should equal at least 75% of total revenue of the entity. If this threshold is not met, additional operating segments should be disclosed until at least 75% of reported revenue is included in operating segments.

Disclosure requirements

General information about operating segments must be disclosed as follows:

1. The factors used to identify the reportable segments, including the basis on which they have been identified – for example, geographical areas, types of product or service.
2. The types of product or services from which each reportable segment derives its revenues.

The entity must disclose for each segment measures of profit or loss AND total assets. The extent of other disclosures depends to some extent on the nature and content of information that is reviewed by the 'chief operating decision maker' (probably the CEO or equivalent). A measure of liabilities must be disclosed for each segment if that information is regularly made available to the chief operating decision maker. If the following information is regularly reviewed by the chief operating decision maker it must be disclosed:

- Revenues from external customers
- Revenues from transactions with other operating segments
- Interest revenue
- Interest expense
- Depreciation and amortisation
- Material items of income and expense
- Interests in profit or loss of associates and joint ventures
- Income tax expense or income
- Material non-cash items other than depreciation or amortisation
- The amount of investment in associates and joint ventures
- The amounts of additions to non-current assets (with some exclusions).

Information about products and services

In addition to the information requirements set out above, an entity must make the following disclosures (unless these are already made via the disclosures described above):

Information about products and services: the revenues from external customers for each product and service, or similar groups of products and services.

Information about geographical areas:

1. Revenues from external customers attributable to the entity's country of domicile and the total of revenues attributable to all foreign countries.
2. Non-current assets located in the entity's country of domicile and the total of non-current assets located in all foreign countries.

Information about major customers:
If revenues in respect of a single customer amount to 10% or more of total revenues this should be disclosed (there is no requirement to disclose the name of the customer). In respect of information about products, services and geographical areas, the disclosure requirement is waived if the cost to develop the information would be 'excessive'.

Long answer questions

Question 1 – DM (May '05)

DM, a listed entity, has just published its financial statements for the year ended 31 December 2004. DM operates a chain of 42 supermarkets in one of the six major provinces of its country of operation. During 2004, there has been speculation in the financial press that the entity was likely to be a takeover target for one of the larger national chains of supermarkets that is currently under-represented in DM's province. A recent newspaper report has suggested that DM's directors are unlikely to resist a takeover. The six board members are all nearing retirement, and all own significant minority shareholdings in the business.

You have been approached by a private shareholder in DM. She is concerned that the directors have a conflict of interests and that the financial statements for 2004 may have been manipulated.

The income statement and summarised statement of changes in equity of DM, with comparatives, for the year ended 31 December 2004, and a statement of financial position, with comparatives, at that date are as follows:

DM: Income statement for the year ended 31 December 2004

	2004 $ million	2003 $ million
Revenue, net of sales tax	1,255	1,220
Cost of sales	(1,177)	(1,145)
Gross profit	78	75
Operating expenses	(21)	(29)
Profit from operations	57	46
Finance cost	(10)	(10)
Profit before tax	47	36
Income tax expense	(14)	(13)
Profit for the period	33	23

DM: Summarised statement of changes in equity for the year ended 31 December 2004

	2004 $ million	2003 $ million
Opening balance	276	261
Profit for the period	33	23
Dividends	(8)	(8)
Closing balance	301	276

DM: Statement of financial position at 31 December 2004

	2004 $ million	$ million	2003 $ million	$ million
Non-current assets:				
Property, plant and equipment	580		575	
Goodwill	100		100	
		680		675
Current assets:				
Inventories	47		46	
Trade receivables	12		13	
Cash	46		12	
		105		71
		785		746
Equity:				
Share capital	150		150	
Accumulated profits	151		126	
		301		276
Non-current liabilities:				
Interest-bearing borrowings	142		140	
Deferred tax	25		21	
		167		161
Current liabilities:				
Trade and other payables	297		273	
Short-term borrowings	20		36	
		317		309
		785		746

Notes:

1. DM's directors have undertaken a reassessment of the useful lives of non-current tangible assets during the year. In most cases, they estimate that the useful lives have increased and the depreciation charges in 2004 have been adjusted accordingly.
2. Six new stores have been opened during 2004, bringing the total to 42.
3. Four key ratios for the supermarket sector (based on the latest available financial statements of twelve listed entities in the sector) are as follows:

 (i) Annual sales per store: $27.6m
 (ii) Gross profit margin: 5.9%
 (iii) Net profit margin: 3.9%
 (iv) Non-current asset turnover (including both tangible and intangible non-current assets): 1·93

Requirements

(a) Prepare a report, addressed to the investor, analysing the performance and position of DM based on the financial statements and supplementary information provided above. The report should also include comparisons with the key sector ratios, and it should address the investor's concerns about the possible manipulation of the 2004 financial statements.

(20 marks)

(b) Explain the limitations of the use of sector comparatives in financial analysis.

(5 marks)
(Total = 25 marks)

Question 2 – STV (Nov '05)

One of your colleagues has recently inherited investments in several listed entities and she frequently asks for your advice on accounting issues. She has recently received the consolidated financial statements of STV, an entity that provides haulage and freight services in several countries. She has noticed that note 3 to the financial statements is headed 'Segment information'.

Note 3 explains that STV's primary segment reporting format is business segments of which there are three: in addition to road and air freight, the entity provides secure transportation services for smaller items of high value. STV's *Operating and Financial Review* provides further background information; the secure transport services segment was established only three years ago. This new operation required a sizeable investment in infrastructure which was principally funded through borrowing. However, the segment has experienced rapid revenue growth in that time, and has become a significant competitor in the industry sector.

Extracts from STV's segment report for the year ended 31 August 2005 are as follows:

	Road haulage		Air freight		Secure transport		Group	
	2005 $million	2004 $million	2005 $million	2004 $million	2005 $million	2004 $million	2005 $million	2004 $million
Revenue	653	642	208	199	98	63	959	904
Segment result	169	168	68	62	6	(16)	243	214
Unallocated corporate expenses							(35)	(37)
Operating profit							208	177
Interest expense							(22)	(21)
Share of profits of associates	16	12					16	12
Profit before tax							202	168
Income tax							(65)	(49)
Profit							137	119
Other information								
Segment assets	805	796	306	287	437	422	1,548	1,505
Investment in equity method Associates	85	84					85	84
Unallocated corporate assets							573	522
Consolidated total assets							2,206	2,111
Segment liabilities	345	349	176	178	197	184	718	711
Unallocated corporate liabilities							37	12
Consolidated total liabilities							755	723

Your colleague finds several aspects of this note confusing:

'I thought I'd understood what you told me about consolidated financial statements; the idea of aggregating several pieces of information to provide an overall view of the activities of the group makes sense. But the segment report seems to be trying to disaggregate the information all over again: what is the point of doing this? Does this information actually tell me anything useful about STV? I know from talking to you previously that financial information does not always tell us everything we need to know. So, what are the limitations in this statement?'

Requirements

(a) Explain the reasons for including disaggregated information about business segments in the notes to the consolidated financial statements.

(5 marks)

(b) Analyse and interpret STV's segment disclosures for the benefit of your colleague, explaining your findings in a brief report.

(12 marks)

(c) Explain the general limitations of segment reporting, illustrating your answer where applicable with references to STV's segment report.

(8 marks)
(Total = 25 marks)

Question 3 – ABC (May '06)

You are the assistant to the Chief Financial Officer (CFO) of ABC, a light engineering business based in Bolandia. ABC, a listed entity, has expanded over the last few years with the successful introduction of innovative new products. In order to further expand its product range and to increase market share, it has taken over several small, unlisted, entities within its own country.

ABC's directors have recently decided to expand its markets by taking over entities based in neighbouring countries. As the first step in the appraisal of available investment opportunities the CFO has asked you to prepare a brief report on the position and performance of three possible takeover targets: entity W based in Winlandia, entity Y based in Yolandia and entity Z based in Zeelandia. These three countries share a common currency with Bolandia, and all three target entities identify their principal activity as being the provision of light engineering products and services. The report is to comprise a one page summary of key data and a brief written report providing an initial assessment of the targets. The format of the summary is to be based upon the one generally used by ABC for its first-stage assessment of takeover targets, but with the addition of:

(i) price/earnings ratio information (because all three target entities are listed in their own countries); and
(ii) some relevant country-specific information.

You have produced the one-page summary of key data, given below, together with comparative information for ABC itself, based on its financial statements for the year ended 31 March 2006.

	ABC	W	Y	Z
Country of operation	Bolandia	Winlandia	Yolandia	Zeelandia
Date of most recent annual report	31 March 2006	31 January 2006	30 June 2005	30 June 2005
Financial statements prepared in compliance with:	IFRS	IFRS	Yolandian GAAP	IFRS
Revenue	$263.4m	$28.2m	$24.7m	$26.3m
Gross profit margin	19.7%	16.8%	17.3%	21.4%
Operating profit margin	9.2%	6.3%	4.7%	8.3%
Return on total capital employed	11.3%	7.1%	6.6%	12.3%
Equity	$197.8m	$13.6m	$14.7m	$16.7m
Long-term borrowings	$10.4m	$6>2m	$1.3m	$0.6m
Average interest rate applicable to long-term borrowings by listed entities	7.5%	6%	8%	10%
Income tax rate	30%	28%	31%	38%
Inventories turnover	47 days	68 days	52 days	60 days
Receivables turnover	44 days	42 days	46 days	47 days
Payables turnover	46 days	50 days	59 days	73 days
Current ratio	1.4 : 1	0.7 : 1	1.1 : 1	0.9 : 1
P/E ratio	18.6	12.6	18.3	15.2

ABC has a cash surplus and would seek to purchase outright between 90% and 100% of the share capital of one of the three entities. The directors of ABC do not intend to increase the gearing of the group above its existing level. Upon acquisition they would, as far as possible, retain the acquired entity's management and its existing product range. However, they would also seek to extend market share by introducing ABC's own products.

Requirements

Prepare a report to accompany the summary of key data. The report should:

(a) analyse the key data, comparing and contrasting the potential takeover targets with each other and with ABC itself.

(13 marks)

(b) discuss the extent to which the entities can be validly compared with each other, identifying the limitations of inter-firm and international comparisons.

(12 marks)
(Total = 25 marks)

Question 4 (May '08)

Several years ago, on leaving university, Fay, Jay and Kay set up a business, FJK, designing and manufacturing furniture for sale to retailers. When FJK was established, Fay and Jay each took 45% of the share capital, with Kay holding the remaining 10%. This arrangement has remained unchanged. Fay and Jay have always worked full-time in the business and remain its sole directors. Kay's role was initially part-time, but after the first two years she transferred to full-time work in her own consultancy business. Her contribution to FJK in recent years has been limited to occasionally providing advice. The relationship between the three shareholders has remained good, but all three are so busy that Kay rarely meets the others. FJK has been successful, and in February of each year, with the exception of 2008, has paid a substantial dividend to its three shareholders.

Kay's consultancy business has also been successful and she now employs 20 staff. You are Kay's financial adviser.

During 2006, the two directors decided to expand FJK's international sales, by establishing sales forces in two neighbouring countries. By early 2007, orders were starting to come in from the new countries. The expansion strategy has been very successful. Last week, Kay attended a meeting with Fay and Jay, to discuss the future of FJK. Fay and Jay explained that the business now requires more capital in order to fund further expansion, and the purpose of the meeting with Kay was to request her to inject capital of $250,000 into the business.

Kay was provided with a draft income statement for the year ended 31 March 2008 and a statement of financial position at that date (given below). The draft statements are unaudited, but the figures are not expected to change, except for the income tax expense figure for 2008. FJK's accountant has not yet completed a tax calculation and so the 2007 figure of $164,000 has been used as an estimate. No statement of changes in equity has been provided, but the only movements on it would be in respect of a revaluation of property, plant and equipment that took place during the year, and the movement on retained earnings for profit for the period.

Kay, who has a reasonably good understanding of financial statements, is impressed by the revenue and profit growth. However, she has asked you, as her financial adviser, to look at the figures, in order to identify possible risks and problem areas.

FJK: Draft income statement for the year ended 31 March 2008

	2008 $000	2007 $000
Revenue	5,973	3,886
Cost of sales	(4,318)	(2,868)
Gross profit	1,655	1,018
Distribution costs	(270)	(106)
Administrative expenses	(320)	(201)
Finance costs	(97)	(40)
Profit before tax	968	671
Income tax expense	(164)	(164)
Profit for the period	804	507

FJK: Draft statement of financial position at 31 March 2008

	2008		2007	
	$000	$000	$000	$000
ASSETS				
Non-current assets				
Property, plant and equipment		3,413		1,586
Current assets				
Inventories	677		510	
Trade and other receivables	725		553	
Cash	-		12	
		1,402		1,075
		4,815		2,661
EQUITY AND LIABILITIES				
Equity				
Called up share capital ($1 shares)		1		1
Retained earnings		2,166		1,362
Revaluation reserve		167		–
		2,334		1,363
Non-current liabilities				
Long-term borrowings		763		453
Current liabilities				
Loans and borrowings	327		103	
Trade and other payables	1,227		578	
Income tax	164		164	
		1,718		845
		4,815		2,661

Requirements

Prepare a report for Kay that

(a) analyses and interprets the draft financial statements and discusses FJK's performance and position.

(19 marks)

(b) discusses possible risks and problem areas revealed by the financial statements, and the actions that the directors could take to address these risks and problems.

(6 marks)

(Up to 8 marks are available for the calculation of relevant accounting ratios).

(Total = 25 marks)

Question 5 – SBD (Nov '06)

A friend of yours has recently been left a portfolio of investments by a relative. The portfolio includes 150 shares in SDB, a listed entity that designs, manufactures and supplies houses in kit form for export to developing countries. Having recently received the financial statements of the entity for the financial year ended 31 July 2006, your friend, who has some basic knowledge of accounting, has asked you to clarify certain points for him, and to provide him with a brief report on the position of the business.

The income statement, statement of changes in equity and statement of financial position are as follows:

SDB: Consolidated income statement for the year ended 31 July 2006

	2006 $000	2005 $000
Revenue	25,200	25,300
Cost of sales	(18,400)	(18,000)
Gross profit	6,800	7,300
Distribution costs	(970)	(1,030)
Administrative expenses	(1,750)	(1,720)
Finance costs	(1,220)	(1,140)
Share of losses of joint venture	(1,670)	–
Profit before tax	1,190	3,410
Income tax expense	(250)	(780)
Profit for the period	940	2,630
Attributable to:		
Equity holders of the parent	810	2,230
Non-controlling interest	130	400
	940	2,630

SDB: Consolidated statement of changes in equity for the year ended 31 July 2006

	Share capital $000	Other reserves $000	Retained earnings $000	Non-controlling interest $000	Total equity $000
Balance at 1 August 2005	4,000	–	18,600	540	23,140
Profit for the period			810	130	940
Dividends			(2,470)	(330)	(2,800)
Issue of share capital	1,600	2,000			3,600
Balance at 31 July 2006	5,600	2,000	16,940	340	24,880

SDB: Consolidated statement of financial position at 31 July 2006

	2006 $000	2006 $000	2005 $000	2005 $000
ASSETS				
Non-current assets:				
Property, plant and equipment	19,900		17,800	
Investment in joint venture	7,500		–	
		27,400		17,800
Current assets:				
Inventories	8,300		6,900	
Trade receivables	4,700		4,100	
Cash	3,100		13,000	
		16,100		24,000
		43,500		41,800
EQUITY AND LIABILITIES				
Equity attributable to shareholders of the parent:				
Called up share capital ($1 shares)	5,600		4,000	
Retained earnings	16,940		18,600	
Other reserves	2,000		–	
		24,540		22,600
Non-controlling interest		340		540
Total equity		24,880		23,140
Non-current liabilities:				
Long-term loans		13,600		13,600
Current liabilities:				
Trade payables	4,770		4,280	
Income tax	250		780	
		5,020		5,060
		43,500		41,800

Your friend's queries are as follows:

1. I've looked up IAS 31 *Interests in Joint Ventures*, which mentions proportionate consolidation and equity accounting as possible methods of accounting for joint ventures. I've not previously encountered joint ventures, or proportionate consolidation. Can you explain how IAS 31 affects these financial statements?
2. The long-term loans are described in a note as 'repayable in three equal instalments in each of the years 2008–2010'. What does this mean, and what are the implications for SDB's position?
3. There is a note to the financial statements about a contingent liability of $10 million. Apparently, one of the models of house supplied by SDB has a tendency to collapse in adverse weather conditions, and $10 million is the amount claimed by litigants in a case that is due to be heard within the next 18 months. SDB's directors think it is possible

that the entity will have to pay out. This seems a very large amount of money. How likely is it that the entity will have to pay out, and how bad would the effect be?

4. I can see that the business's profitability has suffered during the year, but if anything, I'm more concerned about the fact that the cash balance has fallen by almost $10 million. I'd very much like to have your opinion on the entity's position.

Requirements

Write a report to your friend that:

(a) Explain the concept of a jointly controlled entity and the permitted approaches to accounting for it, identifying possible reasons for the selection of accounting method by SDB.

(9 marks)

(b) Analyse the financial statements of SDB, focusing as requested upon the entity's position, and including references to the queries about the long-term loans and the contingent liability.

(16 marks)
(Total = 25 marks)

Question 6 – SBD (Nov '07)

DAS, a listed entity, is engaged in house-building activities. It was listed a little over two years ago and it prepares its financial statements in compliance with International Financial Reporting Standards. A business associate of yours is thinking about applying for a job as human resource manager at DAS. The job advertisement promises a 'great future in a rapidly expanding business'. She was made redundant when her last employer went into liquidation, and she is looking for a new role with a more stable and prosperous employer. She has obtained DAS's recently published financial statements for the year ended 31 August 2007 and would like your advice on the entity's prospects for the future. DAS provides several potentially useful voluntary disclosures about the nature of its business and its current work in progress. In the year ended 31 August 2006 DAS sold 1,080 new houses. During the financial year ended 31 August 2007, a major part of the entity's efforts were directed towards the development for housing on the site of a former hospital. This was DAS's largest project to date. By the year end most of the houses on site were nearly complete, and a few were ready for sale. The site contains 225 houses, which are expected to sell for between $425,000 and $600,000 each. DAS's directors consider that the development scheme has been successful; by the year end 100 of the available houses had been reserved by buyers who paid a 10% deposit. None of the hospital site house transactions had been completed by 31 August 2007, although the Chief Executive's report noted that there were several completions during September and October 2007. DAS sold 675 other houses during the year ended 31 August 2007.

DAS's statement of financial position at 31 August 2007 and an income statement for the year then ended, together with comparatives, follow:

DAS: Statement of financial position at 31 August 2007

	2007 $ million	2006 $ million
ASSETS		
Non-current assets:		
Property, plant and equipment	9.3	9.8
Current assets:		
Inventories	270.5	275.0
Trade and other receivables	3.2	3.7
Cash	–	2.8
	273.7	281.5
	283.0	291.3
EQUITY AND LIABILITIES		
Equity		
Called up share capital ($1 shares)	8.2	8.2
Other reserves	16.3	16.3
Retained earnings	61.9	54.7
	86.4	79.2
Non-current liabilities:		
Long-term borrowings	114.7	112.0
Current liabilities:		
Loans and borrowings	52.6	75.4
Trade and other payables	29.3	24.7
	81.9	100.1
	283.0	291.3

DAS: Income statement for the year ended 31 August 2007

	2007 $ million	2006 $ million
Revenue	157.9	243.0
Cost of sales	(126.5)	(192.7)
Gross profit	31.4	50.3
Expenses	(9.2)	(8.6)
Finance costs	(12.2)	(13.4)
Profit before tax	10.0	28.3
Income tax expense	(2.8)	(8.9)
Profit for the period	7.2	19.4

Notes:

1. DAS's policy is to recognise revenue from the sale of houses upon legal completion of the transaction.
2. Most of the house-building work is undertaken by sub-contractors; DAS retains only a small direct labour force. Payments to sub-contractors are included as part of property under construction in inventories until such time as the houses are sold.
3. Inventories comprise the following:

	2007	2006
	$ million	$ million
Land held for development	130.0	210.0
Property under construction	140.5	65.0
	270.5	275.0

4. The statement of changes in equity (not given above) shows that no dividend was paid in the period of a little over two years since DAS was listed.
5. Deposits paid by buyers are included in trade and other payables.
6. Economic conditions are generally buoyant and house prices during 2006 and 2007 have risen at a rate significantly in excess of the general rate of inflation. Bank interest rates in respect of low risk lending have been running at between 5% and 6% throughout the two year period covered by the financial statements shown above.

Requirement

Write a report to your business associate that analyses and interprets the information given above. The report should explain the extent to which DAS can be considered to meet her requirements for a 'stable and prosperous' employer.

Up to eight marks are available for the calculation and explanation of **relevant** accounting ratios.

(Total = 25 marks)

✓ Answers to long answer questions

Answer 1 – DM (May '05)

(a)
Report to Investor on DM

Date: May 2005

Note: The ratio calculations referred to in the report can be found in the Appendix.

In 2004 DM has expanded rapidly, increasing the number of its stores from 36 to 42. The annual sales figure per store has fallen substantially since 2003; however, this may be because the new stores have been open for only part of the year. Even so, DM's annual sales per store is significantly higher than the sector average. However, it may simply have larger stores than average.

Gross profit margin has increased slightly, but the increase in operating profit margin is substantial. Operating expenses have actually fallen by over 27% in the year. The expenses may have been affected by the lengthening of most non-current asset lives, and the consequent decrease in depreciation charges.

The review of depreciation has resulted in higher profits and it is certainly possible that the directors have deliberately manipulated the results. Also, the significant decrease in operating expenses may indicate that some items of expenditure have been classified as capital rather than revenue in nature. This method of creative accounting can be quite difficult to confirm using the information available in a set of financial statements. Nevertheless, it would be sensible to conduct further comparisons using information in the notes to the financial statements.

Net profit margin is significantly lower in both years than the sector average, despite higher than average gross profit margin. It is noticeable, however, that the net profit margin has increased from 1.9% to 2.6% in the year, and this could, for reasons already given, be a result of deliberate manipulation.

The current ratio in both years is low. The cash level is higher in 2004 than in 2003. It appears from the statement of financial position that suppliers may be providing even longer credit than usual. Trade and other payables have increased by over 8%, whereas the increase in cost of sales is only 2.8%. Gearing does not appear to give cause for concern.

Despite several new store openings the level of property, plant and equipment remains almost the same. It may be that the majority of the investment in new stores was made during 2003. Non-current asset turnover has improved although it has not quite reached the sector level.

Summary

DM is a profitable and rapidly expanding entity. Its margins compare reasonably well with the sector average although net profit margin is relatively poor. It is possible that the entity's directors have deliberately manipulated the financial statements in order to produce better results in the hope of affecting the offer price in a takeover bid. They do stand to benefit personally and may be keen to sell the company in order to realise a lump sum upon retirement. However, it is not possible to state conclusively that the financial statements have been manipulated. Further investigation would be required, especially, if sufficient information is available, to ascertain the reasons for the fall in operating expenses.

Appendix: Ratio calculations

Ratio	2004	2003	Sector comparative
Gross profit	78/1,255 × 100 6.2%	75/1,220 × 100 6.1%	5.9%
Operating profit margin	57/1,255 × 100 4.5%	46/1,220 × 100 3.8%	N/A
No of stores	42	36	N/A
Annual sales per store	1,255/42 $29.9m	1,220/36 $33.9m	$27.6m
Net profit margin	33/1,255 × 100 2.6%	23/1220 × 100 1.9%	3.9%
Non-current asset turnover	1,255/680 1.85	1,220/675 1.81	1.93
Current ratio	105/317 0.33 : 1	71/309 0.23 : 1	N/A
Gearing (debt/equity)	142/301 × 100 = 47.2%	140/276 × 100 = 50.7%	N/A

Note: The gearing calculation could also include short-term borrowings as part of debt capital.

(b) Sector comparatives often provide useful information for the analyst, but should be treated with some caution for the following reasons:

- The comparatives are usually, as in this case, based on an average of entities. Averages can be skewed by one or two atypical cases.
- No two entities are completely alike. For example, DM trades in only one of six provinces in its country. Economic conditions may vary between provinces, and so it may not be valid to compare DM using averages based on entities operating in other provinces.
- Although international standard setters have attempted to reduce the range of accounting choices available, there remain, quite legitimately, areas of accounting policy difference between entities.
- There are different ways of calculating some of the common accounting ratios. The analyst must be sure that the method of calculation is consistent.
- Information published for the sector may not contain all the ratios that the analyst would ideally require. For example, in this case, it would be useful to know the average gearing and current ratios.

Answer 2 – STV (Nov '05)

(a)
The overall objective of financial statements is to provide information about the financial position, performance and changes in financial position of an entity that helps users in making economic decisions. In the case of a group of companies, consolidated financial statements help users to see the overall performance of businesses that are often disparate in nature. It is, additionally, helpful to users to see aggregated results for businesses which are under common control, as it permits them to make judgements about the effectiveness of senior management.

However, different types of product or service may be subject to differing rates of return, opportunities for growth, future prospects and risk. Segment reporting allows users to make better informed assessments of the risk profile of a business by examining the performance and position of different major business segments. Users can identify those segments (geographical and/or business segments) that are performing well or badly, and those that are inherently more risky because, for example, they are located in an unstable economic environment. It may thus become clear, for example, that one segment significantly outperforms others, and that it helps to compensate for poor performance in other areas.

(b)
Report on the segment information of STV for the year ended 31 August 2005

The group result as a percentage of revenue shows a sound improvement from 23·7% in 2004 to 25·3% in 2005. However, this hides significant variations which are revealed once the segment result is analysed. The result as a percentage of revenue has fallen slightly in the road haulage segment and has improved slightly in the air freight segment. However, the really significant change has been in the secure transport segment which has turned from loss to profit during the year. Similarly, asset turnover is little changed in the two established segments, but has improved significantly in secure transport. However, asset turnover is very low in secure transport compared to the other two segments, suggesting that the business is only just starting to recoup the significant investment that it made in this segment three years ago. In terms of investment in assets, the investment in secure transport is far greater than that made in air freight, and it seems likely that this segment of the business is expected to grow in importance in the near future.

The best return on investment (measured by segment result as a percentage of net assets) is made by the air freight segment. The move from loss into profit results in a big improvement in this measure in the secure transport segment. However, this segment's overall contribution to group result remains relatively insignificant.

There has been no significant additional investment in the road haulage segment, and its results are slightly worse in 2005 than in 2004. It is possible that the segment's assets are ageing, and/or that competition is eroding margins. STV's management may have decided that it therefore makes sense to diversify its operations and this could explain the move into secure transport services. Nevertheless, road haulage continues at the moment to be the dominant segment, accounting for 68% of total group revenue in 2005.

The return on investments in associates is good in both years. The share of net profits in associates in 2005 accounts for almost 8% of profit before tax.

In summary, STV appears to be performing fairly well. If current trends were to continue, the secure transport segment could become a very important contributor to overall profitability, and could help to make up for slowly declining profitability in the road haulage segment.

Appendix: Key ratios

	Road haulage	Air freight	Secure transport	Group

Segment result as a percentage of revenue

| 2005 | $169/653 \times 100$ = 25.9% | $68/208 \times 100$ = 32.7% | $6/98 \times 100$ = 6.1% | $243/959 \times 100$ = 25.3% |
| 2004 | $168/642 \times 100$ = 26.2% | $62/199 \times 100$ = 31.1% | $(16)/63 \times 100$ = (25.4%) | $214/904 \times 100$ = 23.7% |

Profit before tax as a percentage of revenue

2005 $202/959 \times 100 = 21.1\%$
2004 $168/904 \times 100 = 18.6\%$

Asset turnover (revenue/segment assets)

| 2005 | $653/805 = 0.81$ | $208/306 = 0.68$ | $98/437 = 0.22$ | $959/1,548 = 0.62$ |
| 2004 | $642/796 = 0.81$ | $199/287 = 0.69$ | $63/422 = 0.15$ | $904/1,505 = 0.60$ |

Segment net assets

| 2005 | $805 - 345 = 460$ | $306 - 176 = 130$ | | $437 - 197 = 240$ |
| 2004 | $796 - 349 = 447$ | $287 - 178 = 109$ | | $422 - 184 = 238$ |

Segment result as a percentage of segment net assets

| 2005 | $169/460 \times 100 = 36.7\%$ | $68/130 \times 100 = 52.3\%$ | $6/240 \times 100 = 2.5\%$ |
| 2004 | $168/447 \times 100 = 37.6\%$ | $62/109 \times 100 = 56.9\%$ | $(16)/238 \times 100 = (6.7\%)$ |

Return on investments in associates

2005 $16/85 \times 100 = 18.8\%$
2004 $12/84 \times 100 = 14.3\%$

Contribution of each segment to group revenue and results

	2005	%	2004	%
Revenue – haulage	$653/959 \times 100$	68%	$642/904 \times 100$	71%
Revenue – freight	$208/959 \times 100$	22%	$199/904 \times 100$	22%
Revenue – secure	$98/959 \times 100$	10%	$63/904 \times 100$	7%
Result – haulage	$169/243 \times 100$	70%	$168/214 \times 100$	79%
Result – freight	$68/243 \times 100$	28%	$62/214 \times 100$	29%
Result – secure	$6/243 \times 100$	2%	$(16)/214 \times 100$	(8%)

(c)
Most groups of entities have problems in defining segments and in allocating assets and liabilities to them. It is common to find that segment information includes amounts for unallocated expenses, assets and liabilities, and STV is no exception. The unallocated items in STV's segment information are significant, especially in the case of assets. Unallocated assets account for 26·0% of total assets in 2005 (24·7% in 2004). If the unallocated items were, in reality, found to belong to one or more of the segments, this could significantly alter the accounting ratios based on asset values. Also, of course, unscrupulous managers could classify items as 'unallocated' in order to manipulate the picture presented by the segment information.

IAS 14 *Segment reporting* does not require the allocation of interest expense between segments. In STV's case, it would be informative to see such an allocation; we are told that the sizeable investment in the infrastructure required for the secure transport operation was funded principally through borrowing. However, we do not know how much borrowing was required, and how much of the group interest charge relates to it.

Other general limitations in segment reporting include the definition of segments, which is a matter of judgement on the part of the directors. Also, there may be quite genuine difficulties and ambiguities in allocating elements such as assets to different segments. A further general problem lies in comparability between businesses. Comparisons between STV's segment report and that of another haulage and freight business could be misleading if the segments have been defined differently.

Answer 3 – ABC (May '06)

Report

Takeover targets: W, Y and Z

(a)
The three potential targets are similar in size, each producing revenue at the level of approximately 10% of ABC's revenue. In respect of performance, Z appears superior to the others: its gross profit margin and operating profit margins are significantly higher than those of W and Y. Y's operating profit margin is disappointing at 4·7%; however, there may be scope to improve control over its operating expenses. Z's return on capital employed is also impressive, at almost double that of entity Y, and it is better than that of ABC itself. However, it is relevant to note that the income tax rate in Zeelandia is significantly higher than that of the other countries, and this effect offsets some of its advantages.

The level of gearing in ABC itself is negligible with debt constituting only around 5% of equity.

Gearing is also at a low level in Y and Z, but entity W is relatively more highly geared (debt constitutes 45·6% of equity). However, after takeover ABC's management would be able to control the level of gearing and to repay any long-term debt if it was felt necessary to do so. The economic environments in which the entities operate are, apparently, rather different from each other. As well as the differences in income tax rates already noted, interest rates vary from 6% in Winlandia to 10% in Zeelandia.

Working capital management varies between the entities. For ABC, the turnover in days for inventories, receivables and payables all lie in the mid-40s. Receivables turnover across the four entities is broadly similar, but there are some significant differences in respect of inventories and payables. Entity W appears to hold inventories for much longer than the other entities, and there may be problems with slow-moving or obsolete items. Payables turnover, on the other hand, is relatively fast in entity W, but at 73 days entity Z takes a long time to meet its payables obligations. This may be as a result of poor management, or deliberate policy. ABC has a relatively comfortable current ratio of 1·4 : 1, but the comparable ratio in all three target entities is less impressive.

The P/E ratios of the three targets and of ABC itself lie within a fairly narrow band. W's P/E is the lowest at 12·6; this could indicate that the share is relatively undervalued, that the most recent earnings figure was better than expected and the share price has not yet been adjusted upwards to reflect this, or that the investment is perceived as relatively risky in the market.

On the basis of the preliminary analysis, entity Z appears superior to the others in several aspects of performance. However, a great deal of further analysis will be required before reaching a conclusion, and, as noted below, there are many limitations in the analysis.

(b)
There are several general limitations to any inter-firm comparisons. These limitations become even more important where international comparisons are made. The limitations include the following:

Accounting standards and policies: In this case, entity Y prepares its financial statements in accordance with Yolandian GAAP. This may be very different from the International Standards that the other entities comply with. Even where the same or similar standards are adopted there is often scope for considerable variation in the choice of policies.

For example, an entity can choose between valuing property, plant and equipment at depreciated cost, or at valuation. The policy selected by management may have a significant effect on the financial statements and upon accounting ratios such as return on capital employed.

Accounting reference date: There is a gap of nine months between the accounting reference date of entities Y and Z on the one hand, and the accounting reference date of ABC on the other hand. A great deal of change can take place in a period of several months, both within the economy as a whole and in the activities of a single entity. The figures of Y and Z are, relatively speaking, out of date, and the comparison may be at least partially invalidated because of this effect.

Size of entities: The three target entities are of similar size, and so comparison between them is likely to have some validity. However, ABC is approximately ten times the size of each of the targets. Its expenses, for example, may be subject to economies of scale.

Differences between activities: All of the four entities being compared have the same principal activity. However, it is rarely, if ever, the case that entities are engaged in precisely the same sphere of activity, and there may be relatively minor supplementary activities that distort their performance. For example, one entity may derive part of its income through the hire or leasing of equipment. It is important to examine the details of entities' activities carefully in order to be sure that they areit is comparable with those of each other entities.

Single period comparisons: There is always a risk that the results of a single period are not representative of the underlying trends within the business. Therefore, it is better, wherever possible, to examine the performance and position at several different dates.

Special problems of international comparison: Where entities in different countries are being compared, it is even more important to be cautious about the value of the comparisons and conclusions drawn. National economies often experience cycles of economic growth and decline. These cyclical differences may have a significant effect upon the performance of entities. The entities in this case are, apparently, subject to different tax regimes. Such differences may very well be important factors in making decisions about investment. The size and nature of the stock markets may well differ considerably between different regimes. In a small, illiquid market, for example, share prices may be generally lower, reflecting the lack of liquidity in the investment. Lower prices would, of course, affect the important P/E ratio, which is regarded as important.

Answer 4 (May '08)

Report

To: Kay

From: Management Accountant

FJK draft income statement and statement of financial position – 31 March 2008

(a)
1. *Performance*

The improvement in both revenue and profit between the two years under review is impressive. Revenue has increased by around 54% and profit before tax by over 44%. FJK's new strategy has evidently been very successful in terms of increased profitability. However, it is helpful to break the figures down further. Return on assets (ROA) (pre-tax profit as a percentage of total assets) has actually decreased over the period; it was 26·7% in 2007 and has dropped to 22·9% in 2008 (for calculations see **Appendix**). In order to analyse the change in more detail ROA can be broken down into two constituent parts: net profit margin and total asset turnover. Net profit has reduced from 17·3% to 16·2%, but the more significant change is in total asset turnover which has reduced from 1·46 to 1·29. The most significant change in assets between the two years is in non-current assets. Even after removing the effect of the revaluation, there has been a significant increase in non-current assets. It may be that much of the additional investment in non-current assets has yet to bear fruit in the form of increased profits, and so the deterioration may be reversed in the 2008/9 financial year.

Elsewhere in the income statement, the message is more positive: gross profit margin has actually increased slightly, suggesting good control of manufacturing costs. Both distribution and administrative costs have increased substantially over the year. The large percentage increase in distribution costs might have arisen because of the greater distances involved in product distribution now that sales have expanded internationally. Administrative expenses as a percentage of revenue have hardly increased at all. However, some of those expenses are likely to be fixed in nature, at least within a certain range of activity. It may be, therefore, that this category of expense has not been as well controlled as in previous years.

Finance costs have more than doubled in the period under review, suggesting either a substantial increase in the cost of borrowing, or greatly increased borrowing, or a combination of the two. However, interest is apparently well covered by available profits and is not a source of immediate concern.

2. *Position*

It is immediately apparent from the statement of financial position that the increase in finance cost arises, at least in part, from a greatly increased level of borrowing. Total borrowings at the end of March 2008 were (763 + 327) $1,090,000 compared to (453 + 103) $556,000 a year earlier, an increase of 96%. The fact that a high proportion of borrowings at the statement of financial position date (30% of the total) fall due within one year could be a cause for concern. The gearing ratio has increased over the year, but it is the absolute increase in borrowing that is worrying.

Turning to immediate liquidity, the ratio of current assets to liabilities is substantially below 1 : 1, a significant fall from the previous year. There is no cash in the statement of financial position at 31 March 2008. The calculation takes into account the probability that the

232 Exam Practice Kit: Financial Management

income tax payable balance is understated. Trade payables have greatly increased between the two year ends (by 212·3%). There is insufficient information available to calculate an efficiency ratio using purchases, but it is nevertheless clear that it is taking FJK much longer to meet its trade payables. Efficiency ratio calculations for inventory and trade receivables indicates a significant improvement in both. The figures suggest that receivables are being chased for payment and inventory has been driven down in order to free up some cash to meet liabilities. While reductions in efficiency ratios are usually regarded as evidence of good management, such reductions can go too far. If inventory is driven too low, it may mean that it is not available to fulfil customer orders, thus losing goodwill. Customer goodwill could be further threatened by over-zealous chasing of amounts due.

(b)
Possible risks and problem areas

The overall impression given by the 2008 financial statements is of a business that has grown too quickly. It risks becoming a victim of its own success if it cannot improve liquidity. The proposed cash injection of $250,000 would clearly ease the liquidity problem but it is probably not enough to solve it (it would be sufficient to meet the tax bill but not much more, or alternatively only about 20% of the year end payables). There is a distinct risk that more cash would be required very soon. It is quite possible that now, some seven weeks after the year end, the liquidity position is already significantly worse. The fact that Fay and Jay are calling on Kay for a cash injection may suggest that the limits of the business's borrowing capacity have been reached. The request for more funds should be treated very cautiously. The directors should be advised to prepare budgets, including sensitivity analysis, to determine what the actual level of cash requirement is over the coming year or two, and then should take action to properly fund the business. This may involve further extensive borrowing, a venture capital investment or even a stock market flotation. If action is not taken promptly there is a distinct risk that the business could fail through lack of liquidity.

Appendix

Accounting ratios

1. Return on assets can be broken down into net profit margin and asset turnover. In order to compare like with like, the revaluation amount has been excluded from total assets. The net profit figure before finance costs and tax is used.

Revenue

$$\frac{\text{Profit before finance costs}}{\text{Revenue}} \times \frac{\text{Revenue}}{\text{Total assets}} = \frac{\text{Profit before finance costs}}{\text{Total assets}}$$

2008

$$\frac{968 + 97}{5,973} \times \frac{5,973}{(4,815 - 167)} = \frac{968 + 97}{(4,815 - 167)}$$
$$0.178 \times 1.29 = 22.9$$

2007

$$\frac{671 + 40}{3,886} \times \frac{3,886}{2,661} = \frac{671 + 40}{2,661}$$
$$0.183 \times 1.46 = 26.7$$

	2008	2007

2. *Gross profit margin*

$$\frac{\text{Revenue}}{\text{Gross profit}} \times 100 \qquad \frac{1{,}655}{5{,}973} \times 100 = 27.7\% \qquad \frac{1{,}018}{3{,}886} \times 100 = 26.2\%$$

3. *Distribution costs*
   As a percentage of revenue

$$\frac{\text{Revenue}}{\text{Distribution costs}} \times 100 \qquad \frac{270}{5{,}973} \times 100 = 4.5\% \qquad \frac{106}{3{,}886} \times 100 = 2.7\%$$

4. *Administrative expenses*
   As a percentage of revenue

$$\frac{\text{Revenue}}{\text{Administrative expenses}} \times 100 \qquad \frac{320}{5{,}973} \times 100 = 5.2\% \qquad \frac{201}{3{,}886} \times 100 = 5.4\%$$

5. *Non-current asset turnover*

$$\frac{\text{Revenue}}{\text{Non-current assets}} \qquad \frac{5{,}973}{(3{,}413 - 167)} = 1.8 \qquad \frac{3{,}886}{1{,}586} = 2.5$$

6. *Efficiency : inventory*

$$\frac{\text{Inventory}}{\text{Cost of sales}} \times 365 \text{ days} \qquad \frac{677}{4{,}318} \times 365 = 57.2 \text{ days} \qquad \frac{510}{2{,}868} \times 365 = 64.9 \text{ days}$$

7. *Efficiency: trade receivables*

$$\frac{\text{Revenue}}{\text{Trade receivables}} \times 365 \qquad \frac{725}{5{,}973} \times 365 = 44.3 \text{ days} \qquad \frac{553}{3{,}886} \times 365 = 51.9 \text{ days}$$

8. *Liquidity : current ratio*

$$\frac{\text{Current liabilities}}{\text{Current assets}} \qquad \frac{1{,}402}{1{,}718 + 72^*} = 0.78:1 \qquad \frac{1{,}075}{845} = 1.27:1$$

* Note: The 2008 figure for income tax is almost certainly underestimated. The effective rate of tax reflected in the 2007 income statement is 164/671 × 100 = 24·4%. Applying the same rate to 2008 profit before tax gives a tax charge of 968 × 24·4% = 236. This suggests that an additional liability of (236 − 164) 72 should be taken into account.

9. *Gearing*

$$\frac{\text{Debt}}{\text{Equity}} \times 100 \qquad \frac{763 + 327}{(2{,}334 - 167)} \times 100 = 50.3\% \qquad \frac{453 + 103}{1{,}363} \times 100 = 40.8\%$$

10. *Interest cover*

$$\frac{\text{Profit before interest and tax}}{\text{Interest}} \qquad \frac{968 + 97}{97} = 11.0 \qquad \frac{971 + 40}{40} = 17.8$$

[Examiner's note: As 2008 is a Leap Year, candidates could have chosen to use a denominator of 366 days as applicable in the above calculations.]

Answer 5

Report on the financial statements of SDB for the year ended 31 July 2006

(a) Joint ventures, according to IAS 31, fall into three principal categories: jointly controlled assets, operations and entities.

Joint control arises where decisions must be made unanimously between the controlling parties, and no one party is dominant. It appears that during the year, SDB has invested in a jointly controlled entity. A jointly controlled entity is a venture involving the establishment of an entity in which each venturer has an interest. The entity could be, for example, a partnership or a limited liability corporation. IAS 31 prefers the adoption of the proportionate consolidation method: this involves combining the entity's share of assets, liabilities, income and expenses with its own assets, liabilities and so on. However, it also permits the use of the equity method which involves recognising the investment (at cost plus share of any subsequent profits less amounts distributed) on one line in the statement of financial position, with a one line entry in the income statement showing the share of profits in the joint venture for the period. The proportionate consolidation method has the advantage that it results in financial statements that show the assets, liabilities and profits over which the entity has either control or joint control.

IAS 31 permits the use of equity accounting because it recognises the argument that joint control is not the same as control. In SDB's case, its directors may feel that they exert significant influence rather than joint control. However, it is also possible that the directors wish to avoid augmenting, for example, liabilities by including those under joint control because it would provide a less positive view of the entity.

(*Note:* where equity accounting is adopted, IAS 31 requires extensive disclosure by note of the amounts of assets and liabilities in the joint venture. Therefore, it should be possible to adjust the statement of financial position figures to an approximation of proportionate consolidation).

(b) The position of the entity has deteriorated in some respects between 2005 and 2006. As you pointed out, the cash balance has declined by almost $10 million. This is not necessarily a problem, of course: cash that is not needed in the working capital cycle should be used for investment in profitable opportunities. There appears to have been some investment in property, plant and equipment (the net book value has increased by $2·1 million — 11·8%), but the principal investment has been in the joint venture. The income statement shows that this investment has resulted in substantial losses so far, but it is possible that the venture will show improved results in its second year of operation. Overall, however, it is clear that profitability is reduced, and if this reduction continues into the longer term it will have an effect upon the entity's position and level of risk. The non-current asset turnover ratio has worsened, indicating that the new investment in property, plant and equipment has not yet paid off in terms of higher revenues.

Another substantial outgoing during the year was the payment of a dividend. This was in excess of the profit for the year ended 31 July 2005, and it is likely to be difficult for the entity to sustain a dividend at that level unless profitability improves significantly.

Working capital management has declined in effectiveness. Both inventory and receivables turnover are high in absolute terms and have worsened significantly during the year. Inventory, on average, spends nearly 165 days or five and a half months on the premises. There may be operational reasons for this, but it could also suggest that management is not in full control of the current assets. While the current and quick ratio suggest no immediate problems, both have declined substantially in the year.

The description attached to the long-term loans shows that they are payable between the years 2008 and 2010. It is quite possible that the directors plan to replace them with other long-term loans. However, if the fall in profitability and the deterioration in working capital management were to continue, a lender might require higher interest rates to reflect increased risk. The interest rates on the current loan appear to be around 9%. Interest cover is not a problem at the moment, but, again, this ratio has declined over the year because of the reduction in profitability.

The contingent liability is, indeed, worrying. Such liabilities would be recognised (i.e. would appear in the statement of financial position) only where the assessment of probability of adverse outcome exceeded 50%. The fact that the contingent liability is noted means that the probability of an adverse outcome is assessed at less than 50%. If the full amount of $10 million were to be payable the outlook for the entity could be very poor. If a major product failure were to be proven, it is likely to have a very bad effect on sales of similar products, and could even result in the closure of the entity. Even if other product sales are not affected, the entity would be left with the problem of how to find the very large sum required. It is not immediately clear how this could be done, especially as the outcome of the case may very well coincide with the redemption of loan notes.

Conclusion

While the entity is currently solvent, and, indeed, has a positive cash balance of $3.1 million, the position in the slightly longer term could become very much worse. The product liability case represents a severe threat to the entity. Most indicators already show a worsening position, and the directors need to address, as a matter of urgency, the disappointing joint venture results, the general decline in profitability and the poor working capital management.

Appendix:

	2006	2005
Inventory turnover	$8{,}300/18{,}400 \times 365 = 164.6$ days	$6{,}900/18{,}000 \times 365 = 139.9$ days
Receivables turnover	$4{,}700/25{,}200 \times 365 = 68.1$ days	$4{,}100/25{,}300 \times 365 = 59.1$ days
Current ratio	$16{,}100/5{,}020 = 3.2$	$24{,}000/5{,}060 = 4.7$
Quick ratio	$(16{,}100 - 8{,}300)/5{,}020 = 1.6$	$(24{,}000 - 6{,}900)/5{,}060 = 3.4$
Gearing	$13{,}600/24{,}880 \times 100 = 54.7\%$	$13{,}600/23{,}140 \times 100 = 58.8\%$
Non-current asset turnover	$25{,}200/19{,}900 = 1.27$	$25{,}300/17{,}800 = 1.42$
Interest cover	$(6{,}800 - 970 - 1{,}750)/1{,}220 = 3.3$	$(7{,}300 - 1{,}030 - 1{,}720)/1{,}140 = 4.0$

Answer 6 – SBD (Nov '07)

REPORT

To: A business associate

DAS Financial statements for the year ended 31 August 2007

At first sight the business's performance appears to be in decline. Revenue and net profit in 2007 were much lower than in 2006. However, much is explained by the nature of DAS's business and its policy for recognising revenue).

During 2007 it undertook its largest housing development project to date, and this clearly involved a major commitment of resources.

No revenue was realised from the project in the financial year under review, because DAS adopts the relatively conservative policy of not recognising revenue until the legal formalities relating to the sale of a house are completed.

However, it could be expected that most, if not all, of the revenue from this project will be realised in the course of the current financial year, thus significantly enhancing the business's performance in 2008.

Gross profitability is at a similar level in both years, at 19·9% in 2007 and 20·7% in 2006 (see appendix for this and other calculations). Because DAS uses sub-contract labour and has only a small direct labour force, cost of sales is likely to vary in line with revenue and significant fluctuations in gross profitability would not be expected.

Net profitability is different: the 2007 income statement shows an increased level of expenses most of which are likely to be fixed rather than variable in nature. This helps to explain why profit for the period is very much lower in 2007 than in 2006.

The 2008 performance figures are likely to be much better than those of 2007. Prospects for sales of the hospital site houses seem good, given that almost half of the units were secured by means of a deposit before the 2007 year end.

Assuming that all 225 units are sold in the current financial year, and that the gross profit margin remains at around 20%, gross profit of $23 million can be projected for this development.

Sales of other houses were significantly lower in 2007 than in 2006, probably because resources were diverted to the hospital site project.

However, even if sales in 2008 were to remain at the lower level, an overall improvement in profit for the period could be expected. If, as seems likely, attention is now given to other developments, overall sales could be even better.

The entity appears to be moving into a different sector of the market as the average price of the hospital site houses is much greater than the average price of its other house sales.

The housing market is currently buoyant, so there are grounds for supposing that DAS could do very well.

Turning to the statement of financial position, it is clear that there is only one significant asset: inventories.

Land held for development is classified under current assets, suggesting that it is likely to be moved into the property under construction category, and possibly sold, within the 12 months following the statement of financial position date.

The value of land held for development has decreased substantially between 2006 and 2007, but it would be reasonable to assume that this is accounted for by the development of the hospital site.

However, more development land will have to be acquired at some point if the business is to continue to expand, and further acquisitions will require cash.

In a buoyant housing market it is likely that land values will increase rapidly. The value of property under construction has more than doubled but this can be easily explained by the hospital site development which was almost completed by the year end.

The non-current assets of property, plant and equipment are relatively insignificant which would be expected in a business that sub-contracts most of its work.

Trade and other receivables are very low in both years, which is easily explained by the nature of the business: legal title to a house is likely to pass only upon receipt of cash.

There is no cash in the business at the end of 2007, compared to a balance of $2·8 million a year earlier.

The business's activities are financed principally through borrowings. DAS's gearing ratio (debt/equity $\times$ 100) is 193·6% at the end of August 2007, compared to 236·6% a year earlier.

A substantial portion of the borrowings in each year are classified under current liabilities and so will be payable within the next 12 months.

In many businesses this level of gearing would indicate significant financial distress.

However, this approach to financing appears to be quite routine for DAS. The average interest rate on the entity's borrowing is approximately 6·9% which is very little in excess of the general bank interest rate in respect of low risk lending, and which suggests that lenders do not regard the business as especially risky.

Interest cover has dropped significantly to a level of 1·8 in 2007, but this is less of a worry in the context of the business's conservative revenue recognition policy.

The borrowing figures are undoubtedly very large, but then the business is likely to generate cash inflows of approximately $115 million from the hospital site development alone during the 2008 financial year.

Since listing, DAS has not paid a dividend, although it has generated sufficient profits to do so. Because listing occurred only recently, it is quite likely that equity investors were induced to invest on the promise of capital growth, and that they are not concerned about the absence of a dividend. At the moment the directors' policy appears to be to reinvest earnings.

It is not possible to state with any degree of certainty that DAS is a stable and prosperous business. The high level of gearing is not a cause for concern at the moment, but this could change if the housing market were to slow down.

It is likely that the borrowings are secured on the principal asset of inventories. Lenders might become concerned as the level of inventories falls following sales, especially if some of the proceeds have to be diverted into acquiring more land for development.

Another possible cause for concern is the business's vulnerability to increases in interest rates. A one point increase in the rate of interest charged (i.e. a rate of 7·9% rather than 6·9%) would add almost $2 million to the annual interest charges at the current level of borrowing. Even relatively small changes in conditions can have a disproportionately severe effect upon entities like DAS that rely so heavily on borrowing.

Conclusion

Provided that the housing market continues to flourish and interest rates remain at or below their current level, prospects for DAS look promising.

Appendix

		2007		2006
Gross profit margin	31.4/157.9 × 100	19.9%	50.3/243.0 × 100	20.7%
Profit before tax as a percentage of sales	10.0/157.9 × 100	6.3%	28.3/243.0 × 100	11.6%
Gearing (debt/equity)	(114.7 + 52.6)/86.4 × 100	193.6%	(112.0 + 75.4)/79.2 × 100	236.6%
Interest cover	(31.4 − 9.2)/12.2	1.8 times	(50.3 − 8.6)/13.4	3.1 times

---

Estimated gross profit from hospital site house sales:

Assume average selling price of one house = ($425,000 + 600,000)/2 = $512,500
Estimated revenue = 225 units × $512,500 = $115 million
Estimated gross profit = $115 million × 20% = $23 million

Approximate interest rate applicable to DAS's borrowings:

Average borrowings = [(114·7 + 52·6) + (112·0 + 75·4)]/2 = $177·4 million
Approximate interest rate = 12·2/177·4 × 100 = 6·9%

Effect on profit of an increase in interest rates of 1%:
$177·4 million × 7·9% = $14 million, that is an increase in finance costs of $1·8 million. At current profit levels, profit before tax would drop from $10 million to $8·2 million, a decrease of 18%

Average selling price per 'other' house (to nearest $000):

2006 243 million/1,080 = $225,000
2007 158 million/675 = $234,000
Average selling price of hospital site house: ($425,000 + 600,000)/2 = $512,000

16

Scope of External Reporting

Scope of External Reporting 16

Learning Outcomes

After studying this chapter students should be able to:

- describe pressures for extending the scope and quality of external reports to include prospective and non-financial matters, and narrative reporting generally;
- explain how financial information concerning the interaction of a business with society and the natural environment can be communicated in the published accounts;
- discuss social and environmental issues which are likely to be most important to stakeholders in an organisation;
- explain the process of measuring, recording and disclosing the effects of exchanges between a business and society – human resource accounting.

The operating and financial review

OFR: the ASB's reporting statement of best practice

The ASB specifies that an OFR should be a balanced and comprehensive analysis, consistent with the size and complexity of the business, of:

(a) the development and performance of the entity during the financial year;
(b) the position of the entity at the end of the year;
(c) the main trends and factors underlying the development, performance and position of the business of the entity during the financial year; and
(d) the main trends and factors which are likely to affect the entity's future development, performance and position.

The OFR should be prepared so as to assist members (i.e. shareholders) to assess the strategies adopted by the entity and the potential for those strategies to succeed. It is thus capable, potentially, of addressing some of the traditional limitations of financial statements, in that it specifically examines future business developments.

The ASB sets out the following principles for the preparation of an OFR.

The OFR shall:

(a) set out an analysis of the business through the eyes of the board of directors;
(b) focus on matters that are relevant to the interests of members (i.e. shareholders);
(c) have a forward-looking orientation, identifying those trends and factors relevant to the members' assessment of the current and future performance of the business and the progress towards the achievement of long-term business objectives;
(d) complement, as well as supplement, the financial statements in order to enhance the overall corporate disclosure;
(e) be comprehensive and understandable;
(f) be balanced and neutral, dealing even-handedly both with good and bad aspects;
(g) be comparable over time.

The principal disclosure requirements are as follows:

(a) the nature of the business, including a description of the market, competitive and regulatory environment in which the entity operates, and the entity's objectives and strategies;
(b) the development and performance of the business, both in the financial year under review and in the future;
(c) the resources, principal risks and uncertainties, and relationships that may affect the entity's long-term value;
(d) the position of the business including a description of the capital structure, treasury policies and objectives and liquidity of the entity, both in the financial year under review and the future.

Some more specific requirements relating to particular matters are added to this broad, general description of disclosures. The statement specifies that information should be included about:

(a) environmental matters (including the impact of the business on the environment);
(b) the entity's employees;
(c) social and community issues;
(d) persons with whom the entity has contractual or other arrangements which are essential to the business of the entity;
(e) receipts from, and returns to, members of the entity in respect of shares held by them; and
(f) all other matters directors consider to be relevant.

It can be seen, therefore, that a mandatory OFR would have added very materially to the disclosures of many listed businesses, and that some aspects of the disclosures (notably the environmental and social aspects) would have represented a major development in disclosure for many businesses.

Advantages and drawbacks of the OFR

The advantages of including an OFR as part of the annual report are as follows:

> Such a statement is a useful summary of information that can be found in a more complex form elsewhere in the financial statements.
> It may provide genuinely useful statements of management's intended business strategy, and sufficient information to be able to assess the relative success of business strategies to date.
> It may be more likely to be read and absorbed than some other parts of the annual report.

There are, however, some potential drawbacks:

> Users may rely too heavily on the OFR, and may read it in preference to a thorough examination of the detailed figures.
>
> Even though there is a basic template for the OFR, these statements may vary significantly in practice and may not be readily comparable.
>
> OFRs currently (both in the UK and elsewhere) have the status of voluntary disclosures and so they suffer from all the general drawbacks of voluntary disclosure (e.g. they may not be prepared on an entirely consistent basis, bad news may be underplayed and so on).

Mangement commentary

- Discussion paper on 'Management commentary' (this is a term synonymous with 'Operating and financial review' in the UK or 'Management discussion and analysis' which is the term commonly used in the USA).
- Objective of the management commentary is to assist current and potential investors in assessing the strategies adopted by the entity and the potential for achieving these strategies.
- Initial indications are that the management commentary would not be included in IFRS but would have a voluntary but best practice status.
- The terms 'neutral' and 'balanced' are obviously less onerous than achieving fair presentation, which is what the auditor is charged with ensuring.
- The issue of verifiability of the information that is included in the management commentary will be a difficult one as much of what is likely to be covered will be forward looking and so not necessarily verifiable.
- Intended to be 'through the management's eyes' and so the term 'balanced' is used to reflect the fact that the commentary is unlikely to avoid some element of bias as the management are likely to have a positive outlook on their strategies.

Social accounting and reporting

- *The natural environment.* A business uses physical resources such as coal, gas, water, air but the full cost of this usage is not reflected in the financial statements. Firms may have adverse impacts on the environment, but until recently, these effects were not recognised at all in the financial statements.
- *The sociological environment.* The way in which firms attract human resources, and the use of those resources, has an impact on society. For example, a decision to close a large division will have an adverse impact on local society. On a global level, certain groups of consumers are likely to express preferences against those firms that exploit child labour in developing countries.
- Social accounting and reporting covers both financial and non-financial aspects of reporting. It is potentially very wide-ranging in its coverage, and might encompass such matters as:
- reporting on the environmental impacts of an entity's policies;
- measuring and reporting the expected value of future obligations related to rectification of environmental damage;
- measuring and reporting on the value of human assets in an entity;

- reporting policies and measurements relating to the workforce, for example, the policy on employment of disabled people, and statistics reporting on the numbers of disabled staff employed;
- reporting on an entity's intellectual capital;
- reports on an entity's policies on ethical issues.

Accounting for the impact of an entity on the environment around it

Taxation-related matters
1. *Climate change levy*: This may have the effect of encouraging businesses to improve energy efficiency and to reduce emissions of carbon dioxide.
2. *Landfill tax*: A landfill tax was introduced in 1996. This may have significant financial impacts on the profitability of those businesses that dispose of large volumes of waste.
3. *Capital allowances*: For example, there are currently 100 per cent first year allowances for capital expenditure on natural gas refuelling infrastructure.

Accounting for additional costs related to the environment
Significant costs may be incurred by, for example, house-builders who build on brownfield land that has previously been contaminated. Highly restrictive planning policies limit the use of greenfield sites for building, and so in very densely populated areas (such as England) significant decontamination activity may be required before land can be built on.

Increasingly stringent laws may involve business entities in incurring additional costs in respect of environmental damage they have caused. Where sites are polluted by, for example, mining activities, local legislation is increasingly likely to require reinstatement.

Environmental provisions
Sometimes anticipated costs related to environmental damage require provisions. Provisions required in respect of environmental costs are no different from any other provisions, in that they must follow the requirements of IAS 37 *Provisions, contingent liabilities and contingent assets*. Students should remember the recognition rules in respect of provisions.

A provision should be recognised when:

(a) an entity has a present obligation (legal or constructive) as a result of a past event;
(b) it is probable that an outflow of resources embodying economic benefits will be required to settle the obligation;
(c) a reliable estimate can be made of the amount of the obligation.

Accounting for human resource issues

Social reporting could take many forms. It could include a 'social income statement' which would report social costs and benefits to different areas of society, and a social statement of financial position disclosing human assets, organisational assets, and the use of public goods, and of financial and physical assets.

One of the most important documents to be produced on the subject was *The Corporate Report*, published in the UK in 1975. This was, both for its time and ours, a radical document that advocated not only the publication of financial statements, but also of supplementary reports to serve the needs of users other than the investor group. Supplementary reports would include:

1. *Statement of corporate objectives.* The statement could take many forms, but would include objectives relating to all stakeholders.

2. *Employment report.* This would give information about the number of employees, wage rates and training.

3. *Statement of future prospects.* Although *The Corporate Report* acknowledged the difficulty of reporting about future prospects, this would provide welcome information to all types of stakeholder.

4. *Value-added reports.* This would show the development of resources throughout the entity, demonstrating the interdependency of all parties (employee, government and the providers of capital). A typical value-added statement would show a split of 'value added' between the various providers of resources to the business.

Intellectual capital reporting

Knowledge which can be used to create value. Intellectual capital includes.

(i) *Human resources*: The collective skills, experience and knowledge of employees.
(ii) *Intellectual assets*: Knowledge which is defined and codified such as a drawing, computer program or collection of data.
(iii) *Intellectual property*: Intellectual assets which can be legally protected, such as patents or copyrights.

Human asset accounting

- Attempt to identify the intangible components of the very large gap that exists between market capitalisation and book value in many 'people' businesses.
- Many barriers to adopting this approach. The IASB in its *Framework for the Preparation and Presentation of Financial Statements* defines an asset thus:

> An asset is a resource controlled by the entity as a result of past events and from which future economic benefits are expected to flow to the entity. (para. 49)

- Reliable measurement is a problem.

The global reporting initiative

The GRI's intention is that reporting on economic, environmental and social performance by organisations becomes as routine and comparable as financial reporting. To this end it has created a Sustainability Reporting Framework, some details of which are given below.

The Framework sets out a series of key stages that are involved in the sustainability reporting process:

- defining report content
- defining report quality
- setting the report boundary
- profile
- disclosure on management approach
- performance indicators
- sector supplements.

The 'Profile' stage identifies the base content that should appear in a sustainability report, which can be briefly summarised as follows:

1. *Strategy and analysis*

This section provides a strategic view of the organisation's relationship to sustainability. It should include a statement from the most senior decision-maker in the organisation (typically, the CEO in a commercial organisation) which should present the overall vision and strategy of the organisation in relation to sustainability. The report should then describe the key impacts, risks and opportunities in relation to sustainability.

2. *Organisation profile*

This section should provide information on the principal brands, products and services offered, the countries in which the organisation operates, markets service, scale of the organisation (e.g. number of employees, capitalisation) and any significant changes during the reporting period.

3. *Report profile*

This section should include information on the process for defining report content (e.g. how materiality has been defined), the boundary of the report, the basis for reporting on joint ventures, subsidiaries and other related organisations, data measurement techniques, and the policy and current practice for seeking assurance on the report.

4. *Governance*

The report should describe under this heading the entity's governance arrangements, including the mandate and composition of boards and committees, processes in place to avoid conflicts of interest, internally developed statements of mission, values, codes of conduct and stakeholder engagement.

The disclosure on management approach should report on the following aspects:

1. *Economic*. Performance, market presence and indirect economic aspects, goals, policies and any other relevant contextual information.
2. *Environmental*. A concise disclosure should be provided on materials, energy, water, biodiversity, emissions, effluent and waste, products and services, compliance, transport and any other relevant items. Details should also be provided of policies, goals and performance.
3. *Social*. This area of the report should report under the headings of Labour Practices and Decent Work, Human Rights and Society. For each of these the report should discuss goals and performance, policies, organisational responsibility, training and awareness, monitoring and any other relevant contextual information.

Extensive guidance is also offered in respect of the choice of performance indicators.

Medium answer questions

Question 1 (May '06)

You are the assistant to the Finance Director of MNO, a medium-sized listed entity that complies with International Accounting Standards. One of MNO's directors has proposed the publication of an Operating and Financial Review (OFR) as part of the annual financial statements. Most of the directors know very little about the OFR, and the Finance Director has asked you to produce a short briefing paper on the topic for their benefit.

Requirement
Write the briefing paper, which should discuss the following issues:

- Any relevant regulatory requirements for an OFR.
- The purpose and, in outline, the typical content of an OFR.

The advantages and drawbacks of publishing an OFR from the entity's point of view.

(Total = 10 marks)

Question 2 (Nov '06)

In many industries there is a large gap between the market capitalisation of listed entities and the statement of financial position value of their net assets. Some commentators have suggested that the gap comprises unrecognised intangible assets in the form of intellectual capital obtained through the employment of human resources, and that these assets should be capitalised.

Requirement
Identify the principal arguments for and against the proposal to capitalise intellectual capital.

(Total = 10 marks)

Question 3 (Nov '07)

It is becoming increasingly common for listed entities to provide non-financial disclosures intended to inform stakeholders about the business's environmental policies, impacts and practices. Supporters of such voluntary disclosures argue that stakeholders have a right to be informed about environmental issues in this way. However, there are also arguments against this type of disclosure.

Requirement
Identify and explain the principal arguments **against** voluntary disclosures by businesses of their environmental policies, impacts and practices.

(Total = 10 marks)

Question 4 (Nov '08)

CIMA's *Official Terminology* defines intellectual capital as 'knowledge which can be used to create value'.

Currently, IFRS permit the recognition of only a limited range of internally generated intellectual assets including, for example, copyrights.

Requirement

(a) Explain the advantages that could be gained by entities and their stakeholders if the scope of IFRS were expanded to permit the recognition in the statement of financial position of a wider range of intellectual assets, such as know-how, the value of the workforce and employee skills. **(5 marks)**

(b) Explain the principal reasons why IFRS do not currently permit the recognition in the statement of financial position of intellectual assets such as know-how, the value of the workforce and employee skills. **(5 marks)**
(Total = 10 marks)

Answers to medium answer questions

Answer 1

Briefing paper to the directors of MNO

The Operating and Financial Review
Many international entities are choosing to expand the scope of their reporting in the form of an Operating and Financial Review (OFR). There is no formal regulatory requirement to publish such a review, although IAS 1 *Presentation of Financial Statements* encourages entities to present a financial review by management that would ideally cover some of the areas that are commonly covered by the OFR. Any such publication, however, would constitute a set of voluntary disclosures.

The principal source of guidance on the purpose and content of an OFR is the UK Accounting Standards Board (ASB) Reporting Statement of Best Practice which was issued in January 2006. However, this is the topic. A statement has no international application, except as a source of general guidance. In October 2005, the IASB isisued a discussion paper on 'Management Commentary'. The topic is on the IASB's research agenda, but does not, at the moment, constitute an active project, and so it may be some time before an exposure draft is issued.

Form of disclosure was first issued in 1993, and was revised in 2003. More recently, the UK government has proposed that publication of an OFR should be mandatory for UK listed entities.

However, this proposal and the exposure draft issued by the ASB in 2004 has no international application, except as a source of general guidance. The IASB has set up a working group to undertake a project on 'Management Commentary', but as yet no exposure draft has been published on the topic.

The purpose of an OFR is to assist users, principally investors, in making a forward-looking assessment of the performance of the business by setting out management's analysis and discussion of the principal factors underlying the entity's performance and financial position.

Typically, an OFR would comprise some or all of the following:
- Description of the business and its objectives
- Management's strategy for achieving the objectives
- Review of operations
- Commentary on the strengths and resources of the business

- Commentary about such issues as human capital, research and development activities, development of new products and services
- Financial review with discussion of treasury management, cash inflows and outflows and current liquidity levels.

The publication of such a statement would have the following advantages for MNO:

- It could be helpful in promoting the entity as progressive and as eager to communicate as fully as possible with investors.
- It could be a genuinely helpful medium of communicating the entity's plans and management's outlook on the future.
- If the IASB were to introduce a compulsory requirement for management commentary by listed entities, MNO would already have established the necessary reporting systems and practices.

However, there could be some drawbacks:

- If an OFR is to be genuinely helpful to investors, it will require a considerable input of senior management time. This could be costly, and it may be that the benefits of publishing an OFR would not outweigh the costs.
- There is a risk in publishing this type of statement that investors will read it in preference to the financial statements, and that they may therefore fail to read or miss important information.

Answer 2 (Nov '06)

The principal arguments for the proposal are as follows:

1. Those organisations that depend upon human resources, know-how and intellectual capabilities to generate revenue, often have a relatively low level of traditional capital investment. The statement of financial positions of such entities do not reflect the true value of the capital used in revenue generation: indeed, as noted in the question, the gap between market capitalisation and the book value of net assets may be very substantial. The mismatch between statement of financial position and revenue generation could be addressed by recognising a wider range of intangible assets, including intellectual capital.
2. At present, financial statements fail to provide sufficient information to permit interested parties to assess the full range of resources available to the organisation. Their information content suffers because of low levels of intangible asset recognition.
3. It is also argued that the recognition of intellectual capital would encourage better management of human resources because it would make visible resources that have tended to be hidden and under-valued.

The principal arguments against the proposal are as follows:

1. The recognition of intellectual capital would present problems in that it does not fulfil all aspects of the definition of an asset. The Framework defines an asset as: '... *a resource controlled by an entity as a result of past events and from which future economic benefits are expected to flow*'. The problem lies in the area of control: human resources cannot be fully controlled, because staff are free to leave their employment whenever they wish.
2. The measurement of intellectual capital would present many practical difficulties. It is unlikely that the fair value of a group of employees could ever be measured reliably.
3. Recognition and measurement of such intangible factors as know-how and skills would allow for considerable latitude in practice, and it would be possible for the unscrupulous to exploit the element of judgement involved in making valuations in order to manipulate their financial statements.

Answer 3 (Nov '07)

Arguments against voluntary disclosures by businesses in respect of their environmental policies, impacts and practices might include the following principal points.

The traditional view of the corporation is that it exists solely to increase shareholder wealth. In this view business executives have no responsibility to broaden the scope or nature of their reporting as doing so reduces returns to shareholders (because there is a cost associated with additional reporting).

From a public policy perspective, if governments wish corporations and similar entities to bear the responsibility for their environmental impacts, they should legislate accordingly. In the absence of such legislation, however, businesses bear no responsibility for environmental impacts, and in consequence there is no reporting responsibility either.

Voluntary disclosures of any type are of limited usefulness because they are not readily comparable with those of other entities. Therefore, it is likely that the costs of producing such disclosures outweigh the benefits to stakeholders.

The audit of voluntary disclosures is not regulated. Even where such disclosures are audited, the scope of the audit may be relatively limited, and moreover, its scope may not be clearly laid out in the voluntary report. Voluntary reports are not necessarily, therefore, reliable from a stakeholder's point of view.

Especially where voluntary disclosures are included as part of the annual report package, there is a risk of information overload: stakeholders are less able to identify in a very lengthy report the information that is relevant and useful to them.

Voluntary disclosures by business organisations, because they are at best lightly regulated, may be treated by the organisation in a cynical fashion as public relations opportunities. The view of the business's activities could very well be biased, but it would be quite difficult for most stakeholders to detect such bias.

It is questionable whether voluntary disclosures about environmental policies, impacts and practices would meet the qualitative characteristics of useful information set out in the IASB's Framework. The key characteristics are: understandability, reliability, relevance and comparability. Voluntary environmental disclosures might well fail to meet any of these characteristics and, if this is the case, it is highly questionable whether or not they merit publication.

Answer 4 (Nov '08)

(a)
The recognition of intangible assets, and of intellectual capital assets in particular, has been much discussed in recent years. The traditional business model involving exploitation of physical assets in the form of tangible non-current assets and inventory is no longer so prevalent. For many service businesses, the most significant category of 'asset' relates to the skills and talents of the people who work for them. If accounting regulation and practice permitted the recognition of such assets as part of the business statement of financial position, there could be some positive effects.

Under current accounting practice, the statement of financial positions of many types of business recognise few intangible assets. Recognition of a wider range of assets would provide a more realistic view of the productive capacity of the business, which could be helpful to many categories of stakeholder. For example, existing and potential investors would find it easier to relate the flow of revenue to the 'assets' that had produced it, thus improving understanding of the nature of the business and its ability to generate positive income streams.

A related point is that realistic analysis of the financial statements would be much easier where a greater range of assets was recognised. Under current IFRS many of the standard accounting ratios make little sense because the recognised asset base is so low. Accounting ratios such as asset turnover, return on assets and return on capital employed are essentially meaningless in businesses that rely principally on intellectual capital assets. With full recognition of intellectual assets, comparisons between the productivity of different types of business would become more realistic.

From the point of view of the employee stakeholder group, recognition of intellectual assets would increase the prominence of the value they add to the organisation. Instead of being viewed as a cost to be borne by the business, the amounts incurred in remunerating and training employees could be seen as an investment by the business. If a formal valuation process were adopted in respect of individuals their status and prospects could be improved.

(b)

The principal problems relating to the recognition of intellectual assets are as follows:

Intellectual assets such as know-how and skills do not usually fall into the Framework definition of an asset ('a resource controlled by the entity as a result of past events and from which future economic benefits are expected to flow to the entity').

The problem is one of control: skills are in the possession of the individual employee who has the option to cease working for the entity and to take his or her skills elsewhere. Where resources cannot be controlled their value to the entity is questionable.

Realistic measurement of intellectual assets presents a challenge that may well be insuperable in practice. Although some guidance is provided by market salary rates from which a capital value could in theory be extrapolated, any such values would necessarily be vague and imprecise. The difficulties involved in reaching realistic values would rule out valid inter-firm comparability.

Finally, because of the problems of arriving at consistent and robust measurement techniques, there would be scope for creative accounting by the unscrupulous.

17

International Issues in Financial Reporting

International Issues in Financial Reporting

17

LEARNING OUTCOMES

After studying this chapter students should be able to:

► discuss major differences between IFRS and US GAAP and the measures designed to contribute towards their convergence.

Progress towards convergence

The IASB and FASB have lost no time in pursuing their convergence programme. The fruits of it to date include the following:

- An extensively revised version of IFRS 3 *Business Combinations* issued in January 2008.
- The standard on segment reporting (IFRS 8 *Operating segments*) issued in November 2006.
- IFRS 5 *Non-current Assets Held for Sale and Discontinued Operations*.
- An extensively revised version of IAS 1 *Presentation of Financial Statements*, issued in September 2007.

As well as the projects currently under way which have reached the exposure draft stage (business combinations, non-financial liabilities and segment reporting), there are several other active projects:

Short-term convergence projects

- IAS 12 income taxes
- impairment.

Long-term projects

- revenue recognition
- the conceptual framework
- post-retirement benefits.

Despite all this activity, many significant differences remain between IFRS and US GAAP. These are the subject of the following section.

Remaining differences between US GAAP and IFRS

The set of differences between the two sets of regulations changes frequently with the issue of new standards. Significant recent changes have included the issue of IFRS 8 *Operating Segments*, and the updated versions of IFRS 3, IAS 27 and IAS 1. All of these have significantly reduced differences between US GAAP and IFRS.

This means that any list of differences is soon out of date, and all such lists should be treated with caution. Nevertheless, the list provided by, for example, the accounting firm PricewaterhouseCoopers is helpful. It was last updated (at the time of the update of this *Learning System*) in August 2007, and is available at www.pwc.com.

The table below summarises some of the significant remaining differences:

Issue	IFRS	US GAAP
General approach	Broadly, principles-based	Broadly, rule-based
Comparative information	One year of comparative information is required	No specific requirement, but SEC rules required 3 years of comparative information (2 years for the statement of financial position)
Extraordinary items	Prohibited	Defined as being both infrequent and unusual, and are rare
Jointly controlled entities	Both proportionate consolidation and equity method are permitted	Equity method is required except in certain circumstances
Revenue recognition	IAS 18 contains general principles only	While principles are similar to IFRS, there is extensive industry-specific guidance
Development costs	Are capitalised and amortised when specific criteria are met	Development costs are expensed as incurred
Property, plant and equipment	Either cost or revaluation bases are permitted	Historical cost is used; revaluation is not permitted
Inventories	Use of LIFO is not permitted	Use of LIFO is permitted
Investment property	Measured at fair value or depreciated cost	Depreciated historical cost is the only permitted measurement

International Issues in Financial Reporting

Detailed knowledge of the differences is not required for Paper 8 *Financial Analysis*. However, it is expected that candidates will be able to identify some of the principal differences that still exist between IFRS and US GAAP. Questions are quite frequently set in this area, and are often badly handled by candidates.

Barriers to harmonisation

- The drive towards international harmonisation has gathered pace in recent years and from 2005 onwards listed companies within the EU will have to produce their consolidated financial statements in compliance with international standards.

    However, those aiming for a single set of global accounting standards still have some significant hurdles to overcome:

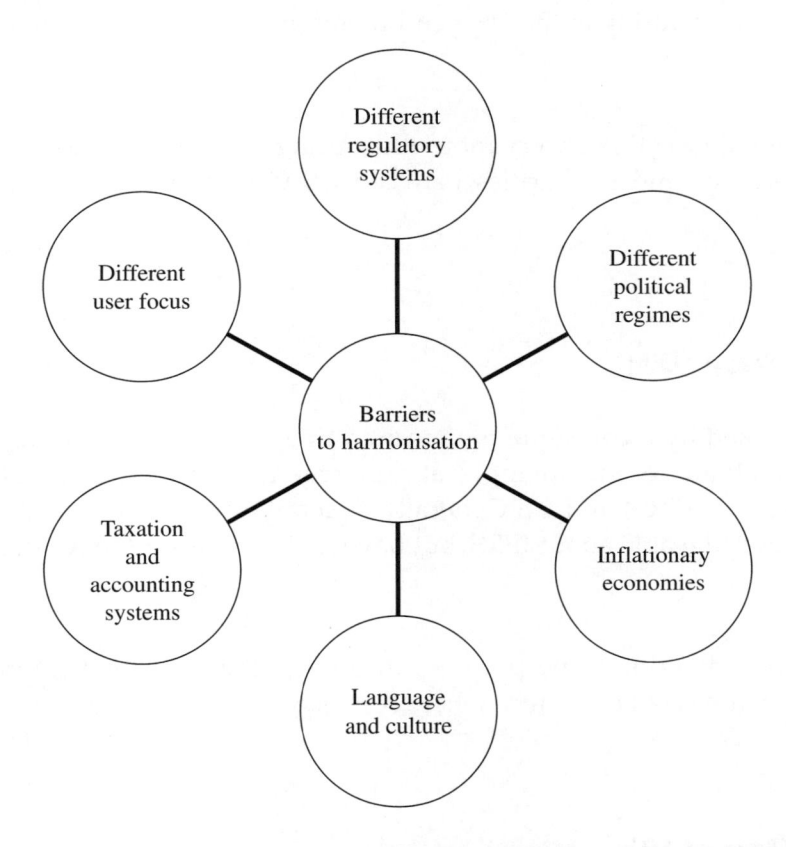

```
                    Different
                   regulatory
                    systems

   Different                      Different
   user focus                     political
                                  regimes

              Barriers
           to harmonisation

   Taxation                       Inflationary
   and                             economies
   accounting
   systems

                    Language
                   and culture
```

- The rewards of harmonisation will be high for multinational entities who will see cost reductions and easier access to finance.
- Stakeholders will find comparison of financial statements easier.

Note: The following question on the convergence process between IFRS and US GAAP are by nature out of date as progress is made. These questions past examples of the way in which this area has been examined to give an indication of the level of knowledge required.

Medium answer questions

Question 1 (Nov '05)

At a recent staff seminar on Accounting Standards, a senior member of your firm's accounting staff made the following observation:

'International Standards have now been adopted in many countries across the world. Unfortunately though, they can never be truly international because US GAAP will continue to dominate accounting in the USA and therefore in many multinational businesses'.

Requirement

Explain the rationale for this observation, illustrating your explanation with examples of significant differences and similarities between US GAAP and International Accounting Standards.

(Total = 10 marks)

Question 2 (May '07)

You have been asked by a colleague to present a brief paper to accounting students at the local university about recent attempts at convergence between International Financial Reporting Standards (IFRS) and US Generally Accepted Accounting Practice (GAAP). The students are knowledgeable about IFRS, but have not studied US GAAP in any detail.

Requirement

Prepare the paper, describing the progress to date of the convergence project, including some examples of areas of accounting where convergence has taken place.

(Total = 10 marks)

Question 3 (May '08)

An important development in international accounting in recent years has been the convergence project between the IASB and the US standard setter, the Financial Accounting Standards Board (FASB).

Requirements

(a) Describe the objectives, and progress to date, of the convergence project, illustrating your response with examples of the work that has been successfully undertaken.

(6 marks)

(b) Identify four continuing, and significant, areas of difference that exist between IFRS and US GAAP.

(4 marks)

(Total = 10 marks)

Question 4 (Nov '07)

It is becoming increasingly common for listed entities to provide non-financial disclosures intended to inform stakeholders about the business's environmental policies, impacts and practices. Supporters of such voluntary disclosures argue that stakeholders have a right to be informed about environmental issues in this way. However, there are also arguments against this type of disclosure.

Requirement

Identify and explain the principal arguments **against** voluntary disclosures by businesses of their environmental policies, impacts and practices.

(Total = 10 marks)

Question 5 – Titanium plc

Chas Patel is a senior partner with DHN & Co, a medium sized accountancy practice that has a large portfolio of small and medium sized clients. The firm has always found it difficult to break through into the 'blue chip' sector, although they believe they have the expertise to provide high quality advise if requested.

Chas has recently received a letter from the finance director of Titanium plc, and recognises that this could represent the opportunity that the firm requires. Titanium plc is an unusual company in that it has a full public listing, but has never diversified away from its core business, and hence has no subsidiaries or associates.

The finance director is aware that listed companies in the European Union will have to prepare consolidated financial statements that are compliant with IAS for financial periods commencing on or after 1 January 2005. Technically the company is not caught by these regulations as it does not produce consolidated statements, but the finance director is keen to convince the senior management team that it would be better to transfer to the new accounting rules sooner rather than later.

He has invited Chas, who is well known as an expert in this field, to put a presentation to the directors explaining the pros and cons. Although he wants to transfer to IAS he believes that it is better to get the 'buy in' of his peers rather than pushing through changes.

Additional factors to be considered are:

- Titanium plc's financial year end is 30 September
- The company trades around the World
- It has always favoured the principles based accounting guidance issued in the UK.

Requirements

Prepare a maximum of four slides on the arguments for and against the transfer to IAS for the presentation, and include brief notes with each to support the points made.

(10 marks)

Answers to medium answer questions

Answer 1 (Nov '05)

International Standards have, indeed, been adopted in many countries across the world: for example, compliance with them is compulsory in companies listed on a Stock Exchange within the European Union, and their adoption in Australia and New Zealand is well under way.

Nevertheless, it is certainly the case that accounting in accordance with International Standards continues to differ from US GAAP in many respects. To this extent, the observation by the senior staff member has some validity. Examples of important areas of difference are:

- *Performance reporting*. In the US a comprehensive income model is used whereas international practice has not, to date, developed performance reporting requirements beyond IAS 1. Performance reporting has been on the agenda of the IASB since 2001, but it has not yet published an exposure draft on the topic.
- *Valuation*. International accounting practice allows the option to value property, plant and equipment at either depreciated cost or fair value. US GAAP is more restrictive in this respect and reporting at depreciated cost is much more prevalent.

On the other hand, convergence between US and international practice is becoming increasingly common. For example, a significant area of difference in the past has been that of business combinations: it was common in the US until recently to account for many business combinations as pooling of interests. While international practice did not outlaw pooling of interests its use was far less common. However, developments in US and International Standards have now resulted in a position where pooling of interests accounting is no longer available.

The senior staff member does not mention the 'Norwalk agreement', which established a formal convergence project between the IASB and its US counterpart, the Financial Accounting Standards Board (FASB). Under the terms of this agreement, the IASB and FASB agreed to work together to remove differences between their respective sets of Standards, and to coordinate their future programmes of work. The agreement has already resulted in a narrowing of differences: for example, IFRS 5 *Non-current assets held for sale and discontinued operations* brings international practice into line with US GAAP. The two boards are working together on a project on performance reporting which is likely to produce convergence in the form of a comprehensive income reporting requirement.

There is a great deal of work to be done before US GAAP and international practice can be described as 'convergent'. However, much has already been achieved in a short time. The view expressed by the senior staff member would have been widely regarded as valid until very recently, but it has been overtaken by events. The convergence project has undoubtedly been given additional impetus by the recent, spectacular, corporate and accounting failures in the USA. These have resulted in a period of introspection and self-criticism among US regulators and in a push towards significant improvement in financial reporting.

Traditionally, the US approach to accounting regulation has been 'rules-based'; this has resulted in the production of very lengthy, detailed Accounting Standards. By contrast, International Accounting Standards have tended to be 'principles-based'. For example, instead of having a very detailed international Standard addressing substance over form, international accounting practice relies much more upon promulgation and acceptance of the general principle of substance over form. The recent US accounting scandals have led to a great deal of criticism of the 'rules-based' approach and greater acceptance of the value of the 'principles-based' approach.

On the other hand, international regulation appears to be moving to some extent in the opposite direction, as International Standards become lengthier and more prescriptive (e.g. IAS 39 *Financial instruments: recognition and measurement*). Therefore, it seems likely that US and international regulators will find it easier to occupy common ground in their approach to Standard setting.

Answer 2 (May '07)

The convergence project: progress to date

Traditionally, the US has adopted a 'rule-book' approach to financial reporting standard setting, whereas the approach taken by the IASB, and its predecessor body, has been to encourage adherence to principles. This fundamental difference in approach made it appear, for a long time, as though the US would never accept International Standards. However, the rule-book approach was found wanting in a series of financial scandals in the US in the late 1990s and early years of the 21st century. The climate was therefore amenable to a change in approach which would make convergence possible between US and International Financial Reporting Standards.

In September 2002, the US standard setter Financial Accounting Standards Board (FASB) and the IASB agreed to undertake a project which would have the objective of converging their accounting practices, reducing the number of differences between US GAAP and IFRS. This agreement (the 'Norwalk agreement') committed the parties to making their existing standards fully compatible as soon as practicable, and to co-ordinating their future work programs. In order to address the first commitment, a short-term project was undertaken to remove some of the differences between existing standards. The second commitment was to be met by collaborating on the development of standards.

A memorandum of understanding between FASB and the IASB sets out a 'Roadmap of Convergence between IFRS and US GAAP 2006–8'. This is aimed at removing the need for a reconciliation to US GAAP requirement for those companies that use IFRS and are registered in the USA.

Progress to date has been impressive. Projects undertaken jointly between FASB and IASB have produced the following:

- IFRS 5 *Non-current Assets Held for Sale and Discontinued Operations*.
- The exposure drafts on business combinations issued in June 2005.
- IFRS 8 *Operating Segments*, issued in November 2006.
- ED Proposed amendment to IAS 1 *Presentation of Financial Statements: a Revised Presentation*, issued in March 2006.

There are several on-going projects that will run into the longer-term. For example, the amendment to IAS 1 noted above represents just a first phase in a larger project on financial statement presentation. Subsequent phases will address fundamental issues in presenting information and the issue of interim reporting.

Other longer-term projects include convergence of the conceptual frameworks and revenue recognition.

Finally, despite the high level of activity on convergence, it should be noted that many significant differences remain between US GAAP and IFRS.

Answer 3 (May '08)

(a)

In September 2002, FASB and IASB agreed to undertake a project with the objective of converging international standards and US GAAP, thus reducing the number of differences between the two sets of conventions. The 2002 agreement (the 'Norwalk agreement') committed the two parties to making their existing standards fully compatible as soon as practicable, and to co-ordinating their future work programs. To date, the Boards have undertaken a short-term project to address, and where possible, remove some of the differences between standards. The longer-term issues have been tackled by undertaking work jointly on the development of new standards.

A memorandum of understanding between FASB and IASB set out a 'Roadmap of convergence between IFRS and US GAAP 2006–8'. This was aimed at removing the need for a reconciliation to US GAAP requirement for foreign registrants in the USA which use IFRS.

Recently, the Securities and Exchange Commission in the USA announced that it intends to consider the removal of the reconciliation requirement, and even to permit US registrants the option to adopt IFRS if they wish to do so.

The convergence project has produced several tangible results, including the following:

- IFRS 5 *Non-current Assets Held for Sale and Discontinued Operations*.
- The exposure drafts on business combinations issued in June 2005.
- IFRS 8 *Operating Segments*, issued in November 2006.
- ED Proposed amendment to IAS 1 *Presentation of Financial Statements: a Revised Presentation*, issued in March 2006.

(b)

Many differences between US GAAP and IFRS continue to exist. Examples include:

- The general approach to IFRS is principles-based; whereas US GAAP follows a more prescriptive rules-based approach.
- Inventory cost: IFRS prohibits the use of the LIFO method of valuation, whereas it is permitted by US GAAP.
- Accounting for investments in joint ventures: IFRS permits the use of either proportionate consolidation (the preferred method) or the equity method. US GAAP permits only the equity method.
- Development costs: IFRS requires that development costs be capitalised, provided that a set of conditions are met. US GAAP stipulates that development costs must be written off when incurred.

(Examiner's note: there were several other acceptable examples.)

Answer 4 (Nov '07)

Arguments against voluntary disclosures by businesses in respect of their environmental policies, impacts and practices might include the following principal points.

The traditional view of the corporation is that it exists solely to increase shareholder wealth. In this view business executives have no responsibility to broaden the scope or nature of their reporting as doing so reduces returns to shareholders (because there is a cost associated with additional reporting).

From a public policy perspective, if governments wish corporations and similar entities to bear the responsibility for their environmental impacts, they should legislate accordingly. In the absence of such legislation, however, businesses bear no responsibility for environmental impacts, and in consequence there is no reporting responsibility either.

Voluntary disclosures of any type are of limited usefulness because they are not readily comparable with those of other entities. Therefore, it is likely that the costs of producing such disclosures outweigh the benefits to stakeholders.

The audit of voluntary disclosures is not regulated. Even where such disclosures are audited, the scope of the audit may be relatively limited, and moreover, its scope may not be clearly laid out in the voluntary report. Voluntary reports are not necessarily, therefore, reliable from a stakeholder's point of view.

Especially where voluntary disclosures are included as part of the annual report package, there is a risk of information overload: stakeholders are less able to identify in a very lengthy report the information that is relevant and useful to them.

Voluntary disclosures by business organisations, because they are at best lightly regulated, may be treated by the organisation in a cynical fashion as public relations opportunities. The view of the business's activities could very well be biased, but it would be quite difficult for most stakeholders to detect such bias.

It is questionable whether voluntary disclosures about environmental policies, impacts and practices would meet the qualitative characteristics of useful information set out in the IASB's Framework. The key characteristics are: understandability, reliability, relevance and comparability. Voluntary environmental disclosures might well fail to meet any of these characteristics and, if this is the case, it is highly questionable whether or not they merit publication.

Answer 5 – Titanium plc

Slide 1: Advantages of global harmonisation

- Raising financial capital
- Helping stakeholders
- The Internet.

Notes: A major advantage for listed companies will be better access to foreign investor funds, and a greater variety of markets upon which financial capital can be raised.

The fact that all financial statements will be prepared using a common rule set also makes it easier for different stakeholder groups to make comparisons between entities. A potential investor based in one country will be able to evaluate the relative merits of entities in different geographic locations.

Increasingly large organisations are releasing their financial results on the Internet. This means that users in any location have access to this information.

Slide 2: Further advantages

- Cost savings and efficiency
- Improved analysis.

Notes: Although transfer from national GAAP to IAS will have to be funded (e.g. new accounting systems, etc.), in the longer term there should be significant cost savings. For international companies it will no longer be necessary to prepare financial information using local GAAP for each subsidiary, and this in turn should reduce the costs incurred using professional advisers.

Inter-group and inter-company comparisons will be easier and faster; thereby allowing decisions to be made more efficiently.

Slide 3: Global barriers to harmonisation

- Different cultures and regulatory environments
- Different purposes of financial reporting.

Notes: The regulatory environment under which entities prepare financial information is not restricted to accounting standards. It is unlikely that uniformity will ever be achieved with all legislation and hence this makes the smooth implementation of IAS more difficult. Furthermore there will be resistance to change from local cultures that have evolved over extended periods.

The primary purpose of financial statements also differs in different countries. In the USA and UK the main user of financial statements is perceived to be the shareholders, whereas in other locations the government or creditors take first place. It is impossible for one accounting system to provide complete information to all users without making financial statements too unwieldy.

Slide 4: Specific barriers to harmonisation

- Unique status
- Unproven.

Notes: Some countries are exposed to unique circumstances that influence every stakeholder group. Typical examples would be hyperinflation or government expropriation of assets. These tend to override all other factors, and make it difficult for IAS or any other accounting regime to give parity with users elsewhere across the globe.

Some commentators also argue that the implementation of accounting standards on this scale is an unproven concept. However, the IAS are now recognised as a very resilient accounting regime, and after some initial teething difficulties a successful introduction is expected.

Exam Q & As

At the time of publication there are no exam Q & As available for the 2010 syllabus. However, the latest specimen exam papers are available on the CIMA website. Actual exam Q & As will be available free of charge to CIMA students on the CIMA website from summer 2010 onwards.